OPPOSABLE TRUTHS

OPPOSABLE
TRUTHS

MARTIN YOUNG

Matador
9 Priory Business Park,
Wistow Road, Kibworth Beauchamp,
Leicestershire. LE8 0RX
Tel: 0116 279 2299
Email: books@troubador.co.uk
Web: www.troubador.co.uk/matador
Twitter: @matadorbooks

ISBN 978 1784623 890

British Library Cataloguing in Publication Data.
A catalogue record for this book is available from the British Library.

Printed and bound in the UK by TJ International, Padstow, Cornwall
Typeset in 11pt Aldine401 BT Roman by Troubador Publishing Ltd, Leicester, UK

Matador is an imprint of Troubador Publishing Ltd

For: Susan, Jonathan & Lynsey, Annabel & Steve, Molly,
George and Jessica.

CONTENTS

FOREWORD

Who would you rather trust? The East African maned rat or a journalist? Tough call. But the rat only has partially opposable thumbs. Old World Monkeys and all great apes have opposable thumbs like ours. So, on this more equitable comparison, journalist or ape? This is getting trickier.

Then there is the matter of speech. Animals have been clambering onto YouTube making various noises that affect to mimic human speech. But Wikipedia, the fount of all unopposable truth, tells us that these sounds are not a language because they lack "grammar, syntax, recursion and displacement". Now, journalists can and do speak, some would say ad nauseam. But I've never seen a decent op-ed column from an East African rat.

In the race to rule the jungle the man with the trilby and the belted trench coat, hunched over his keyboard, chattering incessantly with his recursions and displacements is bound to be king.

Ah, I hear you, my Greek chorus, cry, "Does the scribbler bring us Truth? What is Truth? Is this journalistic 'false memory' merely hubris?" It brought forth a dreadful Nemesis for the demigod of the American network, NBC, Brian Williams, who fell from the Pantheon of the Gods, from Walter Cronkite and Ed Murrow to Pinocchio in just a few short sentences. Under fire in Iraq he claimed to have been a passenger in a Chinook helicopter that was hit by a SAM missile and forced to land, which was a great story until the pilot of the stricken Chinook pointed out that Williams was actually in a following, unscathed helicopter. If you can shake off the Schadenfreude for a second you might be able to strike up some sympathy for the fallen hack. Throughout his career a series of benign or malign despots have despatched him to war zones, knowing that colourful stories will chatter digitally back to their news desks. He's a celeb. He sits on brightly-lit sofas and tells his heroic story again and again. The memory fades, the embellishment burgeons, the SAM missile really gets him this time. He falls to earth.

Take all that follows with a pinch of cordite. It's as near the Truth as I can manage. As anyone can manage.

This is my one chance at an autobiography. The first thing you should know about me is that I only have one life. If I were Wayne Rooney or David Beckham I'd be on my fourth or fifth autobiography by now. So, if you bought this because you thought it was by Didier Drogba I apologise and suggest you see an optometrist. Nope, sorry, never scored a goal in my life, not even at school. Oh well, he must be a celebrity then. If you read Kim Kardashian or Katie Price on the cover then Specsavers are in for a healthy profit this month.

Did you misunderstand the title on the cover? If it had been "BBC correspondent and chancer for thirty years" would you have snatched it up so readily? Would "The BBC, blackmail, lesbians and me" have aroused the voyeur that had, thus far, lain dormant within you? All autobiographies of course ought to be called "Me, Me, Me", would the unabashed candour of such an approach have appealed to you? I've always wondered why Stephen Fry called his book *Moab is my Washpot*. I now realise it was out of sheer desperation. Of course Clive James came up with the best: *Unreliable Memoirs* which I can't nick because he was a friend from Cambridge days and because posses of lawyers stalk the land. I could have joined the honourable ranks of "How To" books: "How to present yourself on television", since I now teach these black arts to youthful executives who seem to think that I am either Marconi or John Logie Baird.

If you are detecting an existential crisis in the author as a result of these musings then, with respect, you'd be wrong. Try Albert Camus instead. No, these are the ramblings of the congenital freelance, bounced from one place to another and one catastrophe to another, from the tyrant to the weeping widow, from princes to paupers by the shifting sands of news and fashion. "Send Young" the cry goes out from the editor behind the comfy desk and "Young Goes". He goes, normally by air. Not for him the folding canoe and the forked sticks of William Boot (fictional) or the months of steaming up the Amazon to somewhere unpronounceable of James Cameron (real), nor the digital dash of daring Alex Crawford of *Sky News* bringing you instant high-tech gore straight from the battlefield. I fall somewhere in the middle. I have been shelled in a low-tech kind of way on the battlefield but I was fully napalmed in the more august surroundings of the Court of Appeal by a man in a wig.

I thoroughly enjoyed writing this book. It was cathartic and it made me laugh at the folly of it all. I hope you like it too. As they used to say in *The Goon Show*: "This is where the story really starts…"

I WANTED ADVENTURE

Fast forward to the lift of the Intercontinental Hotel in Tehran in 1980. Here I am, in the thick of the adventure at last. My BBC TV pass in my wallet along with a wedge of currency and about to go to war. The lift doors open and I am presented by a bedraggled, dusty American film crew. Forgetting momentarily that the Americans totally lack irony I say brightly: "it must be wonderful for you chaps to be here in Tehran now that spring is here." The tall, rangy and very shop-soiled cameraman fixes me with a Clint Eastwood unyielding stare: "Tehran fucking sucks."

And it did.

Hot news to us British boys, fresh off the plane: the Foreign Minister, Sadegh Ghotbzadeh, is giving a Press Conference in the next hour. The scene is familiar, a tangle of camera crews, wishing they were back home at the Dog and Duck or Le Café Rene but thinking of the overtime and the danger money; lots of print hacks wearing their crumpled 'presidents' suit'; a hair gel of lesser television hacks and a machismo of TV's finest, the seasoned travellers bringing blood and guts into your lounge or kitchen.

The questioning was mundane, mostly about the Kurdish insurrection in the North (go to any exotic, chaotic country there is always a Kurdish insurrection in the North). Mundane that is until America spoke. Mr America was tall, good-looking with night club hair and perfect orthodontics. He finally stretched out the legs of his two thousand pound suit and delivered himself of the following: "Mr Ghotbzadeh, could you give me one good reason why I should not think that you are one big, fucking liar?"

I looked around for the Revolutionary Guards to step in and rush him to Evin Prison for a spot of torture. I had always thought that I would be the man who spoke truth unto power.

However there was a story going on. In 1979 the guardians of the revolution had overthrown the Shah of Persia and taken power. The Ayatollah Khomeini returned from exile in Paris to become the Supreme Leader and to denounce the Great Satans of America and Israel. He didn't like Britain much either. The implications for the US were rapidly apparent when a bunch of revolutionary students stormed the US embassy in Tehran and took a couple of hundred hostages. The Brits in London were the next to be hit when hostages were held in the Iranian embassy.

At this point the big guns swung into action. Her Majesty's Britannic Government sent in "our brave boys" of the SAS to create some whiz-bang footage for the television news and generally to save the day. Her Majesty's BBC sent ingénue foreign correspondent, Martin Young and producer Eric Abrahams to save the day for British journalism.

Eric and I set out for the prison near Tehran where the main action appeared to be. We arrived there in two taxis (nobody was hiring cars to media people because they came back all shot up – the cars, not necessarily the media people) and emerged into the crowd with all our film gear. If you did this in Stockton on Tees you were guaranteed a hero's welcome but here in Iran we were one of the Great Satans and the crowd turned on us. They may not have known much before about the modern film camera but they had learned rapidly that the bit they wanted was the take-up reel of exposed film. The trick for us was to change the reel to blank film, secrete the actual exposed film and give the blank reel to the angry crowd. But during this procedure one little man caught on to what we were doing and tried to grab the exposed reel from me.

A fight between him and me was inevitable. Fortunately the Iranians are a small nation so I pulled myself up to my full 5ft 7ins and won the struggle. The crowd, now rapidly becoming a mob, pursued us as we climbed the nearby hill to get a top shot of the prison complex. They began to hurl rocks and stones at us and it was all getting very ugly when a car arrived bearing a group of Pasdaran and we were duly arrested. This was my first arrest but by no means would it be my only one. We were taken back to a jail and put in a cell along with a grumpy crew from NBC so that was the second Great Satan safely incarcerated. The Americans' interpreter, a well-heeled, slick young man with perfect English was despatched to try to secure our release. In remarkably quick time we were free to return to Tehran. It only later occurred to us that the interpreter you would assign to the Americans would of course be a spy. I have no idea what he promised in return for our release and I didn't care. We had our footage and I had a prize spot on the following morning's *Today* programme on Radio 4. I managed to get through to my wife, Susan, and tried to reassure her that, whatever she heard that morning on the *Today* programme, I was quite safe. No, I wasn't. The London film editors at Lime Grove were deeply unimpressed by my 'heroics' but thrilled that I had finally admitted that I was 'stoned' outside the jail. They had always assumed that that was my permanent state but had never expected me to admit to it on air.

A HILLTOP TOO FAR

We had broken the rules by going to film at the jail so, continuing to work on Rule One, which states there are no rules, we decided to break a bigger rule. No media were allowed in the north-west of Iran where the Kurdish insurgency was raging. Rumour had it that Khomeini's troops were using heavy weaponry and helicopter gunships against the Kurds who had the occasional AK 47 Kalashnikov. After a period of haggling which involved paying thousands of pounds to two taxi drivers we set off for forbidden territory. We didn't resent paying all those licence fees to the two drivers because they might very well come back with no taxis or, indeed, dead. We suffered too because it took us eighteen hours to get to the action, huddled down in the back of the cabs so that our western faces could not readily be seen. We found out where the action was and drove towards it. You may not think of journalism as a very distinguished career but what does distinguish us from sensible people is that, while they are running away we are running towards the danger. In Bob Poole, the cameraman, we had a good runner. He had shot his way through two Middle Eastern wars and several other conflicts and his first piece of advice was to get on to the high ground above the village that was being bombarded by the troops operating on behalf of the Supreme Leader. The first shell from the artillery came impressively close to us but Bob knew that the process was to 'bracket' the target to establish the necessary range for the guns. This bracketing process went on for an hour or so and then we learned that a curfew had been called until 4.00pm to allow people to leave the village and for the army presumably to regroup. At this stage a shell landed very close to us and I said to Bob

"Gosh! That was really close. Did you get it on film?"

Bob replied "Yes it was bloody close. If the next one comes any closer we're fucking off out of here". It did and we did.

It was quiet now and the curfew seemed to be holding. We gathered our taxis and drove into the village with our frightened drivers. The village was deserted except for one exotic scene – a group of Kurdish rebels dressed in turbans, baggy trousers and bandoliers were mounted on an old Bedford flat-bed truck. Also mounted on the truck was an antique anti-aircraft gun which had been unconvincingly bolted to the metal of the flat-bed.

I heard the sound first as a low, chuntering roar and looked up to see that the curfew had been broken by a small number of helicopter gunships. They are awesome in the true sense of the word and, stopping for a moment from admiring their power and menace, I looked around at my surroundings and asked myself a simple question: if I were a pilot flying over a deserted village and there was nothing to aim at except a Bedford truck and an anti-aircraft gun where would I be firing my rockets? I screamed at the crew to get back into the taxis and go. Three of them jumped into one taxi and disappeared leaving me with the other taxi and the driver who was now terrified for his life. He didn't speak any English and I didn't speak any Farsi – the archetypal Englishman abroad. We screamed at each other in our respective languages until the driver got the message and raced away from the village. No heroics, just a blue funk.

It was now important for us to establish that the Ayatollah's troops were killing and maiming their own people, so we went to a nearby hospital to film the innocents who had become "collateral damage" in all the fighting. I had always thought that terms like "gut-wrenching" and "stomach-turning" were just lazy journalese. Now we were to experience both in real life, and death. The children are the hardest to deal with. They have never touched a Kalashnikov in their young lives. Now they lay strewn across blood-spattered sheets in crammed wards, where good nurses and doctors tried to help them with whatever inadequate drugs they had. I had seen blood before but never the blood of innocent children running free in a bomb-shaken hospital ward. (I only need to get accreditation into Syria or Iraq in 2015 to see the same scenes all over again. "When will they ever learn?") While that question was still awaiting an answer that was blowin' in the wind, I was still there in a ward full of broken and bent children. I wanted to weep but I mustn't. My distress was insignificant compared to theirs. I fell back on an old acting technique taught to me on the stage of the Arts Theatre, Cambridge in the 1960s. In order to convey false, fictional emotion you can take a deep breath far down into your system, tauten your stomach muscles into a knot, and then let the breath escape very slowly. It seemed fraudulent and effete to be practising this technique in the bloody mess of that hospital ward. But it worked and I came out into the fresh air with Bob who, of course, had filmed such scenes many times before. My producer, Eric, had not been so fortunate. He was throwing up on the scrubland and was very visibly upset. The whole tragic scene ended in farce as the overstretched medics had to come away from the chaos inside to revive a Hampstead Liberal who was being sick as a dog.

CAVE PICTURES

Still operating on Rule 1 we looked around for the next rule we ought to break. Near the top of the regime's rules would surely be a complete prohibition on the western media interviewing the insurgents. So we decided to interview the leader of the insurgents, Abdul Rahman Ghassemlou. We made contact with one of his lieutenants and were told to go back to our flea-bitten hotel and wait for the call. On the way we stopped at the obligatory "colourful market scene" where the carpet salesmen brandished guns at us which made it seem less colourful and distinctly threatening until we learned that this was their way of expressing their machismo, or willy-waving to put it more colloquially. It also transpired that when not selling carpets they sold guns. Eric bought a carpet; none of us bought any guns. Having survived the bellicose carpet men I went in search of alcohol, largely unobtainable in Tehran. I found a bottle of Black & White whisky for £15.00. Eric and I returned to the room we were sharing to drink the whisky. Manfully we polished it off and fell asleep until woken by the aforesaid lieutenant. He had an old Land Rover but hardly any fuel. Just enough in fact to get us to an illicit fuel dump where we filled the Land Rover and took on a giant tin can of extra fuel to get us home to the hotel again with our interview.

Our journey to the mountains took us first along a beautiful lakeside road. Beautiful that is until our driver casually mentioned that the army regularly posted snipers along the way in order to deter visitors they didn't like or want. Where was the fuel can? Ah, there it was nestling between my legs. This was not reassuring but the snipers must have been having a tea-break because we got through unscathed.

In order to reach the terrorists' hideout we had to climb a steep slope to the top of the mountain. The sound recordist, who is the one of our quartet I have not yet mentioned, was struggling with the effort. So far, his only real contribution had been on the plane out from London where he had asked:

"How many days have the hostages been held in the Tehran embassy?" We told him that it was 147 days. There was a pause while he worked on his calculator.

"Christ! If only we'd been in there filming when they stormed the embassy. At £30 a day BBC subsistence we'd each be due £4410." Satisfied at the thought he settled back in his airline seat and ordered another drink. Now, however, he was suffering halfway up the mountain from what we all thought was 'a dickey ticker'. Fortunately he survived and we reached the leader's hideout, which was a cave. We sat cross-legged on the floor and were invited to share a meal with him. I was prepared to eat anything to get the interview but I wasn't prepared for a feast of lamb, rice and yoghurt and flat, unleavened bread. This was a terrorist democracy. All the henchmen sat down to eat with us and the chatter in Farsi was incessant. Ghassemlou himself had been educated at the Sorbonne and spoke very good English amid the gloom. The gloom was very important. I have not filmed in a great number of caves but a minimum for adequate lighting would be a blonde and two redheads. No, it was an all-male cave. I refer to the main powerful light which is blonde in colour and the two small ones which are red. Bob Poole had the answer. As he had struggled up the mountain carrying his film gear he had also been carrying a calor gas lamp. It cast just enough light on the interviewee for you to be able to make him out at home. So what did he say? To be honest, I don't really remember and I don't really care. I had the exclusive with the leader of the Kurdistan Democratic Party, a man who criticised the revolution and the Supreme Leader and told us about the 'atrocities' that Khomeini's army was carrying out. That was plenty good enough and we were off to our waiting Land Rover.

This was 1980; by 1989 I would be filming the first series of *Rough Justice* for the BBC, where my main protagonist would be the Lord Chief Justice. By 1989 Abdul Ghassemlou would be dead. He was still fighting for Iranian autonomy in talks in Vienna when he was apparently assassinated by members of the Iranian Security Forces. Apparently. Three bullets at close range to his head was a clue. This civilized child of the Sorbonne, who spoke eight languages and fought diligently for the benighted Kurds, was almost certainly murdered by the theocracy. At the beginning of the Iranian Revolution Ghassemlou must have thought that out of the post Shah chaos he could create a new state of Kurdistan. The current leader of our friends and allies, the Iraqi Kurds, must believe that he too can grab a bit of land for his people out of the current ongoing crises in Syria and Iraq. High stakes.

As it transpired our elation after the interview with Ghassemlou was short-lived. While we were away the most dramatic story of the hostage crisis had broken. President Carter had launched "Desert One", a helicopter invasion of Iran in an attempt to rescue the trapped Americans. It went disastrously wrong and Jon Snow, then of ITN news was there to speak to the nation, while we were hundreds of miles away luxuriating in a terrorists' lair, scoffing lamb and flat bread with the Kurdish leader. That pesky Jon Snow, the same age as me but so much older at the foreign correspondent's game. I had wondered for some time why Jon could get through to

London by phone from the Intercon whereas some of my calls were taking up to five hours to connect. Could a sum of money have changed hands between Jon and the switchboard operator? I had foolishly assumed that the enemy was the Revolutionary Guards, the Pasdaran. Now I realised it was also my esteemed colleagues who were out to get me.

The next time I met Jon Snow was at the Edinburgh Television Festival just after my suspension from the BBC, of which much more anon, when I had been assigned to *BBC Breakfast*. That morning *Breakfast* had screened a trivial film I had made about the boy scouts. When I went down to the lobby of the hotel Jon said Hello and "I saw your film this morning. The BBC certainly knows how to punish a guy, don't they".

Nonetheless Jon's moment had gone and we still had our exclusive interview with the terrorist leader. The problem was: how to get it back to London unscathed. Bob Poole, as usual, had the answer. We couldn't take exposed film out of the country because the revolutionary guards would insist on processing it there in Iran. Not only would it come out sepia coloured but rather more terminally it would be destroyed once they saw the contents. We could, however, take unexposed film back home with us. First of all we borrowed twelve cans of unexposed film from various friendly film crews. We took that to the Iranian censor who wrapped it round with yards of gaffer tape and scribbled a message on it to Iranian Customs in Farsi. We took the unexposed film back to the Intercon and very carefully unwrapped all the tape, substituting the exposed film for the unexposed film. Then meticulously we rewrapped the package making sure that the Farsi writing matched up all the way around the cylinder of reels. One problem solved but another rapidly appeared. We had several thousand pounds in American dollars and British sterling on us. If we declared that to the authorities at Mehrabad Airport the lucky customs officials would simply steal it. Bob set about dismantling half the film gear and hiding the currency under various circuit boards. There were still several hundred US dollars that we couldn't find a place for. Bob unscrewed the back of his much travelled transistor radio and secreted about 800 dollars in the little machine. He closed it up and turning round said to us all: "Now, the chances are that all they'll want to do is check that the radio works." He switched it on and out came some wailing Farsi music. "That's pretty smart isn't it?" "There's only one problem, Bob, – George Washington is winking at me through the radio dial". We made the necessary adjustment and set off for the airport.

There is a scene in the recent film *Argo* in which a group of Americans with fake passports and papers are trying to get out of Iran flying to Zurich from Mehrabad Airport. The director, Ben Affleck, has exactly represented the tension and fears the four of us felt as we came to the Customs Check with our heretical film and dodgy currency. Customs men, in my experience, are rarely bathed in smiles. The bearded Iranian who checked in my briefcase had done extra lessons at the Revolutionary School for Scowling. This was long before the days when all my research would have been hidden away on a laptop or memory stick. He began rifling through a stack of news cuttings about the Shah and the revolution. He went into extra grim mode when confronted by a photograph of the Shah's wife sitting in some luxurious palace. He started pointing and jabbering at me, clearly attacking the Shah and all he stood for. I am nodding vigorously in agreement. He pushed his fingers into the centre of the picture, tore it out, spat on it and threw it to the floor. I am now nodding so vigorously I think my head may fall off. Nobody, thank God, sorry thank Allah has been monitoring my heartbeat and the sweat could be a result of the Iranian climate. The customs official though has clearly decided that I am a bosom pal of the revolution and lets me through. Eric has brought from the gun-toting carpet sellers a kilim and this helpfully deflects the tension while the customs officers deprive him of a load of money in 'taxes'. We reached the aircraft and settled into our seats. I am very conscious that we are still in Iran but we have almost escaped. A real sense of relief hits us when the cabin crew announces that we have left Iranian airspace. It is almost drowned out by the urgent call for alcohol.

We were met at Heathrow by a man from BBC Shipping who magically whisks away our precious film for processing. Once safely landside I see a very attractive young woman coming towards me with a baby in a push-chair and a little boy clutching Mummy's hand. It is, of course, my family. I have been away for just a month, even though it seemed like a year. But children change quickly when they are very young and as they came towards me I had to recalibrate their faces in my mind. It was a precious moment, to be repeated many times during their early childhood. The fact that neither Jonathan nor Annabel grew up to be raging, psychological wrecks was a credit to Sue who brought them up so well while their father was abroad inviting strange men to fire bullets at him.

The BBC had sent a Ford Granada camera-car to take us and all our equipment back to Lime Grove. But, first, we had to complete the perfect crime. The BBC could only operate in any State using the official exchange rate on the currency in question. We, on the other hand, could sell our dollars and pounds for wheelbarrow loads of Iranian currency which we carted back to the safe deposit boxes which stood behind the front desk of the Intercon. Indeed one night when we learned that armed terrorists had stormed the front desk and threatened to shoot the German reporters from *Stern* magazine for some blasphemy they had put in their paper, we sympathised with our fellow hacks but were more worried that the gunmen might have emptied the rack of safety deposit boxes. When we came to submit our expenses to the BBC that process could only be done according to the official rate of exchange during our visit. The result was that the money we had smuggled home was ours. We duly opened up the camera gear and Bob's radio and spread out the loot on the bonnet of the

Granada. I walked back to my family about two thousand pounds richer. We were happy. The Beeb would be pleased with the speed of our expenses submissions; the shady currency dealers squatting on the roadside in Tehran would be pleased. All was well with the world. As I say, the perfect crime.

Sue and I and the family went to the Holiday Inn, Heathrow, for lunch. The Dorchester Grill it is not but it catered for us royally and became a regular family haunt when I returned from similar jaunts in the future. I noticed in passing that there were no armed terrorists in the foyer.

RELUCTANT JUSTICE

The gestation of the *Rough Justice* scandal was six or seven years long. Peter Hill and I had made investigative films for both *Newsnight* and *Panorama* in the late seventies, one of which *Video Piracy* was repeated on BBC1. The management no doubt regarded us as maverick and dangerous but at least original and successful. We went to see the Head of News and Current Affairs, John Gau, who had not been swallowed by the maw of the conventional BBC management beast. We had met a marvellous man called Tom Sargant who ran the *Justice* organisation from an eyrie in Chancery Lane, piled high with past court cases. Tom said that he knew of at least two hundred and fifty cases of false imprisonment from petty crimes all the way to rape and murder. Tom was just too good for this world. He believed that everybody who wrote to him was innocent. He would gladly give us access to all he knew and the investigative arm of the BBC could provide the money and the manpower to prepare the case for the plaintiff, when lawyers would take over to plead the case in the Court of Appeal. The manpower was easy but the money bit required pleading our own case in front of the Head of News and Current Affairs. We could not, as yet, prove a single case. We were asking John to sign a blank cheque. We waited anxiously for a response.

John was immediately enthusiastic and gave us the go-ahead. Peter then felt able to say: "we were worried that you might think this was 'trial by television'. "No, no" said John with glee "this is re-trial by television".

This was the BBC operating at its very best (we shall see it working at its very worst later on). Can you imagine going to the fiftieth storey of the NBC building in New York and making a pitch like this to the commissioning editors: "If you give us an unspecified sum of money we may be able to offer you some miscarriages of justice cases at some point in the future. Of course, we may research a case for some weeks and then decide that it isn't true". I think you would be kicked back down all the fifty floors and thrown into the street like Otis B. Driftwood in *A Night at the Opera*.

That's the proposition that the publicly funded BBC was prepared to go along with. For the next five years they were to be vindicated and rewarded with record audiences for a Current Affairs programme. We won three awards including a Special Award for Journalism from the Royal Television Society. More of year six later.

There had always, of course, been revelations of a single miscarriage of justice case in the quality newspapers and on television. The beauty of Peter's idea was that we would present four or five cases, one a week, as a series highlighting the malfunction of the police and the judicial system. If a viewer watched the first one and was unconvinced the following week he might begin to wonder, by week five he might be thinking that perhaps there really was something wrong. As it turned out our first miscarriage was so blatant that people immediately took it to be the truth. It was the injustice meted out to Jock Russell.

We realised that we were onto a winner when Ludovic Kennedy, himself a great champion of legal justice, told us in the middle of Russell's Appeal Court Hearing that he had been playing golf with Lord Lane, the Lord Chief Justice, who was trying the case. Geoffrey Lane had said to him "We're going to have to let this chap out, aren't we?"

The easiest way to understand the impact of this combination of the BBC and the lawyers is to look at the summary of our first three cases in the introduction to our first book on *Rough Justice* in 1983:

> *In the first of our cases, that of Jock Russell, the man whose hair did not match the handful clutched in the dead girl's hand, a whole stream of contradictory and unconvincing evidence has still not led to an early release or a free pardon, although at the time of writing the Home Office have agreed to refer the case back to the Court of Appeal.*
>
> *(Russell was subsequently acquitted).*
>
> *In the second of our cases, that of Michael and Patrick McDonagh, the two men have served their full term in prison and are currently on parole. For a year now the Home Office has known that new testimony claims that another man confessed to the murder for which the McDonaghs served ten years in prison. Yet the Home Office has neither released them early nor pardoned them.*
>
> *In the third of our cases, John Walters remains in Broadmoor. For some months the Home Office has known that the main forensic evidence against him has been thoroughly discredited. The evidence of description, as outlined, should never have been credited in the first place. Yet John Walters is not pardoned.*
>
> *And that surely, is rough justice.*

At the end of the third series Peter and I investigated the most extraordinary case yet. A woman called Anne Fitzpatrick claimed that she had been assaulted in her flat and had all her goods stolen by a man called Antony Mycock whom she had identified both in an identity parade and subsequently in the High Court. 'That's the man' she said as Anthony Mycock stood in the dock. He was jailed and Fitzpatrick went to work in California as a nanny. Peter and I found her ex-flatmates and interviewed them about the alleged assault and robbery. We emerged from the meeting with the flatmates and looked at each other and, almost in unison said 'I don't think there was actually any crime. I think she made it up'. If we could trace her and show her to be a liar not only would we prove that a man had been falsely imprisoned but we could prove that the crime itself had never actually happened. This would be sensational.

We knew from her flatmates that she had gone to Orange County, Los Angeles. After a short search we found an address and tipped up at the front door of the family house where she was working as a nanny. We now began the cat and mouse game that Peter and I were so familiar with: trying to persuade people to talk. We kept asking for a meeting and, after a few days, she agreed to a face-to-face meeting but without cameras. She arrived with a friend and all four of us sat down at a table in the hotel where Peter and I were staying. He produced a small tape recorder and they agreed that we could record the meeting. Fitzpatrick stuck firmly to the story she would tell in Court, omitting the ludicrous assertion that we had blackmailed her with threats to reveal her as a lesbian if she would not give us an interview. Back in the mid-1980s being "outed" as gay no longer had any shock element in civilized Western societies. And in California it was a completely accepted way of life. Quite what effect our alleged blackmail was supposed to have was a mystery to us both. It should also be added that neither Peter nor I would ever countenance using someone's sexuality against them. Fitzpatrick was presumably reassured that we had had no new questions for her and agreed to do a filmed interview for the programme.

When she arrived for the critical interview she was very nervous and tearful. I appealed to her better nature – she had spoken the words that condemned a man to false imprisonment, now she could set that man free at last by telling the truth. Investigative interviews can be very long. I had done some interviews with conmen that had gone on for half an hour or more as they twisted and turned their way out of the truth. As the interview progresses and they sense they are winning they get over-confident and that can be what catches them out. Anne Fitzpatrick was no conman. She was just an accomplished playground liar. The truth came tumbling out. She admitted that Mycock was not the man who had attacked her. "So, there was no crime?" I asked. "No", she confessed, "I made it all up".

We parted amicably enough. She would return to nannying some unfortunate American children. We would head for Los Angeles International Airport with her confession. There could be no doubt now that this case would be heading for the Court of Appeal.

The case would be heard by Lord Lane, who had presided over the eventual release of Jock Russell. During that first hearing his Lordship had averred that television was just a vehicle for fun, implying that it had no place in the adult world of The Law. As he read his brief for the Fitzpatrick case I can only hope that he began to realise that the medium was there in Lord Reith's stirring words to inform and to educate as well as to entertain.

Had the circumstances been different I could imagine sitting in a distressed leather armchair in the warmth of his Lordship's club, while he talked of his days as a paratrooper and how he made his way from humble lawyer to one of the highest Offices in the land. I am sure that, as the cognac flowed and the Montecristo smoke curled, he would have been a most genial companion. But the situation was quite different. He and the BBC were at war and we had backed Lane into a corner. Anne Fitzpatrick's confession in California had changed everything. If she had lied about Anthony Mycock in the original hearing, then Lane must allow his appeal and set him free. If she had lied to me in America then she was a liar and an untrustworthy witness. Bear in mind that there was no forensic evidence against Mycock. He had been convicted on her word alone. Lane would have to declare the original verdict unsafe and unsatisfactory and allow the appeal. Either way Anthony Mycock would be a free man.

What to do when confronted by such a black and white choice? Reach for the civil service book entitled "How to get out of a screw-up" by Sir Humphrey Appleby. Chapter one is a neat little essay "Create a Diversion". Despite the fact that we had proved beyond doubt that Fitzpatrick was a liar, Lord Lane chose to believe every word of her fantastical story that we had attempted to blackmail her as a lesbian. He knew that every newspaper in the Street of Shame would be salivating at the idea of a headline combining BBC, blackmail and lesbian. For the *Daily Mail*, a long time hater of the Beeb, it was as if all their Christmases had come at once. If only they could work in a line about immigrants go home. Instead they splashed it on the front page and set their attack dog, Paul Johnson, to dip his stylus in a vat of vitriol about all the pinkoes and perverts running the BBC. I didn't read it but then I didn't need to. Woodrow Wyatt also foamed at the mouth. With enemies like that I felt quite pleased. While the knives were still out we went for a rare family outing to the cinema in Oxford to see *Back to the Future* where there is a scene in a car park involving Libyan terrorists. My young daughter Annabel enjoyed the film and said afterwards "Daddy, were they the same Lesbian terrorists that you were chasing?" It was a very welcome laugh before I returned to BBC "meeting land" the following morning to be dragged further down the path to betrayal.

What annoyed us both very much was one word in Lane's final judgement. Having outlined the evidence he had sat through he affected totally to believe Fitzpatrick's outrageous lie about our behaviour. He said that he reluctantly allowed the appeal. Reluctantly? How dare he dispense justice in that way? A person is either innocent or guilty before the Law. He cannot be called reluctantly innocent.

Finally we were able to leave the Court. My wife, Susan, teaches full time and couldn't be there to see my triumph or was it my demise? Our life-long friends, Richard and Annabel Stilgoe were there and, as I emerged from the ordeal, Annabel gave me the best hug ever. I had not been on trial, I was simply a witness but I felt I had just been treated like a serial killer. We trooped back to Chancery Lane for a Press conference in the Justice offices. This was normally a happy occasion but this time we all knew that tomorrow's front pages would be all about Fitzpatrick's allegations, not just about the release of an innocent man for a crime that had never even been committed.

MEETING LAND

The trial at the BBC was about to begin.

I ascended to the sacred turf of the sixth floor of Television Centre and entered a different world. It was sacred because it was where power lay and turf because it was the field of battle between rival factions. A sixth floor insider, who had been a successful editor, told me two things about the sixth floor that I have never forgotten. Mid-morning on Day One, as he was still settling his bum into the Leather Chair (Executives for the Use Of), a secretary arrived, bearing a glass of chilled Chardonnay and a message from the egregious Brian Wenham, who had been Head of News and Current Affairs but was now Head of Rubber Bands and Allied Paper Clips. It read simply: "Welcome. You are one of us now". I would never be one of them and would have to buy my own Chardonnay. The second thing my insider told me was that the single most difficult task of his day was to find enough work for his secretary to do. For I had now entered "meeting land", a surreal place where clever, talented people who could otherwise be doing something creative, chose instead to sit around grey tables in grey rooms having grey thoughts, only brightening the opaque nature of their quasi-Socratic dialogue by clever, barbed attacks on their rivals for High Office. Whenever I am tempted by the thought of a big, fat BBC pension I think of all the butt-numbing, useless meetings I would have had to endure to earn it.

There were many meetings, few I remember. One of the first was with Alan Protheroe, Head of something or other, about our method of persuasion to get Anne Fitzpatrick to talk to us on camera in California. Of course, he mused, you had been living in the gutter for five years or more. Some of that dirt must have rubbed off on you. He was accepting that Hill and I had indeed threatened to blackmail Fitzpatrick. I strenuously denied this on behalf of us both. The fact that he took it seriously showed just how out of touch he was with his staff.

Onwards and downwards. Her lies vindicated by the Lord Chief Justice in Britain, Fitzpatrick chose to take Hill and Young and the BBC to court in California. Sensing a quick buck and knowing that the American courts were notorious for awarding huge damages, she sued us for $17.2 million dollars for blackmail and harassment. I shall never forget the $0.2 million. That in itself could wipe me out completely. In meeting land this was no time for Socratic dialogue, it was time for action. Two hot-shot American lawyers were flown in from California. One was to defend the BBC, the other to represent Hill and Young. Why were they splitting the defence? I could see us poor saps being left to cling to some flotsam and jetsam while HMS BBC bobbed innocently away over the horizon. The two lawyers were hilarious. One had Californian Surfer's blonde hair and looked just like the young Robert Redford. This Aryan, Ivy League God was to act for the BBC. The lawyer acting for the sacrificial lambs was a tall version of Dustin Hoffman who looked like he might be good in a street fight but not in the rarefied air of Broadcasting House. Butch Cassidy and the Sundance Kid. As they read their briefs Robert came up with a plan of attack. "Look, Dustin," he said happily, "It's clear from this that she's got some hick lawyer with a small practice. He's probably doing a no win, no fee deal and hoping we'll go for a settlement figure. I suggest that we deluge him with demands for disclosures, harass him into so much work that we can then, effectively, blackmail him into pulling out or settling for a tiny amount." I swear he used the words "harass" and "blackmail", the two crimes of which we were being charged.

Every situation in life is designed to make lawyers richer. The Californian case was to drag on for months but Robert "harass and blackmail" Redford was right. The case was settled for a very small amount and I could breathe again without the prospect of $17.2 million dollars hanging over me.

In the meantime the Beeb's official investigation had reached its grisly conclusion. Peter and I were summoned to a meeting with the Great Panjandrum, Bill Cotton. I had never had much time for his Dad, but at least he could lead a band and play the trumpet. His son's talents were harder to identify, save for one. "Wait until the shit hits the fan," said my sixth floor insider "then you'll see Bill in his white suit striding through the mess, deflecting the brown stuff this way and that and emerging spotless from the morass of floundering executives".

We were ushered into his presence and offered expensive-looking mineral water. Cotton actually began by saying "This is going to hurt me more than it does you". When I was subsequently involved with Michael Grade's autobiography, I told him that opening gambit and he didn't believe that Cotton could come up with such a crass cliché. But now, in the heart of "meeting land" clichés were not our major concern. Survival was. We were not to be sacked. We were to be suspended without pay for three months. We were asked if the condemned men had anything to say. We said we thought it very unjust. The cartoonist, Ken Mahood, got it right: he had us emerging from Cotton's office and saying to each other "I think this is a case for *Rough Justice*".

In just five years, Peter and I had delivered audiences of ten to eleven million viewers, won three awards and even forced an editorial condemning hanging from the nasty "hang 'em and flog 'em" *Daily Mail.* More importantly we had forced the Law into retreats on five of our cases, resulting in successful appeals or early release. We had paved the way for the new Criminal Cases Review Board to be established by Parliament, offering a proper safety net to catch those who had been in the wrong place at the wrong time or those who had been accused of murder like Jock Russell because he had "form". In his case his greatest offence had been "begging in a public place". And our reward was the sack. Justice, no. Rough, yes.

My biggest regret is that I should have resigned. I was caught, though, in that familiar old problem: wife, two young children and huge mortgage to sustain. Many years later I was talking about investigative journalism to the City University School of Journalism. One fresh-faced young thing asked me: "If the BBC treated you so badly, why did you carry on working for them?" "Because I owed the Halifax Building Society an awful lot of money." I replied, crushing a little of his youthful idealism. He was right, though. By accepting the suspension I had also accepted a vow of silence. I should have resigned, spoken out about the ludicrous treatment from the BBC and the sheer wrongness of their judgement about our behaviour. I could have said that, confronted by a much bigger story, the Watergate scandal, the late Ben Bradlee, the editor of the *Washington Post*, had uttered just five words:"We stand by our story".

Among our many misjudgements was that we thought we were the free press fighting The Establishment without realising that the BBC was itself very much a part of the Establishment. If you kick the Establishment hard enough for five years, they are inevitably going to kick you back and they are better at it. I never thought that I would find myself being supported by Lord Norman Tebbit, the Chingford Skinhead of the Thatcher governments, but there he was on the Andrew Marr show talking about the next scandal waiting to happen, the allegations of a paedophile ring operating within Westminster in the 1980s, exactly the period when we were uncovering cases of wrongful imprisonment. Norman Tebbit said there "may well have been" a cover up of organised child abuse by Westminster figures in the 1980s.

"At that time I think that most people would have thought that the establishment, the system, was to be protected and if a few things had gone wrong here and there that it was more important to protect the system than to delve too far into it... That view, I think, was wrong then and it is spectacularly shown to be wrong because the abuses have grown."

Andrew asked him if he thought there had been "a big political cover-up" and Lord Tebbit said: "I think there may well have been...it was almost unconscious. It was the thing that people did at that time."

It was the thing that people did at that time.

I rest my case.

I rest my case, except for this sweet, little coda. The Great Panjandrum, Bill Cotton, subsequently published his own memoirs, *Double Bill* which fleetingly dealt with the *Rough Justice* scandal. As the in-depth investigator of the high-powered, stringent BBC inquiry he wrote:

"On the programme front, in the autumn of 1985 we ran into trouble with one of the programmes in the *Rough Justice* series. The purpose of the series, presented by David Jessel (sic), was to investigate apparent miscarriages of justice in the courts."

One of the important considerations when conducting a high-powered, stringent inquiry is to get your own facts right. The eagle-eyed among you will have noticed that David Jessel did not present the programme that so enraged the Lord Chief Justice. This was prima facie libel on my friend, David, who took over the poisoned chalice after 1985. He told me he'd only do it if I consented. I said it was important work and he would be very good at it, adding the proviso that he should be very careful not to get stitched up either by the police or by his own management. The police had taken to re-investigating our witnesses and encouraging them to retract what they had told us. They got little homilies on the law of perjury.

Cotton's book also reveals much more than his carelessness with the facts. After praise of our "resounding victory" in the Mycock case, he turns to realpolitik:

"But things were not what they seemed. It turned out that the methods the team had used to extract the confession from the woman in California were so irregular that the Lord Chief Justice vigorously condemned both the BBC and the programme in the High Court. (The Court of Appeal, actually, Bill). Alasdair Milne (then the Director-General) was furious...I suspended them... the producer and reporter... for three months without pay. Alasdair thought I had been too lenient – he thought they should have been fired". We never saw Alasdair Milne throughout the entire debacle. Of course, the DG can't involve himself in every little controversy but this one was across the front pages of every national newspaper, tabloid and broadsheet. Also, please note that what Lord Lane said was never questioned at all, despite the fact that the appeal had revealed that Anne Fitzpatrick was a liar and the lesbian slur was so gross that even a junior clerk in Chambers would have questioned its veracity.

And Cotton's libellous book? This from Harper Collins, the publishers, to Peter Hill:

"Please be advised that we have already arranged for the withdrawal and destruction of all the unsold copies of the book that are in circulation, and we are also in the process of destroying all the hardback and paperback editions of the book in our warehouse."

I have written six books and I can only guess how soul-destroying it must be to see your book pulped.

BEING IN "TRADE"

So, what do I do now?

There may have been a plot forming in my fuzzy mind but there was a rather more practical and pressing question that I had to address before taking to the barricades. The BBC sentence on me represented a fine of about £9,000, the effect of three months of unpaid suspension. I needed to make this money up and do it quickly. I had, in theory, been a freelance for twelve years but my rolling contract was renewed every twelve months. This came with restrictions: if I wished to make money elsewhere I would have to ask my Editor for permission. This was a bit like "being in trade" within the otherwise elitist salon of the BBC. I remember once going to see my BBC *Nationwide* editor, John Gau, and asking whether I might have permission to do some work for Ford. He looked me up and down in my flared trouser suit with wide lapels and said: "What are you going to be doing, selling second-hand Ford Escorts?" However, knowing I would be suitably humbled by his response, he agreed to let me take the filthy Ford lucre. The job was hilarious. The "Man from Frankfurt" wanted me to rewrite the Ford Escort induction manual in real English, eliminating as much "Fordspeak" as possible. I did this;

they paid me and promptly wrote most of the "Fordspeak" back into the manual. They were happy, poor souls, speaking their own native patois than recognising the language of Shakespeare and Dickens. But this was not about High Art; it was about six hundred quid. The Man from Frankfurt must have sussed me as a dangerous revolutionary when I had looked out on the enormous staff car park below, with Escorts for junior managers, Cortinas for middle pen-pushers and Granadas for the Top Brass. "If I were you I'd give the next promotion to the man who came in the Renault 16" I said pointing out the offending vehicle down below.

Now, however, my contract had been suspended and there could be no restriction on further ventures into dirty trade. So the atavistic hunter took over and I hung my arse out for hire. A gay friend of mine did say that he didn't think I'd get many takers but, nonetheless, the lure of Soho was beckoning. I had always loved Soho; the mixture of porn theatres and film companies, exotic restaurants and bars, the thrill of seeing some old actor staggering from one voice-over studio to another, even the thrill of someone recognising me. One was Stephen Tomkinson who, at that time in the eighties was starring as Damien in a seminal series *Drop the Dead Donkey*. He played the young 'scoop reporter' who was not averse to adding some colour to his war zone scoops. He carried certain helpful artefacts with him on the battlefield. A bloodstained plimsoll and a child's torn teddy bear lying abandoned amid the rubble of war. Damien's hand would come into view and scoop it up as the camera shot widened to show our brave and compassionate correspondent bending to his grim task. Cue the blockbuster piece to camera, ending "Nothing much is left of this tiny village after the vicious bombardment by government troops, nothing that is except the grim sight of a little girl's torn teddy bear, broken amid the rubble of war." Meaningful look from teddy to camera…and Cut. He was delighted that I thought his portrayal of dodgy Damien was so good and I was delighted that he had recognised me. Ah, the deep insecurity of those in the spotlight. I went on that morning to Silk Sound in Berwick Street to record a voice over for ready money. There I bumped into Tom Baker, the most recent *Doctor Who*. He was regularly there in Soho. His agent would fix up a whole series of voice-overs for that deep brown voice. Tom would deliver for one client or another in fifteen minute sessions and then the Time Lord would be whisked back to his Retirement Tardis, considerably richer and await the next call from his agent.

Throughout that three month period of suspension the work kept flowing and you found out who your true friends were. John Gau, who was now part of dirty trade himself, found me some work training MPs on how to handle television interviews. Mike & Jeannie Marshall, who ran a very successful film company, Cinecosse, out of Aberdeen hired me immediately to film another tranche of a documentary I had been making about the electrification of the East Coast Main Line for British Rail in York. The client, Bert Porter, was a delightful, bibulous old Scot who conducted a very successful career from the warm and gentle surroundings of the cocktail bar in the Royal York Hotel. If he actually had an office at the Rail Headquarters I never saw it. Bert had phoned up Mike as soon as he read about my treatment by the BBC and demanded that I be employed immediately for the next part of the BR film. Despite all the bravura I was displaying I was bruised and needed the TLC that Mike, Jeannie and Bert bestowed on me. Indeed, I even won the silver tankard for *BR's Favourite Man* and you can't say fairer than that. To cut to the chase, I made £27,000 in the three months suspension period. Having made the mistake of not resigning, this excess of cash was my only weapon against the bastards who had let me down so badly.

LIFE ON *NATIONWIDE*

old fast while I try to explain the phenomenon that was *Nationwide* to my grandchildren. It's 1969. It's a desert out there, kids. No mobiles, no iPads, no knowledge on demand. To make a phone call you needed a pocketful of coins and a public telephone box; to find your way you used a map; to see a film you went to a cinema and chose from one option; to find out when the Franco-Prussian war was you opened an encyclopaedia and to eat you had meat and two veg. 'Connectivity' was an unheard of word, waiting for its ugly multi syllables to be dragged into the language.

Then, over the sand dunes galloped *Nationwide* with its revolutionary technology. Just a few years beforehand the BBC news was so serious it had to be presented by men in dinner suits. Penetrative questions were asked: "Tell me, Prime Minister, which way are your thoughts turning in terms of foreign policy?" Now, suddenly, there was a new kid on the block, a magic child who could whisk you instantly to such exotic places as Cardiff and Newcastle and excoriate the local councillors for their misdemeanours in their outposts of Empire. At six o'clock the nation tuned in for twenty minutes of local news and forty minutes of national and international news. And tune in they did, twelve million viewers on a good night. For remember, there were just two main television channels and BBC 2.

Nationwide was the place to be. I began my modest contributions on the twenty minutes of local news from the North East, eager to catch the eye of the main editor, the Big Banana, in London. Michael Bunce was that man. He had taken over from the colourful Derrick Amoore who would from time to time divert himself by firing air pellets into the newsroom from the roof of Lime Grove studios. As you do. Michael was a rather more avuncular editor, and unarmed. He was, in the ancient and honourable BBC tradition "a legend in his own lunchtime". To be "bunced" was to be stood up on a lunch appointment by Michael because he'd had a better offer. When I finally caught his eye as a promising provincial wannabe I was invited to lunch and, yes, duly bunced. He did, though turn up for the desserts and I got the job. Michael ran *Nationwide* like a happy family. Testament to his spirit is that that family still assembles for anniversaries.

I remember my six years with *Nationwide* as a series of playlets, small dramas, some serious, many silly, designed to amuse the nation over its tea and homework. In true Reithian principles we set out to entertain, educate and inform, but really to entertain. His Lordship was probably whirling in his grave as he watched us "dumb-down" his grand corporation, but as everyone in the media finds out, it is a monster, a chameleon demanding constant change. Put another, more cynical way, BBC management always seemed to be saying: "Ah, here's something excellent, let's destroy it". *Nationwide* survived longer than most. Each summer we would produce a series of films designed to help us stagger through the "silly season" when there is little real news from Parliament and other institutions where the boss men are enjoying their Tuscan villas. The Balance of Payments, which was a big issue at the time, had also gone on holiday, so there was little doom to be dispensed. Hence the summer series. Richard Stilgoe piloted his own family on a trip down the Thames. This was with his wife Annabel, several months pregnant at the time and their two other children, Holly, my goddaughter and Jack, already training to be a clown at a young age. Dickey claimed that he was taking the typical family on holiday, – Mum, Dad and 2.4 children. We learned a lot about our great Southern river, much of it through Dickey's songs. Philip Tibenham explored the canal system of Britain in his simple, elegant prose and we learned a lot about the birth of the industrial revolution which inspired canal building and the exponential growth of that revolution with the birth of the steam train that killed the canal system. And we ate our tea. Someone came up with the wizard idea that one of the reporters should be transported to a remote, uninhabited island on a succeed-or-starve expedition. They cast around for a suitable mug. Bernie Falk would be no good. Even on an uninhabited island he'd find someone to bribe, someone who'd bring him bottles of Glenmorangie and an escape boat back to the fleshpots. Dickey would be no good either, with his building skills he'd have constructed a small village, complete with post office and music hall by the time the crew returned to film. No, the editor's evil eye fell on James Hogg or Gentleman Jim as we knew him, a man more at home in the leather embrace of a Reform Club armchair in Pall Mall than anywhere North of Watford, let alone a God-forsaken island with no Balkan Sobranie or Courvoisier. The editor's bony finger pointed shakily at James. He was to go far beyond Watford to the uncivilised unknown. The crew returned after each visit with alarming tales of how James was "going native". He had built himself a lean-to shelter with a rock for its base. Howard, the world's most clumsy assistant cameraman, dropped the camera on the rock and everyone held their breath while they checked whether several thousand pounds' worth of cine camera would still work. Everyone, that is, except for James, who screamed out: "Mind my rock". That autumn, when a thinner, wiser Jim had returned from his ordeal to Lime Grove I was having a chat with him and casually said; "How was your year?" What this really means, in presenter speak is how much are you earning outside your contract? James said in his well-spoken way: "It's all been great, apart from that fucking island". When my turn arrived for the summer extravaganza, we returned to the trip around Britain format, but I was to do this by stagecoach following the old coaching routes that Jane Austen's characters would have used in the eighteenth century. The director was my friend, Alan Scales and the cameraman was Colin Munn, who went on to film lots of drama like *Morse*. We needed a conceit to use throughout our mini-series and we decided that I should play two characters, the *Nationwide* reporter and Passenger Young, the eighteenth-century gent in frock coat, knee breeches and stock. In order to make this conceit work it was important to have the two characters together in the same shot from time to time. Our solutions ranged from the simple to the impossible. In the first double take, as it were, we had a life-size picture of Passenger Young sitting at the window looking out as the coach rumbled slowly by Reporter Young talking to camera about the stage route from London to Stamford. A much more complicated deception followed in Stamford itself where we contrived to have Reporter Young asleep in his bed and Passenger Young rose like a ghost and walked from the room. A simple, digital trick these days but then a small sensation as I tried to explain to my nine year old granddaughter, Molly, without success. We spent a lot of our time in friendly, but cold country houses, where the only warm things were enormous gin and tonics. We could use their private roads and lanes to drive the coaches and film them in their natural habitat. In one of these grand residences we found an enormous stable yard and an opportunity to make another double-take. We set the camera up in the centre of the piazza and Colin filmed me as Passenger Young walking along, admiring the Georgian stables. The camera left him and lingered slowly across the stable architecture until, magically in one shot, Reporter Young appeared and began talking to camera about the next stage of the journey north. A wider shot would have been more fun. You would have seen me rapidly throwing off my frock coat and breeches and pipe and wig and scrambling in my rather crumpled reporter clothes to the spot where Colin's camera would find me. After this frenetic quick change act I had about three seconds to compose myself and remember the lines I had to say when the camera reached me. It all went well, despite the fact that Colin, the only one to have seen the sequence though the lens, had trouble keeping the camera steady since he was giggling so much. Whether any of the viewers noticed all this chicanery as they ate their fish fingers and chips we shall never know. But we had a lot of fun doing it.

It was incidental to what appeared on screen but I got a lesson in how the other half lives. They are nothing like a half of the population of course, just a highly unrepresentative few per cent of what might be called the aristocratic poor. As long as you could afford a distressed Barbour coat but couldn't afford to heat the aged family pile, you qualified as poor aristo.

One night we were invited to stay at the stately home in preparation for an early start with the coach and four the following morning. The rules were simple in this eighteenth century milieu; I was the surrogate "star". Alan the director was obviously an Officer and the crew were "other ranks". In other words the four posters in the Big House went to Alan and me, while the crew were to be billeted in town with faithful old Mrs Bloggins. Alan, to his credit, was having none of it. He politely explained that we did not operate a class divide in a travelling film crew, – either we all descended on the redoubtable Mrs B in the village or we all stayed at the Big House. Grudgingly, the owner, Sir Roly Rotund, agreed that further four posters should be turned down for the BBC's below stairs staff. Perhaps he thought that *Upstairs, Downstairs* was a true reflection of BBC values, not a work of fiction. Perhaps he thought that Alan and I were just ghastly pinkoes. Perhaps Sir Roly didn't think at all. The family motto might be "non cogito, ergo sum". Anyway, we prevailed and even our "trade" personnel were invited to the *Downton Abbey* dinner. The unseemly tussle over the sleeping arrangements had upset the balance and the decorum of the occasion and Colin, the cameraman, and I reverted to Rule One and tucked into the best wines that Sir Roly's cellar could provide and the best brandy and the best port and… I don't know what else. What I do remember is the outdoor swimming pool. A headstrong young filly among the poor aristos dragged us out to the pool and took off all her clothes, revealing some very sexy pale lime silk underwear. (I should state formally here that no marriage vows were harmed during the making of this feature film). When Colin and I, demure in our Y-fronts, hit the cold water we took a big meal and a vat full of alcohol with us. The knot that forms in the stomach is a spectacular experience. We splashed around for a while with Miss Lime Green and her toff friends and then dried off in the freezing cold. As Colin and I made our teeth-chattering way to our rooms, we passed the dining room and the array of post prandial drinks on a silver salver. Well, it would be rude not to, wouldn't it? So we had a few more brandies and staggered off to bed, still clutching our balloon glasses of Courvoisier. The dawn came ridiculously soon and I woke up to the sight of a half finished glass of brandy and the sounds of a coach and four being rigged in the yard. When I got there, Colin was already filming carrying his heavy camera on his shoulder and betraying the signs of our night of debauchery. Even Nixon didn't sweat that much. We were, as my Dad would say "no very handy" but Colin had the heavy lifting to do while I could slop about, thinking great thoughts about the script. There were, as we've established no rules, but there were conventions. You could drink as much as you like, but you must be available for work the morning after, and you mustn't whinge about your self-inflicted injury. Alan, as an ex-cameraman with NATO in Paris, understood this. Shortly after the stately home debacle I could have done with Alan's more fluent French in my next TV confrontation in Paris.

Venue La Defense, Paris

Dramatis Personae: director, Peter Bate, the entire French Cabinet and me.

Peter and I were despatched to Paris to investigate an alleged miscarriage of justice. A group of young students had been arrested and beaten by the feared CRS riot control police during a demonstration in the centre of Paris. In those days any film crew that went to Paris was almost certain to encounter left-wing marches from Place de La Republique to Place de L'Opera. In order to avoid getting embroiled in the demo and given a good whacking by the CRS, the preferred method was to find some high point to film from. This involved a trek up to the fourth or fifth floor of an adjoining apartment. If you could manage enough French and loads of charm and some francs, you could inveigle your way into the family home and film the march from the safety of their balcony. Sadly for the young students who were now in jail on public order offences they didn't know this and had become caught up in the struggle between the left wingers and the Right in the visors, flak jackets and truncheons of the CRS. We had library footage of the march, we had evidence that the students were innocent, what we now needed was an interview with the French Minister of Justice, Alain Peyrefitte. Peyrefitte was no mere minister; he was a writer and a philosopher, conforming to that singular, typically French style "intellectuel". In other words, he was no fool and saw no percentage in talking to the BBC. We tried everything. Indeed I got to know his suave personal assistant so well over the telephone I thought I'd have to propose marriage to explain my constant pestering of her. But answer from Alain came there none.

We were reduced to background footage of the French government, over which I would attempt to explain their silence on this emotive issue. We discovered that, while we were in Paris, the national celebration of the Liberation was to be celebrated at La Defense, the fabulous new banlieu that had been created in Paris as another example of how good the French are at "les grands projets". We trooped along, uninvited, and I prepared for the usual battle with the authorities: *"Nous sommes une equipe de BBC de Londres at nous voulons filmer La Liberation, s'il vous plait"*. I awaited a torrent of red tape and all manner of reasons why that would be *"tout a fait impossible"*. No, far from it, we were whisked to the best camera position at the ceremony and given a warm welcome. It was only then that I remembered de Gaulle's stirring speech rousing the French to create La Resistance against the German invaders. He had of course delivered that call to arms from a BBC microphone in the BBC headquarters, London. This day was the French equivalent of our annual ceremony at the Cenotaph in Whitehall, with French President, Giscard d'Estaing and all his dignitaries in attendance. The Cabinet were all forming up in their Crombie overcoats and M. Peyrefitte came to join them. Peter Bate was an excellent film director and a driven man. Partly as a result of that drive and determination and partly to wind me up, Peter said; "Go on then, there's Peyrefitte at last, go and ask him for an interview". I was aghast. This was like some jumped-up little French reporter barging into the line-up beside the Cenotaph on Armistice Day and demanding an interview with a senior government minister. I looked at Peter and said: "You're doing this for a bet aren't you?"

I set off across the huge square and reached Peyrefitte, who was busy greeting his fellow ministers. Given the circumstances, Peyrefitte was every inch the gentleman and proceeded to introduce me to each member of the French government as they arrived. I've never been much good at small talk, but small talk in French with a bunch of politicians who are wondering what on earth I'm doing there in the first place, was a whole new delight. I finally got a chance to pop the question to my quarry. Would he grant us an interview about *"les evenements du vingt-trois mars"*, the day on which the students were arrested.

"Pas a ce moment-ci"

"Entendu, mais plus tard, s'il vous plaît?"

"On va voir et maintenant il me faut attendre au ceremonie".

It was my cue to leave, having been treated with great courtesy, given my cheek in being there in the first place.

We never got that interview. I never did consummate my affair with Alain's secretary and I was left to reflect that in life you have to kiss a lot of frogs.

NOT ANOTHER STATELY HOME...

just couldn't escape from poor aristo land, although my next aristocrat, with 123,000 acres of land in the Highlands and his very own castle, probably wasn't claiming Castle benefit from the local council. Oh, did I mention his private army? He's got one of those too. He was the then Duke of Atholl and ruled his fiefdom from his lands around Blair Atholl in Scotland. A nicer feudal duke you couldn't hope to meet. Like any good Scotsman he had been educated in England and came to the party as the archetypal "Fa,fa,fa" English toff. He stood over six feet tall and wore his Savile Row tweeds with style. There was one problem for television: he had no chin. He did indeed look a dead ringer for the original chinless wonder. The director, Ian Taylor and I liked him a lot but both sadly agreed that, however hard we tried, he was going to come across on prime-time telly as a twit – Upper Class Twit of the Year. He was a definite contender for the Monty Python title.

We met His Grace at the drawing room in his forbidding-looking castle. The Scots didn't ponce about with mini-Versailles or Loire valley phantasmagoria. If your castle didn't have enormous blank walls and all the grace of a medieval Maginot Line, it just wasn't up to snuff. His butler was, satisfyingly, called Snape and seemed to have missed the finer points of his trade. He brought us enormous whiskies in lager glasses to stave off the Highland chill and we settled down to plan our filming. The Duke's land was mostly tended by tenant farmers. He would make a visit to one of his tenants for us to film. Yes, the private army would turn out in full, kilted glory for the BBC. And finally, our visit had coincided with the annual pibroch, where Highland pipe bands competed in Blair Atholl castle. To us, the Metropolitan elite and *Guardian* readers from London this all looked most promising. First, the tenant farmer:

Venue: a field on the Atholl estate, Scotland

Dramatis personae: His Grace, the Duke of Atholl, a bunch of "heeland coos" and Johnny, the tenant farmer.

It's a day for the green wellies as we step out into Johnny's fields.

"Good morning, Your Grace" says Johnny, just stopping short of tugging his forelock and bowing.

"Morning, Johnny". Some ersatz Archers scripting ensues about weather and yields and new birthing techniques, as the Duke surveys his flock with Johnny.

"That's a fine looking cow over there by the stockade, Johnny".

"That cow is a heifer Your Grace".

Oh dear, you just know that, back in his London Club, the Duke would have no trouble distinguishing between a MacCallan and a Laphroig, but the finer points of stock breeding seem to have passed him by. Nonetheless, the Duke is unfailingly polite and considerate to those in his employ and exhibits all the best traits of a feudal monarch. We return to a fine lunch of Aberdeen Angus beef and more of Snape's lager pints of whisky. It will not have passed you by that a great deal of Scotland's greatest export has been consumed by all and sundry during our first day at

Atholl Castle, and there is no way that this trend is about to change, since tonight's pibroch is being sponsored by Grant's whisky.

The scene was quite splendid in the castle's baronial hall. The candles flickered against the high, vaulted ceiling. The pipes were skirling away in the background like so many Formula One thoroughbreds, pawing the ground in their paddocks. The audience in full Highland evening dress, His Grace dispensing his hospitality and hot and cold running Grant's whisky on tap for the thirsty Highlanders and the equally thirsty London film crew. The stage is empty, expectant. Onto it strides a figure who might as well have "Metropolitan Elite" stamped on his forehead. He is dressed entirely in black, from designer T-shirt and jeans to the latest black patent leather winkle-pickers. Standing alone on this stage he produces a light meter and balletically bends his back and holds the meter up to gauge the ambient light. Is this spectre a guest appearance by Nureyev? No. This is our cameraman, reinforcing the image that there are English ponces among the elegantly-dressed but hairy-arsed Highlanders awaiting the first serious notes of the pibroch. At a pibroch you do spend a lot of time waiting. The Highland Pipes are delicate instruments, despite their apparent crudity to the soft southern ear. You must wait until they have fully warmed up. This involves a great deal of wailing and screeching and skirling before each performance begins. The problem is that the warm-up sounds just about the same as the performance. You just cannot make the transition from limp-wristed Hampstead liberal to muscle bound pipes' aficionado in just one night. We took a chance and filmed anyway. There were compensations that noisy night, not least a vat of Grant's whisky round every corner.

The scene shifts to exterior, night time. We have said our farewells and are backing the large Peugeot estate camera car out of the piazza in front of the Castle. Unfortunately we are not aware that the piazza is raised above ground level and we back the car's rear wheels over the edge in dramatic and noisy fashion. An agglomeration of clan kilts and hairy legs is required to hoist Hampstead back onto its Highland perch. We leave, not with a bang, but a whimper.

Perambulations

It is my proud boast that I never had a desk at the BBC. I didn't want or need a desk, because most of my productive time was spent in Workington, Washington or Waikiki. All right, mostly Workington. On *Nationwide* the editor called us the Border Barons. The editor had a Big Desk from which he dispatched his yeoman troops to disparate tranches of the Kingdom. We went ravaging and pillaging for stories, both serious and silly and, from time to time returned to his Court to lay our booty at his feet.

For me, the life of the travelling hack had moved from perambulations through Geordieland to trips to every corner of the British Isles. Later still it would take in the whole globe. I was not the first. A hero of mine is James Cameron, who captured it all decades ago when he was the doyen of foreign correspondents. Here he is in his great book *Point of Departure*:

"Reporters' lore is full of such things: correspondents' archives are full of cables instructing them to take taxis from Khartoum to Johannesburg; demanding weekend coverage from Patagonia of the man in Trinidad. It was my own speciality; for years I had laboured at the whims of a charming and travelled executive whose official conception of the world, nevertheless, was the terrestrial globe he kept on his desk, a thing the size of a grapefruit; from this he was able to demonstrate incontrovertibly that there was no place on the earth's surface that was more than five inches from any other. This godlike attitude caused his principal minions to dart madly from country to country, from continent to continent, indeed from hemisphere to hemisphere, spinning through the airways, burning up the roads, queuing up for visas, wiring home in greater and greater desperation for more varieties of currency with which to pay for their fares, their ham sandwiches, their bottles of whisky. And always, as they stumbled exhausted from the place in Bangkok, the cable announcing that their destination was Hong Kong; the arrival in Cairo for the inevitable re-routing to Damascus; the brooding knowledge as they touched down in Durban that they would be told the story was in Algiers".

My canvas, for now, was much smaller; the demands from London though often just as daft.

Among a kaleidoscope of black, vinyl sofas, bad tea and squelchy carpets and, by contrast posh offices with Meissen china and elegant PAs a few days stand out. This particular day began with a rare visit to the House of Lords. There is always something special about entering the Palace of Westminster, where you feel a cloak of power envelope you. But we were not to sit with Lord Denning inside the great chamber of the Lords itself. Instead we perched precariously on the narrow red benches outside, where his Lordship would meet lesser beings like ourselves. We talked over the rights and wrongs of the forthcoming Police and Criminal Evidence Act, which we were investigating for *Panorama*. As we were leaving the House through St. Stephen's Gate I remembered that there was a pay phone in a lobby on the left. Susan and I had been negotiating to buy a lovely old farmhouse near Oxford. In a quiet village, Old Upper Farm in Woodeaton had six bedrooms, five reception rooms and sat in half an acre of gardens. Poor, young couples today struggling to get on the property ladder, look away now. We had bid £125,000 for it. I duly phoned the agent, yes, we had been accepted. We were to live in Upper Farm for twenty-eight years.

I said to the director, Peter Ceresole, "I'm buying you lunch because it's your birthday and I've just bought a three hundred year old farmhouse." We found a hostelry on our way to our next interview in Deptford and I plied Peter with cheap champagne. He doesn't normally drink, so was a bit tiddly after just a glass. The flat in Deptford was not quite as grand as the Palace of

Westminster but we were greeted warmly by the owner, a flamboyant West Indian with an ample belly and a wooden leg. I am not making this stuff up. The radical lawyer had the pinched unsmiling look of a man permanently campaigning and permanently losing. It didn't matter, my friend with the wooden leg had taken a bit of a shine to me and said: "I like you man, you have to share a drink with me" he said, reaching around the back of an MFI unit and producing a tall, thin bottle of evil looking green liquid with a plant growing inside it. The shot I took by-passed my stomach entirely and went straight into my brain. Call me naïve if you will but it was only then that I realised the plant must be marijuana. Thankfully, Peter had settled for a cup of tea so his utter depravation after the champagne lunch could be avoided. I had another couple of shots and, being unused to drugs, I became very giggly. Our final appointment was at the Old Bailey to interview a human rights lawyer. She was austere and unsmiling and must have wondered why the BBC man kept giggling. Ah, the highs and lows of life on the road.

I loved the sheer variety that life offered. Another filming day, this time for *Panorama* began in Cadiz beside the US Naval Base. I had always resented the people who regarded my foreign trips as going on holiday. My director, Dave Rowley, however, really did think he was on holiday at the licence fee payers' expense. I should add that we only used the licence fees from rich people, never from little old ladies.

"A high today of thirty-two, a low of twenty-five. You all have a nice day." The US army radio implored us. We drove back from America into Spain and headed for Gibraltar. Dave particularly liked "holidays" in Spain, because he was a great gourmet so we had to stop at a roadside tapas bar to refuel. In Scotland you would have called this emporium a "Johnny Aw Things", a general purpose store serving this one-horse town. Amid the spread of tapas dishes Ford radiators and exhaust systems hung from the walls and detergent bottles mixed with the Carlos brandy and the

44

San Miguels. Subliminally, I was writing an Alan Whicker report for the marvellous old *Tonight* programme. Whicker is strolling down the dusty, deserted street of San Erewhon. Cue Whicker drawl and piece to camera: "here in the swirling dust of San Erewhon you might be wondering how the natives manage to survive and get their food and provisions. Well, the answer lies here behind the unprepossessing façade of the one shop in town: "Tapas Terrifico". (Whicker enters through the bat-wing doors – Lime Grove sound recordists will add some Sergio Leone music back in London.) Whicker, in his Gieves and Hawke suit, saunters to the bar as if he were at the Casino in Monte Carlo: "a gin and tonic and a Ford Cortina radiator, por favor." I was brought up on Alan Whicker's reports and I know how it would have gone on: "a bottle of Sangria and a litre of Flash Extra Strong", "a pack of toilet rolls and a San Miguel". Final shot of Whicker staggering back up the dusty road, laden down with exhaust systems, bog rolls and a ton of spare parts.

We ate some very good tapas and headed off for Gibraltar. It was one of those regular occasions when the Spanish Government gets fed up with three hundred years of British occupation of Gibraltar and throws all their toys out of the pram, closing the border between Algeciras and the Rock. We have come armed with an important looking missive from Her Majesty's Foreign & Commonwealth Office requesting our swift admittance to the colony. The Spanish put us in a prison cell and, three hours later we are allowed to cross the border and enter England in the 1950s. We filmed all the touristy sights: the English-style shops, the British pubs and the British Bobbies on the beat. Then to Government House to watch the Changing of the Guard. Just across the road the Gibraltarians have kindly placed a pub, the Angry Friar, so we were forced, naturally to go in there for a couple of pints of Guinness.

We negotiated our way back through Spanish Customs. No jail cell this time presumably because the more Brits they could get off the Rock the better. We headed for Puerto Banus, a small port town the Spaniards were busy trying to transform into Monte Carlo. From the quayside it looked quaint, with row upon row of white, stucco buildings and red-tiled roofs piled on top of each other. When you walked around the back of this ancient agglomeration, however, it turned out to be nothing more than a façade with stage props holding it up. It reminded me of a family holiday we had recently taken with Mick and Heather Dutfield in California. As we travelled around the Universal lot in our "Glam tram" the vacuous American guide said: "If you look down into the valley you can see the facades of Wild West towns and other filming locations. Façade is a French word meaning the front of". On to the glitzy bay of Puerto Banus and an array of restaurants from all over the world. Dave and I chose an Indian emporium and settled down to King Prawn Jalfrezi and a Tarka Dhal and pondered on a day that had taken us from America to Spain to Britain and back to Spain and Delhi. That was the kind of day that Dave really enjoyed. He truly felt on holiday. However, there was a downside. We had toured the length and breadth of the country from the ETA terrorist conflict in the Basque country to the conflict over Gibraltar and we had interviewed the Spanish Prime Minister, Felipe Gonzalez. When we served up this delicious confection to the editor of *Panorama*, Peter Ibbotson declared it the biggest Eton Mess he had ever seen. I didn't mind the mess bit but the suggestion that I had been to Eton really rankled. I have never met a nice Etonian. It was only a few months later when I served up an excellent film about the Mafia in Sicily and America that Peter forgave me, describing the Mafia film as my apology for the Spanish mess.

The Mafia film was to become a problem in its own right. The family were on a skiing trip to Val d'Isere when I ran out of money, so I went to the bank to raise some funds on my Barclaycard. The snotty blonde handed the card back and said with a Gallic sneer: "Ils ont refuse." I had deliberately paid off my card before leaving home but reckoned without the Post Office workers going on strike. I went back to the chalet a broken man. My literary agent, the wonderful Jim Reynolds, rang me to say that I had just been offered a £40,000 advance for a book on the Mafia, called *The Confessions of Tomasso Buscetta*. I was stunned; this was way ahead of any advance I had received for the previous two books I had written. It also turned out be the most difficult book I had ever written. (A nice trusting English couple lent me eighty pounds, by the way, against my promised £40,000 and we got home still solvent. I did pay them back).

FREDDIE STARR ATE MY HAMSTER

I had six happy years on BBC *Nationwide*. We never reached the giddy heights of *The Sun* as exemplified by the front page headline above although my friend and colleague, John Stapleton, came close with his film about the skateboarding duck. We never did the Weather in Norwegian as *The Sun* editor, Kelvin Mackenzie, did in a subsequent TV show nor, of course did we have tits and bums on page three.

Yet *Nationwide* was *The Sun*. It had nightly ratings from ten to twelve million people. If modern commissioning editors could guarantee those figures they would sell their souls for it, if they had any souls. I recognise that there is now a much more fragmented market with hundreds of channels. The truth is that there is unmitigated rubbish on most of them and tiny audiences watching. But *Nationwide* offered plenty of silliness and, crucially, plenty of seriousness on social matters, politics and economics. It was our presenter, Sue Lawley, who hosted the programme that put Mrs Thatcher on the rack over the sinking of the Argentine warship the *Belgrano*. I helped to expose some shady characters around the Poulson scandal in the North East of England including a builder called Sid McCullough. When we finally caught up with

Sid, getting out of his car, he answered my questions with an extravagant V sign. I was disappointed but my producer, Brian, knew what to do. He froze the offending frame and reused it every time I mentioned Sid's name.

It was my first investigative piece for the programme but filmed in Geordieland, where I had been a local reporter for Tyne Tees and then BBC *Look North*. As a local reporter you get recognised all the time so as I went to buy some Christmas lights in a local store it was no surprise to be approached by a well-built young man who grabbed my arm and said: "Well, hello, Martin". I greeted him and made for the Christmas department. His grip on my arm tightened with all the grace of a nightclub bouncer: "Sid McCullough says he'll cut your balls off". I disengaged my arm and headed for the fairy lights. Merry Christmas indeed.

No doubt one of the highlights of my *Nationwide* career was playing the King of the Munchkins in the *Nationwide* pantomime. We decided that we needed some guest stars. So we phoned Dennis Healey, the Chancellor of the Exchequer in Harold Wilson's Cabinet. He agreed to appear on one condition: that he be allowed to play the piano.

Sue Lawley was a lovely Dorothy and Professor Brian McKenzie of the London School of Economics and a regular contributor to the programme, selling us the elixir of life-giving economics, was the Wizard behind the curtains pedalling like mad to keep the whole incredible fiction on the road. The irony of the situation at that time in the late seventies was not entirely lost on us. Out there in Britain there was economic chaos as the unions failed to collect our rubbish or bury our dead. The Chancellor behind the curtain in Number 11 was indeed pedalling like fury on a rickety bicycle between the IMF and the Gnomes of Zurich. In the benign universe of *Nationwide*, he was just playing the piano.

MORE FOOL ME

ike any decent magazine programme *Nationwide* observed
significant dates and anniversaries. One of my favourites
was always April Fool's Day, when we were released from
the normal constraints of truth. Bob Wellings had noticed the
new building on his way into work; it was a rather grand power
station but distinguished by arched windows which appeared to
be upside down. So, we turned it into the Upside-down Library.
We showed pictures of sprinklers in the carpet tiles on the floor
and electric points which were clearly upside-down. My favourite
quote was an interview with one of our researchers Di Milward
who was posing as a librarian. "The worse thing of the lot is that
the books keep falling off the shelves', she said dolefully. We, the
champions of justice, set out to investigate this blatant waste of
tax payers' money. We 'discovered' that the architect had copied
his drawings the wrong way up and the builder had done what the
drawings required. My next door neighbour at the time, Roger
Hingley, was actually a chartered surveyor but more importantly
he had a flamboyant Alfa Romeo and was very happy to play the
errant architect. We lived in a lovely country lane in Oxfordshire
with a ford running across it. He made his escape in the Alfa and

I ran after him shouting questions and sticking a microphone through his car window. He splashed at speed into the ford and was gone. At the end of the film we cut back to Michael Barrett in the studio and as he was back referencing the film the studio director flipped his image upside-down. Only a fool would have thought that the upside-down library was real. Several of them phoned up the BBC switchboard asking where and when they could visit the upside-down library.

The following year we had somehow to top the Library April Fool. My friend and director, Ken Stephinson, had found an idyllic spot in Northumberland called the Lady's Well. Ken and I decided that if we bestowed a magic quality on the well we could make our April Fool Film. We decided that the magic well could cure baldness. It had no effect on the natives already living there but bald men who had moved in, we asserted, had gradually been restored to full heads of hair. Time for BBC makeup to join our team. Jenny Shirgore was a senior makeup artist in London more used to powdering the heaving bosoms of costume drama and rouging the cheeks of duchesses. Jenny travelled to Northumberland and set to with her make-up box and yards of false hair. Her first subject was our assistant cameraman, Howard who had very thin blond hair. She slicked this down until he looked practically bald – the "before" bald shot. Then she turned him into what I can only describe as a Greek god with long flowing flaxen locks and a long Moses beard. Howard was delighted with his new dominant appearance – the "after" shot. I made an initial appearance with my already receding hairline. During my next piece to camera I looked, courtesy of Jenny, a bit hairier and so it continued throughout the film until the final piece to camera in the local pub in Holiwell. Not only did I now look like a werewolf but Jenny had made up all the local drinkers around me in an equally hirsute manner. I curled my werewolf hand around my pint glass saying something about the magic baldness cure available here in Northumberland. On April 1ˢᵗ this all seemed a bit of a jape. However, on subsequent days in early April the tabloids reported that two and a half thousand people had been to the well with all sorts of containers to collect the magic water. The secretaries at *Nationwide* were receiving dozens of calls each day from desperate baldies who wanted information on where to go for their cure. I turned from hero to zero in those few days for having raised the hopes of these poor men who clearly cared so much. All I can say in mitigation is that I am now a slap head myself. Ah, the power of television.

The seeds of spoof film-making had been sown a few years beforehand with a film that David Pritchard and I made in the north-east for *BBC Look North*. David was a film editor keen to become a film director. He came up with a wonderfully ridiculous script maintaining that *Look North* had discovered a Nazi sympathiser Eva von Hofgarten living in Cullercoats, a seaside resort near Newcastle. It turned out that Eva had been Adolf Hitler's housekeeper at Berchtesgarten, Hitler's countryside retreat in Bavaria during the war. It was a ludicrous idea that Hitler's ex housekeeper would talk to us, nearly as daft as choosing to retire to Cullercoats. She could have gone to Rio like the rest of them, for goodness sake.

We could not film the housekeeper's face for security reasons (not to mention the fact that she was being played by David wearing a wig and my wife's cardigan). We filmed the all-revealing interview in my sitting room in Jesmond with the camera pointing over Eva's shoulders and myself in full vision asking the questions. Behind me on the wall we had tacked up a very tasteful poster of a fierce-looking storm trooper under the words 'Der Seig Wird Unser Sein'. Eva/David talked about everyday life in Hitler's hilltop lair and told one particularly affecting story:

"Hitler was such a kind man. I remember one day he came back from the woodlands near Berchtesgarten. He was carrying a tiny little bird with a broken wing. 'Eva' he cried, 'Eva bring me some milch, milch.' He fed the milk to the little wounded bird and I swear there was a tear in his eye. Later on he came back to check on the little bird and, accidentally, he stood on it. Adolf was very upset. He was such a kindly man". When Eva tried to leave after the interview she was arrested by the local police (real police doing us a favour). She was frogmarched to a police car and driven away. It was David's first directing job and it was as inspiring as was his portrayal of Hitler's housekeeper.

Once the furore over the spoof story and the collusion of the local police with the BBC had died down David decided to apply for a place on the Beeb's Film Director Course. The film he decided to make as his magnum opus was a re-run of "Hitler's Housekeeper". He could not play himself in the role of Eva and he came up with the ambitious idea that he would ask Irene Handel to play the part instead. Back in the 1970s Irene Handel had become famous in Britain as a comic actress, appearing as the wife of Peter Sellers' shop steward in *I'm all right, Jack* and many other Ealing comedies of the time. Her agent was rather dismissive of young David's request. David, nonetheless, begged the agent to put the proposition to Irene. She said "Well, dear, if it's for a young man trying to make his way I'll do it for nothing". She played the part and David, in due course, became a fully-fledged film director at the Beeb.

There is a delightful circularity about this story because David Pritchard went on to direct several series of films with Keith Floyd and Rick Stein. Every other celebrity chef should be eternally grateful to Pritchard for his creation of a new genre of cookery programmes. I too am grateful, for these days scanning the daytime schedules, it is such a relief to watch such well-crafted films which are more than just cookery programmes – Floyd is always struggling with the history surrounding his worldwide travels and Stein is always searching the literature and the culture of whichever country he is cooking in. When you look at the wasteland which is most of daytime television it is always a pleasure to watch one of David's films. I hope he negotiated a good repeat fee with the cable channels. When you next see Floyd in Africa or Rick Stein in Indonesia please remember that it all began in my sitting room in Newcastle forty years ago.

REWIND

I n 1969 I emerged from Caius College Cambridge, swathed in
graduation gown and went straight to the Pye Electronics
factory, where I operated a swing press for £13.00 a week. I
had been summoned by the Nat West bank manager in King's
Parade who berated me for my £11.00 unauthorised overdraft. He
wanted to know whether I was going to carry on as a feckless
wastrel or whether I had any plans for self-advancement and,
more importantly, when I would be able to pay off the vast debt I
owed the bank. I explained that my ambition was to go into
television (rather like Miss World wanting to travel around the
globe). I told him that I was already making a start in television by
helping to make TV sets at the Pye Factory in Cambridge. My
wages would eliminate the overdraft in a week or so given that, in
those days, I could live on one pound and ten shillings a week. He
seemed satisfied that this ne'er do well sitting opposite him was at
least prepared to make an effort to pay off his overdraft.

When I reached the Pye Factory it turned out that I would
not be making TV sets but rather police radios which, given my
subsequent legal problems over *Rough Justice*, was just a touch
ironic. I was a whiz with the swing press. It was designed to drill

rivets through the back plate of the car radio. I discovered that if I swung the arm of the press at exactly the right speed I had time to remove the back plate and insert a new one before the swing press returned on its trajectory. I was soon churning out the product faster than anyone else on the production line. In a mirror image of Ian Carmichael in *I'm alright Jack* my super-efficiency was not appreciated by my fellow workers and, once my horrendous overdraft was paid off I quit the grubby surrounds of the Pye factory for the glamour of television. To be more precise I swopped to the Wallfoot Commercial Hotel near Carlisle.

Through a contact of my Dad's I had arranged two week's work at the second smallest of the ITV companies, Border Television. The job was basically emptying wastepaper baskets and being a general dogsbody in the newsroom. I expropriated some Border Television notepaper and wrote to the Programme Controller of Tyne Tees Television in Newcastle. My letter began 'I am currently working for Border Television…' which was true. At the end of my second week with Border they gave me a screen test where I had to interview one of the other reporters on a fictitious story. I was so nervous about keeping the interview flowing that I kept nodding and saying 'yes' throughout; despite this, Border promised me the chance of a job when one came up in the future. The commercial travellers at the Wallfoot hotel were sad at my departure. They couldn't afford to drive to the local pub and risk losing their licence on the return trip. I had been a faithful and sober chauffeur to the men who travelled in everything from ladies' make-up to Ambrosia creamed rice.

After a brief sojourn in London where I shared a flat with Frank Sinatra's bassist, Daryl Runswick and Julie Covington who sang the original Evita song 'Don't cry for me Argentina' and I played a Nelson-age sailor at the Boat Show (don't ask) I set off for Newcastle.

A BONNY LAD

To this day I can still remember the thrill of driving up the A1 (M), past where the Angel of the North now stands dreaming of the fame and riches before me. I had been told by a theatrical agent that I should expect at least £1,800 a year as a reporter on independent television. When I met the news editor there was no prolonged discussion. He said; "You'll be earning the National Union of Journalists minimum wage of £1106 a year". There did not appear to be any debate on this matter and, naturally, I accepted.

All newsrooms are mad, some are madder than others. The usual suspects were in evidence: the drunken Scottish news editor, the sports editor who knew everything about Newcastle United and nothing about anything else, the keen young thing (that was me) and the aging thespian in the sheepskin coat. This was the cast of *Drop the Dead Donkey* sprung into life. There was also one sane reporter called Geoff Druett and, for a time, the two of us shared digs in a let in Jesmond. I was in the attic, he was in the basement. I was seconded to the aging thespian, Roddy, who would show me how to operate on the road. Together we revealed the truth about the broken paving stones in Gosforth and the dreadful disruption that would soon be caused by the construction of the Newcastle Metro. By the time we reached our third story, a young girl who had won a local dressage competition 'My Big Day' had arrived. Roddy let me loose on an expectant Geordie public. Sadly, I cannot remember every word of my first piece to camera; I can only recall the sheer terror of writing it, remembering it and delivering it to camera – much more difficult than simply winning a dressage competition. I was learning. From Roddy I learnt how to sweet-talk nervous Geordies to give interviews to Tyne Tees *Today at Six*, from Geoff Druett, a vicar's son no less, I learnt how to fiddle my expenses, an invaluable lesson that I would refine into an art form in subsequent years at the BBC. Anyway, I must have been doing something right because I rapidly became the co-presenter of *Today at Six* alongside the statuesque figure of Charlotte Allen. Fortunately, with us both sat behind the presentation desk you could not tell that she was several inches taller than I was. It worked in the studio but proved a considerable embarrassment when we were recognised in the streets of Newcastle. I shudder now to think of this callow, college boy interpreting the world for the Geordie audience. I knew nothing other than how to disguise the fact that I knew nothing. Had the *Today at Six* audience wanted an intricate theory about the structure of *Macbeth* or a thesis on Samuel Beckett then I was their man. Discussing the intricacies of Newcastle United's four-four-two system was well beyond me. Indeed I still don't know what I just wrote. I survived well enough though to get a phone call from the rival programme, BBC *Look North*. It hasn't happened very often in my working life but getting a job offer out of the blue is a great feeling. I went to the News Editor at Tyne Tees, told him the BBC wanted me to join them and asked for a pay rise to £2000 a year. They offered me £1900 and I turned them down. The BBC were offering me a guarantee of £2500 and the promise of even more earnings from all or any of the Corporation's many

Current Affairs programmes. Ah, the bravado of youth: I was giving up a secure staff job to become a freelance, Susan and I were about to be married and we had no savings. (Susan reminds me, rather forcefully, that she brought £200.00 into this marriage.)

I did, however, have the beautiful and redoubtable Susan. As our affair at Cambridge had blossomed I delivered myself of the following pomposity; "Look, I like you very much but you must understand that I've got Finals coming up and I'm playing the lead in the Marlowe Society main production. I really can't afford to get tangled up in some love triangle or you going off playing the field. So, if you'll agree not to go out with anyone else, I'd like you to be my girlfriend." Sue looked me straight in the eye and said: "No". A couple of weeks later, just as I was realising what a prat I'd been, she turned up at my room overlooking King's Parade. She was wearing one of those narrow pelmets of cloth that in the seventies passed for a skirt. Looking at this beautiful young woman silhouetted against the neo-classical elegance of the Senate House I now realised I had been a king sized prat to have risked losing her. Mind you, she didn't know that she'd just given up a boyfriend who was to become the director of *Shakespeare in Love*.

Sue and I were now "an item" or going steady, as my parents' generation would have said. For the next two years she had to trust me amid the flesh pots of Newcastle, while I had to hope that she would stick with me despite the allure of the rarefied air of Cambridge and the stark fact that in those days, as I mentioned above, there were ten eager young men for every single woman. We survived and after she had graduated she would come up to my damp little bed-sit as often as she could. On one occasion, just after she had cooked a splendid Hungarian goulash in my squalid kitchen I asked her to marry me. This time she said yes.

By the time we were married in August 1971 we had moved into a nice two-bedroom flat in Kenton Bar just south of Newcastle

Airport and discovered that I was one of Nature's freelances. In the first year at *Look North* I earned a staggering £6000. To give today's generation some sense of the scale of things in 1971 the Kenton flat had cost £3800. A year later we sold it for £5600 and bought a lovely house in the posh bit of Jesmond. Apart from my retainer at the Beeb I would sell the best local stories to the *Today* programme, *The World at One*, *P.M.* and *The World Tonight*, even occasionally national television. I remember saying to Sue that we would never be so rich again: high disposable income, no dependants and a very manageable mortgage. Sue agreed, particularly when we bought a top of the range Bang & Olufsen television and a B&O stereo in the same week.

My life has been full of crazy newsrooms and mad reporters some likeable, some not. I now entered the *Look North* newsroom and the usual cast of characters; the News editor who would shout and scream and eat chunks out of the news desk when the programme went wrong; the drunken old hack who once had a fit directly in front of me; and two deranged but delightful Irishmen. Towering over them all was the ample, impressive frame of Mike Neville. If I go back to Geordieland today and mention that I used to work for Tyne Tees and the BBC I'll get a shrug, if I say I used to work with Mike Neville I suddenly have their undivided attention. He was a consummate broadcaster who told me once over the inevitable large whisky that he used to be physically sick before every broadcast in his early days. By the time I arrived in the newsroom those days were long gone. You could have set off a bomb under Mike's presenter's desk and he wouldn't have blinked. He was trained by a machine, a telecine machine that was on its last legs and constantly breaking down. During one such crisis Mike reached down for the waste paper bin at his feet and, plonking it down on the desk he pulled out a sheaf of paper, smoothed it out and said: "Now for some late news".

He was a great broadcaster and colleague. His daily itinerary was well set: in his local pub for lunch; in the newsroom by 4.30, on air from 6.00 and then to hospitality for rather a lot of whisky, then to the BBC Club for pints of "Heavy", then more whisky. On the rare occasions that I tried to stay with him I never lasted longer than 9.00 and Sue was not amused when I got home.

Mike was a far cry from his opposite number on Tyne Tees *Today at Six*. Earl Bailey was an impossibly good looking Australian. What he may have lacked on the whisky front he made up for on the Sheila front. The girls were queuing up to savour this blonde from Bondi Beach. It was this Oz Adonis I had to interview when I originally auditioned for the Tyne Tees job. He sat there in the interviewee's chair as if he'd been born in a TV studio. He was the essence of cool; sat opposite him was the essence of a quivering wreck. This was, after all, only my second ever attempt at TV interviewing. I knew I had done well writing and presenting my own script, but I knew that a lot would depend on this interview. As I quivered in my seat I had to redress the balance. I leant over towards Earl and tapped him reassuringly on the knee. "Don't worry Mr Bailey, just try to relax." Suddenly I felt more relaxed and the interview went well. I got the job. Later on at a company party in Seahouses an enormous fight broke out. Earl's wife had discovered he was having an affair (just the one?) and was screaming that she was going to do dreadful things to his private parts. She came running to me for help and I could see that I was going to end up in a fight with The Bondi bombshell. In other words I was going to be punished for what he'd been doing with those same private parts. In the words of the great Tabloid Tricksters; "I made an excuse and left".

That's enough of Earl's life with women. What about mine?

MY LIFE WITH WOMEN – ON FILM

Margaret

B ack in the seventies not many global stars beat a track to the North East. When Margaret Lockwood came to Newcastle to play the lead at the Theatre Royal, it was big news and I got the job of interviewing her on the stage. The one condition was that we did not do any BCUs (Big Close-Ups) on Miss Lockwood who, to put it charitably, was no longer in the first flush of youth. She treated me like a bad smell that had drifted onto her stage, totally ignoring me until Jim, the hairy-arsed cameraman, said "turn over". The sound of the camera turning over prompted a sea change in her personality. She was now my best friend and gave me a charming interview. As soon as Jim shouted "cut" her normal rude, surly service was resumed and she was sweeping off stage, when Jim stepped over to her and said: "Divn't worry yourself, hinny, I've kept the camera very wide, so as we cannot see yer wrinkles". God Bless, Jim, he'd recovered some of my dignity.

Marlene

My second encounter with a lady of a certain age took place in Birmingham, where I was waiting for the hotel lift. When the doors opened, there was Marlene Dietrich, dressed in a striking tomato-red trouser suit, looking, I was delighted to note, very sultry. For some reason the lift stopped at every floor on the way to the lobby, while I tried to think of something to say. After all, it's not every day that you share a lift with a living legend. As the lift kept on stopping I realised that what I had taken for alluring sultriness was in fact increasing impatience. Tragic Wagnerian sighs began to emanate from my travelling companion. Eventually, the famous chanteuse erupted: "Zis iz like ze bloody milk train". Not being able to think of something witty to say I mumbled my agreement, the lift arrived in the lobby and she swept away. That was my interview with Marlene in its entirety.

Dolly

Don't say that I don't go to exotic locations for my celebrity interviews. Birmingham one day, Ipswich the next, in fact an old cinema in Ipswich where I was to interview Dolly Parton. At least the sex symbols were getting younger. Dolly was famous for her Country & Western singing and her impossible Barbie Doll figure. Two good reasons for making a film as the lighting man was quick to point out. Dolly suffered from OES, obstructive entourage syndrome. All the people around her who derived a degree of power from their proximity to her fame were uniformly horrid, doing everything they could to deny you access to the star. When I met Dolly herself though she and her spectacular embonpoint were warm and welcoming. The cameraman and his assistant, who was also his wife were a regional BBC crew who looked as though they were both drawing their pensions. Their film gear was pretty ancient too. I was horrified to see that he had fixed an old chunky lanyard mike around Dolly's neck, so nestling between two of the most famous breasts in the world was a big ex-MOD microphone. His idea of lighting the star was equally unsubtle. He bunged a big "blonde", a dazzling 2KW light, straight in front of her. This was not so much "sculpting with light" as sledge-hammering with light. I changed the microphone, salvaged what I could from the lighting set-up and the interview went really well, because Dolly had done dozens of promotional interviews from Dusty Hook, Nevada, to the Gaumont, Ipswich and she was very good at it. She and her OES went off for lunch and the OAPS and I went back to BBC Norwich.

Monica

If I now went on to tell you that my next famous woman encounter was with Madonna or Princess Diana you might not be surprised. But when I tell you that it was with Monica Lewinsky and the venue was my own back garden in Oxfordshire I think you'd raise an eyebrow or think that I had lost my marbles. We had a bunch of predominantly Jewish friends in Highgate, North London, who met regularly at a salon presided over by the ultimate Jewish Momma, Gay Keogh, and her Catholic husband, Mike. We were invited to their son Benjy's wedding to an American girl, Christina. On the day the bride looked lovely as brides are supposed to be, but Christina had done herself no favours by inviting her college friend, Monica Lewinsky to the wedding, who was of course the woman everyone was looking at. The wedding took place in Benjy's old Oxford College, New College. The Chapel there has two sets of pews facing each other like the adversarial lay-out of the House of Commons. Susan and I were on the groom's side as was Monica. On the Opposition benches sat a number of aged Republicans, the sort of men who ought to say "harrumph" a lot and probably do. Their baleful eyes kept swivelling from the ceremony to Miss Lewinsky. You could almost hear them muttering "That's the woman who despoiled the Oval Office." Monica smiled bravely through it, – I imagine by this stage she had a PHD in bravely smiling through.

Since our Highgate friends were all in Oxford on Saturday we threw a party for them on the Sunday at Old Upper Farm. I am glad to say that our Upper Farm parties had become legendary over the years, but when Monica Lewinsky came up the drive this one was forever to be remembered. We welcomed her in and gave her a drink. Next door, in the study our daughter, Annabel asked "Is that who I think it is?" Within seconds she was phoning all her friends: "Monica Lewinsky is standing in my kitchen," she screamed. Within what seemed like minutes the drive was full of Peugeot 205s, the car of choice for well-heeled young women of the time. Annabel and her friends were only a few years younger than Monica and they got on really well. When I told my friends about meeting Monica the first question was always "What is she like?" I said that she was exactly like my daughter, except that Annabel was not called Monica Lewinsky. The second question was usually: "What on earth did you talk about?" assuming that the one thing for which she was famous you couldn't talk about at all. I had had a few drinks and so my first question when we finally talked was about the ethics of the Press. To my surprise she was sanguine about her whole media experience and when I said "You've become a media commodity" she more or less laughed it off. I had recently affected a liking for large, Cuban cigars and I was smoking a Montecristo no. 3, when chatting to Monica who, nonetheless, remained charming throughout and, it seemed to me, she appeared rather lonely.

Margaret again

I had met Monica just after the peak of her fame or notoriety; I first met Margaret Thatcher at the very moment of her triumph as she returned to her home in Flood Street, Chelsea as Britain's first female Prime Minister. I had been keeping watch in Flood Street all night, alongside the impossibly beautiful Anna Ford who was Thatcher-watching for ITN. Mrs Thatcher arrived at about four in the morning and I got the first interview. I have no recollection of what she said but it was one of those occasions where the fact of hearing her speak about her victory for the first time was more important than the text itself. It led the news coverage at 6.00am. I don't think I have ever seen anyone so tired. Everything she did was gruelling and the long, intense campaign was no exception. As I stood close to her that early morning she looked well-groomed and composed as ever but her skin seemed almost translucent with fatigue. She and Dennis disappeared into the Flood Street house and I swapped Chelsea for the exterior of No.10 to answer a swathe of questions like: "Martin Young is there for us this morning at 10 Downing Street. Martin, bring us up to date with all the details of what is happening there". You can't be honest and say: "Nothing actually. I'm standing here with hundreds of other journalists who like me know nothing but are busy making things up to satisfy their editors in Berlin or Buenos Aires". John Stapleton said to me once: "You do realise, Mart, don't you, that people like you and me are paid rather a lot of money for standing on street corners and talking about nothing for forty-five seconds" So I ad-libbed about nothing for the requisite time, hoping that the Downing Street cat might make a life-saving appearance. It didn't, which was just as well, since I didn't even know its name. After subsequent election victories it would have been much easier because by then she would have re-named the cat "Scargill" so that every night as Dennis clutched his post prandial brandy he could say to her: "Have you put the cat out?" and she could open the famous black door and kick Scargill out into the cold, wet night.

The next time I met Margaret Thatcher she was coming to the end of her premiership, though she famously didn't know it yet.

She was paying a State visit to the LBC studios in London and would be arriving during the time that Brian Widlake and I were on air presenting *The Midday News*. She appeared behind the glass in the control room while I was "talking to time". Time was 12.58.30, not a second more, not a second less. A lot of presenting could be done by a trained monkey but this really is a skill, ad-libbing while staring at the studio clock. When I looked at the clock all I could see, just beneath it was the famous Thatcher visage and I was the next one to be smiled at. But I was concentrating so hard that I didn't respond. I came out on time and the programme was over for another day. I looked back through the glass and saw the Thatcher scowl. As Francois Mitterrand said of Margaret: "She has the lips of Marilyn Monroe and the eyes of Caligula". I got the steely gaze of the power crazed Emperor and she turned away. Clearly I was not "one of us".

FROM LORD REITH TO THE LORDS OF MISRULE

My journey from the BBC to LBC had a kind of inevitability about it. In my final months at the Beeb I fronted *The Education Programme* which, let us be generous about it, was worthy, worthy but dull. I was consigned to Religious programmes for a while but it was made very clear to me that anything that smacked of serious journalism was not on offer. It was time to go. Two distinct types of people gravitated to LBC, young, fresh-faced kids on their way up and old, battered faces on the way down. I'll leave it to you to decide which category I fell into. I got the call to go to an interview from my glitzy agent, Annie Sweetbaum, while we, as a family, were on holiday at our modest studio apartment in Denia on the Costa Blanco. While I had been woefully under-employed at the Beeb, I had been earning money hand over fist in the commercial sector, making corporate videos for washing machines, computer companies, insurance firms, you name it. My son, Jonathan, said at the time: "Dad doesn't seem to do much but, when he does, he comes home with shed-loads of money". This chimed neatly with Jack Stilgoe's observation about his father, Dickey, who was pontificating about careers to one of Jack's friends. "You do realise" said Jack "that my Dad has never had a real job in his life." Well I was going for an interview now for a real job as a presenter at a relaunch of LBC, now under new management. The words relaunch and new management were to haunt the next six years. Because LBC was "a game of two halves". On one side were the presenters, Angela Rippon, Michael Parkinson, Andrew Neill and many others who made the actual broadcasting very professional and great fun, on the other side were the management who were all idiots. If you think I am being simplistic about the managers, – read on. The first Management cock-up burst upon us just a few weeks after I joined. The entire staff would have to account for themselves or be sacked. You can call it downsizing the head count, rationalising the workforce or letting people go, but there really is only one old Anglo Saxon term for it. The sack.

Philip Bacon was a slight, unprepossessing man seemingly devoid of talent, but he had power and he was one of those overweening elite I have met in all media organisations; Head of Rubber Bands and Allied Paper Clips. There was a financial flap on so the cry goes out: "Sack some troglodites, sack anybody except us." At the BBC you knew they were really in the deep doo-doo when the cry went out; "Deputy Heads must roll." The big bosses never feel the keen edge of the axe on the nape of their necks. I took my neck and the rest of me up the stairs, having been summoned by the Big Man. I vividly remember looking down at my stomach and seeing not a butterfly in sight. I felt no fear, nothing. Philip Bacon said immediately: "Don't worry (I wasn't worrying) your job is quite secure. We think you are one of our best broadcasters. Carry on with the lunchtime news. Well done." Thus endorsed by the Head of R.B & APC, I made my way back down the managerial stairs. I looked again at my stomach. Nothing. No elation, no emotion and I thought to myself that is great, I've cracked it. They can't hurt me again. It was a moment of pure release. Back to the Dickensian dungeon that was the newsroom in those days. Although Fleet Street had now followed the great God, Murdoch, to the Wapping swamps, LBC's studios still sat in Gough Square just behind the Street of Shame itself. El Vino's and the Olde Cheshire Cheese were within staggering distance and Dr. Johnson's house was cheek by jowl with us modern day digital scribblers in Gough Square itself. I reasoned that if I didn't visit the great Doctor's house in my first few days at LBC I might work there for years and never go. My main memory of my first visit was of the top floor, where there was a large chair for the good doctor's ample frame and a long, oak table. Compiling his innovative and idiosyncratic dictionary would involve him sitting in his large chair and barking his definitions to a phalanx of eager scribes, who would pile up the pages on the oak table. Returning to the LBC newsroom brought me back to earth with a bump. It contained all the usual suspects: the wild news editor for Independent Radio News, Vince McGarry, whose decibel count and expletive quotient would increase dramatically as the sensational story of the moment expanded exponentially. He had an enthusiastic Scottish sidekick who became unnaturally animated by murder and mutilation of all kinds. "Oh, fuck me" he would shout to us all, "I've got a great wee murder for my bully (bulletin). I hope it's a gory one. Plenty of blood for my next bully". Traditionally, those who didn't fit naturally within the Civil Service norms of the BBC had gravitated towards LBC. In due course this intake had formed into a mafia: the Godfather was the LBC Finance Editor, a very important job in a radio station that covered the financial decisions of the City of London. His consigliere was the blonde, perma-tanned Steve Kyte and the Enforcer was Peter Deeley, a vision in black leather who would arrive each day in his very butch Jeep, complete with Rally Cross headlights and black décor. Among the foot soldiers was a man who, allegedly, had his own dungeon in his suburban house, as you do. For a time this colourful crew produced the *Drive Time* show, presented by

Angela Rippon. Angela is a great trooper and works very hard at everything she does. She got on really well with the so-called "gay mafia" and became something of a gay icon herself, rather as Judy Garland did, having played Dorothy in the marvellous *Wizard of Oz.* (Following a group of gossiping old queens down the corridor one day they let me in on the gossip and declared me an honorary gay). That just about covers my new newsroom, apart from honourable mention for the High Tory cross-dresser who was the LBC news editor. I was quite confused by him to begin with, not with stories about him arriving at the studio in full ball gown, but with the endless stream of memos that came through my computer terminal every morning when I logged on. It took me a few days to work out that it was all rubbish, the product of a really sweet man but a strangely disturbed mind. My editor was Lawrie Douglas, – think of that famous photograph of Samuel Beckett and you're almost there. Lawrie had been a merchant seaman and had seen as much of the world as I had, albeit from a different angle. He was a very good producer, I was a decent writer and interviewer and radio is a sweet medium. It was a winning combination and *The Midday News* became a vehicle for good coverage of domestic politics and analysis of world events. Courtesy of Lawrie's address book we built up a fine cadre of correspondents from Anatole Kaletsky, the then economics editor of *The Times*, Peter Hennessey, the suave expert on all things parliamentary and constitutional, and Geoffrey Goodman, who seemed to have been writing about the trades union since Keir Hardie was a boy. They were all highly knowledgeable and great fun to know. Alongside them were some specialists from the various parts of the world that were busy shooting each other at any given time.

Over the years we worked together I interviewed most of the front bench in the last days of the Thatcher government and most of the Major government. Many of you may never have heard of these Colossi of their day or may regard them as historic figures. But make the lateral leap from these various nineties politicians, Yesterday's Men, to today's men and see how nothing changes.

For me, there were many high points. Ken Clarke (still alive and kicking) had recently been elevated to Chancellor of the Exchequer and his aides sent him round the studio tour to help flog off the next tranche of BT shares. His august appearance as a salesman was hedged around with rules. I was not allowed to ask him any questions other than those pertaining directly to the BT share sale. Ken's usual jovial tones came over the airwaves and I asked him two innocuous questions about BT. Then, remembering Rule One, I asked him about fifteen proper questions on the economy as a whole. Ken, of course took it all in his stride while, no doubt his aides were hopping from one well-shod foot to another. When I had finished the interview it fell to Lawrie to thank the Chancellor. A lesser politician might have objected to my cheek but Ken Clarke said "great stuff, haven't enjoyed myself so much in quite a while. Best interview this morning". One antagonist I was particularly frightened of was "The Chingford Skinhead", Norman Tebbit. His natural modus operandi was to get your head on the studio floor and then repeatedly stamp on it. Just once I did get the better of him by backing him into a corner about two completely contradictory statements he had recently made. There was simply no way out for him. I had backed him up to the end of a cul de sac. There was a brief pause and a chuckle and then he said; "That's a very good ball". More disturbing, but in a different, evangelical way was the then Chairman of the Tory party, Cecil Parkinson, Mrs Thatcher's blue-eyed boy. And, what eyes Cecil had. Mrs T's blue eyes were like the scythes on Boadicea's chariot, used to great effect to cut the balls off her ministers. Cecil's blue eyes were those of the believer who wanted you to join the True Path alongside him. It was as if Lawrie had invited a Jehovah's Witness into the studio. I remember how horrified my daughter was when a clean-cut young man with child in push chair knocked on our door at the farmhouse. "Good morning. I'm a Jehovah's Witness" he said. "Oh, no you're not". I said, closing the door. Annabel was appalled that I had just denied the man's very existence. Cecil however had been invited onto the premises and he was ever so keen to spread the word. In the middle of a long interview we needed to go to a commercial break, to sell sanitary towels or bog roll or something equally uplifting. This is normally a time for small talk and arse scratching, a tacit admission that we both know we are playing a tiny role in the Westminster game. Not with Cecil. He carried on with the searching eyes and the Party Line as if we were still on air. Most disturbingly of all Glynn, the driver who had brought Cecil to the studios took me back to Paddington in the afternoon. I asked what he'd been like in the car. Glynn described exactly the same experience that I'd had. The Chairman of the Tory Witnesses had not succeeded. Neither Glynn nor I signed up as true believers. The Tories, though, had no monopoly on stupidity. A woolly-headed Labourite, who was so unimportant I've forgotten his name, came to the LBC studio after an IRA killing because he had said that these people should be "taken out". I asked if he meant they should be killed by the State. He blustered, which I took to be a yes. I then went on to explore ways in which we might kill them. Should we revert to a shoot to kill policy? Should we let the crowd of decent people hang them from the lampposts in London and Belfast? A quick knife to the throat perhaps? He blustered some more and finally came up with the "something must be done" argument. He was looking like a complete fool and I could see the commercial break looming. What was I going to say to this twit by way of mitigation? I needn't have worried. "It's going really well, isn't it?" he said. I hurriedly agreed, thinking send me more numpties like this one, please. He was still bumbling and blustering away as I brought the interview to a close and we parted the best of friends. At least this idiot wasn't going to be Prime Minister but another great blusterer,

Gordon Brown, was. His blustering took the form of steam-rollering the interviewer. On one occasion he was doing this so blatantly that I was on the brink of saying, "Mr Brown it is customary in these interviews for me to get the chance of a second question". Sadly, I didn't. I'd forgotten Rule One and I immediately regretted it. At the same time, in the run-up to John Major's unlikely victory in 1992 I also got the chance on many occasions to interview Michael Heseltine. You couldn't lay a glove on Heseltine. He was at the peak of his intellectual and presentational skills. I only got close to bettering him once. He had come on to promote the Tory scheme for urban renewal and I caught him out with one of his own quotes which contradicted what he was now actually advocating. "Oh, it would be quite unfair to start trading our cheap little sound bites over such an important issue as the future of our major cities". I said, tongue firmly in cheek, "Oh, Mr Heseltine no one would ever accuse you of trading cheap little sound bites" and before I could go on to ask a question he said, "Good I'm glad we agree on that and he was off on a tour of Liverpool, Manchester and points north. It took me about twenty seconds to realise I had been conned by the Right Honourable Member for Henley, my own constituency in Oxfordshire.

It wasn't just politicians I had to deal with. People often used to ask me if I was ever caught out while doing live interviews. I used to struggle to find an example until I remembered the Cezanne Exhibition in London. One of the perks of the job was to go to the press previews of such events. Lawrie had lined up the erudite and often controversial art critic of the *Evening Standard*, Brian Sewell, to give his assessment of Cezanne, so I began confidently enough: "I thought the exhibition, which I was lucky enough to see yesterday was quite magnificent." But, before I could continue Brian cut in with his own question: "really?" he said with camp astonishment "and why on earth would you think that?" I realised that I had just been asked to sum up the life's works of one of the great impressionists of the twentieth century in front of a true critic. He was a mischievous man and he knew perfectly well where he had placed me and just how deeply he had placed me in it. I strove manfully to dig myself out. "Because of the sheer number of paintings stretching throughout his life and because he painted the Mont Sainte Victoire so many times you could see his development from conventional landscape to impressionism, to Cubism and laterally to an early kind of expressionism." Having acquitted myself reasonably well I thought it judicious to stop before I revealed the shallowness of my art appreciation.

"Very well," said Brian in a cursory manner. I felt like a first year student who had just had a successful supervision.

THE AVERAGE LISTENER

I have to confess that I am not at all tolerant of the "average listener's" complaint. In my view nobody who bothers to phone up a radio or television station is "average", they range from the self-important to the plainly deranged. Also Nature in all her wisdom has allowed us to evolve an extra limb, it's called a remote control. With it you can change channels. There is even an on/off switch. During one summer my then sixteen year old son, Jonathan was doing some work experience on various LBC programmes.

Lawrie and I were very busy during the morning finding enough material to fill the lunchtime show, so the extra work from Jonathan was really helpful. Lawrie could land him with the really difficult calls that would take a long time to connect, like calls to Sarajevo in the middle of the Bosnian war. Jonathan's job was to contact General Louis Mackenzie, who was the Canadian leader of the Allied forces in Bosnia. He tried the Sarajevo switchboard dozens of times saying "I want to speak to General Louis McKenzie. This is LBC Radio in London". He tried harder and harder until he sounded at least as important and demanding as Walter Cronkite. Eventually I heard his confident tone reduced to a whimper as he said "Oh, hello…er…General…we'd like to do an interview with you about the war. The interviewer will be (I could hear my son thinking "mustn't say my dad") Martin Young. I got my interview and Jonathan got congratulations from Lawrie and me. Jonathan moved to a new show working with a small, feisty and very bright woman called Jo Philips. She returned to the newsroom after her show to find Jonathan engaged in what had obviously been a long phone call with a complaining listener. Jonathan was saying all the right things about balance and fairness. He was a well-brung up lad, after all. Jo snatched the phone from Jonathan and said: "Fuck Off" before delicately replacing the handset.

Before you could say that again we were back to another round of sackings. One prat walked in from Reuters and sacked sixty human beings from an overall staff of just 163. He stood there in front of us cowering vassals and pledged "This is Reuters, one of the great names of journalism, and we are here for the long haul". Six months later they were gone, leaving behind them a trail of broken lives and shattered promises. Where do they find these people? This Reuters idiot who stood before us in his Crombie overcoat, did he keep his coat on while sacking half the workforce? Good God, we were even "rescued" at one point by Dame Shirley Porter. She had so clearly modelled herself on the Saintly Margaret that she summoned the great and the good to the LBC boardroom and declared her aim of becoming the Voice of Independent Radio in Britain. Today LBC, tomorrow the World. Among the glitterati was Tessa Sanderson who was lovely and bubbly and very good at throwing the javelin though quite what she knew about radio was not explained. More easily explicable was the arrival of David Dimbleby, the very essence of good, public service broadcasting, but what was he doing among this motley crew? David was clearly puzzled himself because he sought me out and suggested that we had lunch after the meeting. I had worked briefly with David on *Panorama*. I remember seeing him at Los Angeles Airport, with his head buried in a huge folder of research. I crept up and said in a matey sort of way "here, you're that bloke from the telly, aren't you?" I saw the look of pain as he shifted his gaze from his work to this oik who was accosting him. He was so relieved when he saw it was me. We settled down to a good, old-fashioned Lime Grove gossip in the buffet of LA International. I was on my way home with what I thought was going to be the greatest triumph yet for *Rough Justice*; David was on his way out to make a film to restore his reputation after a spat with the Beeb. Paradoxically, he triumphed with the film he was off to make and I died a terrible death with what proved to be my last ever *Rough Justice* film. Now, we both found ourselves in the warm embrace of Dame Shirley, albeit for a short time. At lunch, David wanted to know what life was like at LBC. I told him that a BBC colleague had phoned to wish me well at *The Midday News* and he had said: "have you got a good team around you?" I said "yes, he's terrific". Lawrie was terrific, he had, as I've said, an excellent contacts book and would work hard every morning setting up interviewees who would analyse the news of the day, while I would write most of the show. It was challenging, not to say scary some of the time. I told David that I would write a script about the latest Home Office initiative ending with the words: "I'm joined now by the Home Secretary, Michael Howard…." Those dots were important because they signified the fact that I had not had the time to prepare any questions and had no back-up team to do it for me. If the necessary information and quick thinking wasn't there in your head already you were going to be eaten alive by the sinuous Michael Howard QC. David was appalled. He said that when he had to interview Mrs Thatcher he and a dedicated team would spend three days plotting the course of the interview, trying to predict her responses and construct follow up questions to each possible answer. A few miles down the road at Number Ten Mrs Thatcher and her advisers would be doing the same thing. She would, presumably stop from time to time to run the country which was her day job. At one of Mrs Thatcher's election victories (in 1983 I think it was) I watched from the Outside Broadcast scanner in Downing Street as she settled in for her post-election interview with The Beeb's Grand Inquisitor, Robin Day. Both had, of course, been up all night. She looked ice cool and composed and sat down very slowly, every action like a studied Marcel Marceau mime. Very carefully she crossed her legs, held out one hand in front of her and placed it on her knee, then she held the other hand out in front and slowly laid it on top of the first. Satisfied with her pose, the head came up, the fearsome eyes lit up and she waited for her encounter with the great political interviewer. Robin arrived like a Bateman cartoon "the hack in a hurry". He rushed in looking like a badly-tied parcel, clutching a sheaf of notes and cuttings, seemingly tumbling around behind him in a maelstrom as he strode to his seat. The marble statue had not moved an inch.

DRAMA IN DOWNING STREET

Earlier I had been consigned to the wee small hours reporting on the doorstep of Number Ten, you know the bit where you speak as elegantly as you can about nothing for forty-five seconds and then hand back to David Dimbleby in the studio. On this occasion I was wittering on to a bank of cameras and crews waiting to do similar non-pieces for their respective networks. On these occasions, the crews are bored stiff while their camera lenses droop towards the ground. As I was talking live all the cameras came up fast to film something behind me which I couldn't see so I said: "something is clearly happening further along Downing Street, which I can't yet see". I looked behind me to see a young child in a Tory blue sailor suit tramping up the street with a huge bunch of blue flowers, proud Mum walking alongside. I was thinking on my feet: did I have a long enough microphone lead to get down to where Mrs Thatcher's greatest fan was standing? Second thought: never act with children and animals. So I marched off down the street trailing my microphone lead and knelt down in front of the child. "Why had she come to Number Ten that morning?" Clearly she had never been told not to speak to strange men in the street because she piped up: "I've brought these flowers for Mrs Thatcher, 'cos she's just won the election and I think she's good". And there, on my knees in front of a nine year old I got the Downing Street scoop of the day. Flushed with success, I ended the interview with: "And what's your name, little girl?" "Christopher", he said.

The golden days of Number Ten were long gone. Here I was in the Grand Guignol world of LBC and, switching my genres for a moment, like Poe's *The Pit and the Pendulum*, the great sword of sackings was still swinging to and fro over the heads of those wretches who toiled in the slough of despair. This time some idiot bean counter had decided that the presenters were quite expensive so, disregarding the fact that they were the best thing about the station, he set about sacking them all, people as good as Angela Rippon, Frank Bough and myself. Angela invited me to lunch to talk about this great affront. She was incandescent, as well she might be. She had been summoned to the office of the managing director, Peter Thornton, to receive the coup de grace. You may wonder why you have not heard him mentioned before in this black comedy. The answer is simple. You only stir from your executive dungeon when you bring out the axe, dripping with blood and summon suitable heads to bow before you. Angela described the scene and The Speech in teeth grinding detail over our starters. Peter welcomed her in with the usual small talk but then he stood up and put one foot up on his chair. He said: "Angela, you've been our biggest problem because you are our best broadcaster. You have consistently delivered first- class programmes and been highly professional in all that you have done for LBC... " We were now into our main courses and Angela/Peter was well into the Speech. "...you have such a sure touch with the listeners and, particularly with our very life blood, the people who phone in to the station and speak to you live on air..." By now I am thinking this surely cannot be a sacking speech but eventually Angela got to the post-prandial knockout. "... But you have to understand that times are tight and we just can't find space for you in our new schedule, so we'll have to let you go". I said all the right things and agreed what a bunch of bastards the management were. I said this with plenty of conviction, knowing full well that this would soon happen to me as well. But Hell hath no fury and all that and Angela would not be comforted. By chance I was taking the following week off in Cornwall to attend a friend's wedding. Also by chance the house we had rented in Polruan was near Mike Dickin's holiday home. He too had been sacked and turned up with the glad tidings and a bottle of whisky. Mike was our macho motoring expert and had turned himself into one of the early shock-jocks at LBC. Angela may have been elegantly furious, Mike was more like a rumbling volcano as he stalked up and down our little holiday let clutching his first large whisky. By the third large whisky and having travelled the length and breadth of the Dictionary of Cussing, I got a second replay of The Speech. Mike drew up a chair and placed one leg up on it. I decided this must be good form for sacking people, perhaps there is a management book called *How To Bugger Up Your Best People* in which this stance is recommended. "Mike you've been our biggest problem because you are our best broadcaster. Why, only last year you won the Personality of the Year award for Independent radio…" and so on for five minutes of praise for Mike's outstanding talent. Mike stopped for his seventh whisky before delivering the sucker punch, "…but you have to understand, Mike, that times are tough and we're having to downsize the headcount. So we'll have to let you go". It took a few more whiskies to debrief this act of vandalism. Mike left down the steep streets of Polruan. The whisky bottle was empty.

Monday afternoon was my big moment. I had had enough of crap management at the BBC and LBC and had proved to myself that I could survive without them. It was time to confront the management wearing my suicide vest. I was duly summoned to the management floor to suffer death in the afternoon. I felt strangely bullish. Peter was sitting when I entered and made to get up. "No, no," said I, "you sit down, you must be tired after sacking your old friends and colleagues, so I'll do it for you". I cleared my throat and stuck one leg up on the chair I was supposed to be sitting in for my execution. "Martin," I declaimed, "You've been our biggest problem because you are our best broadcaster. You have consistently delivered excellent programmes on the *Midday News* and you have stuck to us faithfully through thick and thin...." On and on I went for about seven minutes, God, I'd definitely have hired me after I'd listened to this paean of praise, this eulogy for such a top-class award-winning broadcaster. "... Martin, you have received great praise from the radio critics, and even a Finalist Award at the New York Radio Festival, we are grateful for all of that but most importantly for the loyalty you have shown over the past five years through many different managements...." I looked at Peter Thornton, he had fidgeted at first but now he was stock still and the colour had drained from his face. After all, he knew what was coming next and, more importantly, he knew that I knew what was coming next. I charged, stuck the horns in and gored the matador. "... But, Martin, you have to understand that we only have two stations running 24/7, 365 days of the year, and we just don't have space for you. So we're sacking you". I sat down. Peter stood up unsteadily. He looked as if someone had shot his puppy. "Well, you've made your speech" he said. "No, no," I replied "I've made your speech, so what are you going to say now?" He muttered something inconsequential and I left.

A PROUD HISTORY OF THE SACK

I n fact I left to a hero's welcome. Nothing travels so fast in a newsroom as internal news. The fact that Martin Young had just sacked himself was common knowledge in seconds. The wine bar across the road became the revolutionary headquarters for the rest of the afternoon. I realised for the first time then that Young family history was repeating itself. No one was more patriotic than my Dad. He had left school at fourteen, because my grandfather and grandmother needed the extra wage to keep the family afloat. So my Dad, George Young, joined *The Glasgow Herald* and began his career running with the newspapers, jumping in and out of a van with bundles of papers for news vendors all over Glasgow. Eventually George Young got promoted to cub reporter not so long after Adolf Hitler got promoted to Chancellor of Germany. That may be the first time that those two names have been linked in a single sentence. My Dad didn't like Adolf one little bit so he lied about his age and enlisted in the Royal Navy, entering as an Ordinary Telegraphist. By 1945 he had been de-mobbed, now Sub Lieutenant George Young. He had had, as they used to say, "a very good war". He returned in his de-mob suit to the *Glasgow Herald* but was given a lowly job as a dogsbody in the newsroom. He kept going to the boss and asking for his old job back as a cub reporter. The boss kept saying that he was far too valuable in his present job and that, in any case, he just couldn't find anybody to replace him. After three attempts, my Dad decided to take things into his own hands and advertised his own job in Glasgow's rival newspaper. He went to see the boss again and got the usual response "I just can't find anyone to replace you". My Dad had just spent five years in Atlantic convoys fighting the Hun. The little man in front of him wielded petty power in the newsroom but as far as my Dad was concerned, if it wasn't for the bravery of himself and all his thousands of comrades, this man would be speaking German by now, editing *Der Glasgow Zeitung*. "Well, sir, I've advertised my job. I got sixty replies and I've selected the best twelve applicants". The boss shuffled through the paperwork, while my father waited to be sacked for insubordination. The boss looked up at him and said: "you're a cheeky wee bugger, Young, but you can have your job back. Now get out of my bloody office". I would like to think that my Dad went out and bought himself a belted raincoat and a trilby with a wide enough hat band to stick a Press tag in but that is not recorded in Young family history.

For all its horrors there is a certain, historic grandeur in the sack. In 1066, King Harold got the sack, right in the eye. Indeed, in Norman times sacking was all the rage. Long before that, the Vikings showed us what a jolly good sacking looked and felt like. In 1536 Anne Boleyn felt the sack, clean in the nape of her shapely neck. In 1945, Adolf Hitler gave himself the sack; a bit like me. Mussolini had his lamp post; Nicolae Ceausescu had his baying crowd and firing squad. You may not feel sorry for the last three but you must empathise with the ordinary decent people who get the sack because the bosses have screwed up big time. Again, James Cameron writes movingly, in this case about the death of *The News Chronicle* and the fate of the sackees:

"*The News Chronicle* staff had no agreement to invoke. There had been no contributory pensions scheme, though for years the staff had urged the establishment of one. Whatever this deal meant to the Cadburys and Rothermeres it was disastrous to many men and women of long service, who in many cases had remained with the paper in spite of far better offers elsewhere. And this was without one agreeable word, without sympathy, without a formal gesture of farewell, and with the prospect of long litigation before they would touch even what compensation was offered... When *The News Chronicle* died this cheapjack death I determined to attach myself to no more newspapers. It was not always easy, but one can breathe".

Young family history

What of Young family history? It was a roll-call of success and honour until you get to me and my serial sackings. For me life began at the age of zero, as it tends to do, in a tenement building in the Maryhill road in Glasgow. By the time I was two my Dad was getting fed up with his daily round of phone calls to the emergency services and the mortuary, seeking ever more tragic detritus for the news pages of the *Glasgow Herald* and so he joined the Highland Hydro Electric Board. We moved to Edinburgh and my father escorted Americans and Japanese around the Highlands of Scotland, urging Company bosses to direct their foreign investment into Scotland. Now, as an executive my Dad was dragging the Youngs into the middle classes. Many years later my new wife was deeply impressed by the George Young tour of the Highlands of Scotland. My Dad was a real enthusiast and he now injected all his drive into the battle for foreign investment, a struggle he would continue for the rest of his working life. I meanwhile got into Daniel Stewart's school in Edinburgh, one of a handful of top Scottish schools like Fettes College and Heriot Watt academy. I was just over four years old and I could have stayed there, under the Scottish system until I was eighteen. But my father applied for and got a rather prestigious job as the London boss of the Scottish Council for Development & Industry, where he could continue his evangelistic crusade to persuade various foreign bosses that the only place in the world to invest was Scotland. At the age of six we flew to London. This was 1953 and only Biggles and really posh people got on planes. I was beside myself with excitement, but my mother was beside herself with fear. My Mum's fear really transmitted to her little boy. The wee boy, nonetheless, continued to fly like Biggles. Indeed, about twenty years later I got my private pilot's licence. My father had now dragged us into the ambassadorial class. He was effectively Scottish Trade Minister in London. I was in a different class too, at the local primary school which believed in "free expression". Now, I was very good at this, culminating in my knocking out a boy I didn't like who happened to be standing on a school desk at the time, as you do. The truth was that I had been too well educated at Daniel Stewart's school and I was bored by my new surroundings. So I went to Greenhayes Prep school and from there won a scholarship to Dulwich College, whose previous alumni included Ernest Shackleton and Bob Monkhouse. I suppose I fitted in well below the first and just above the second, but I did fit in. Indeed, so much so that I became Head Boy. Ella Fitzgerald sang "Into each life a little rain must fall" and the shower that fell on me later in life was the news that another of the Dulwich alumni was Nigel Farage. As Captain of School I had the odious power, never used, to flog another boy. But with Farage who knows what that might have done to my liberal tendencies?

The saga of Queen's bottom

My new position came with real power. I was now the Obergruppenfuhrer of fifty-one prefects, or Gestapo operatives as we liked to call them, with command over 1440 inmates. My first move was swingeing and draconian: I abolished alphabetical order and imposed anti-alphabetical order throughout the school. Well, you try being called Young in a school of 1440 pupils. With one blow I had eliminated the pain and suffering of Zachariah, Vendy and Wyber. I had immediately attracted the opprobrium of Adams, Bazalgette and Bunbury, but I didn't care. They had it coming to them. It's true, absolute power corrupts absolutely. I had one further power which was the ultimate sanction and fixed firmly in the Dotheboys Hall of the nineteenth century. I could summon a persistent offender to the prefect's room and flog his bare bottom in front of fifty-one prefects. The bottom in most danger of this painful humiliation belonged to a boy called Queen. I never beat his bum or anyone else's for that matter. I beat him by acting. Each time I had to talk to him about his latest misdemeanour I became sterner, convincing him that the nuclear option on his rear end was getting ever nearer. Queen will either have gone on to become a multi-millionaire selling villas in Albania or a mass murderer bothering Her Majesty's constabulary. I don't know, all I do know and am so grateful for is that I had the humane good sense not to indulge in the insanity of flogging a boy.

THE PLAYERS IN THE ATTIC

I n my final years at Dulwich I was invited into the Rafter
Players, an ambitious enterprise dreamt up by a number of old
boys from Dulwich who were now in the acting fraternity at
Oxford. The founder, John Young, (No relation) had cleverly
worked out that Shakespeare was a world language and could be
sold to eager English Literature students across the Globe, – well,
across the Channel at least. We toured Denmark, Finland and
Sweden playing *Twelfth Night* at various universities. I gave my
interpretation of Feste, as they say, in Copenhagen, Oslo and
Helsinki. It was rare for the audience to be able to hear Shakespeare
spoken by English actors, albeit callow lads and lassies. The final
tour, in 1966, took us behind the Iron Curtain to what was still
called Leningrad.

It was a truly fascinating experience because in those days of
Cold War fear the young Russian audience had little or no chance
of travelling outside the Soviet Union and few young Brits could
get admitted to the Communist State. The Russian boys and girls
clutched at the fine fabrics of our Marks and Sparks clothing and
were desperate to hear all about our life in the decadent West. Our
Government minder wasn't. Indeed she set up a farewell party

which we reasoned was being recorded, possibly for propaganda purposes. So we set up our own psy ops campaign, downed our vodka and rhapsodised about how perfect life was in glorious Britain.

The professors and students at the university were really kind and appreciative to us. On the second night many returned and brought us gifts. It was clear that the pictures, the books and the artefacts they gave us had come off the walls of their own flats in Leningrad. I was given a book of the Sonnets in Russian and a Shostakovich LP, which appeared to my Western eye to be composed by a man called Moctakobny. For me, he remains Moctakobny to this day.

IT WAS VERY MOVING

So was the ship on the way home. The Rafter Players were nothing if not enterprising. Somehow John Young had managed to get us home on one of Russia's first cruise ships, the *Alexander Pushkin*. The quid pro quo was that the eager young Shakespeareans would present their *Twelfth Night* on board as entertainment on what would now be "this fun-filled cruise of a lifetime".

I say "on board". The play was actually to be performed on the ship's tiny dance floor. It was hardly the Royal Shakespeare stage at Stratford and it did involve a literally hair raising trip from stage right to stage left. In order to make this transition you had to open a bulkhead door, stage right, stagger out onto the fo'c's'le and fight the Baltic wind to another bulkhead door, which would admit you to stage left, with your theatrical hair now stuck out rather than stuck on. Add to that the rolling sensation of the ship and the actors' uncertainty about where any movement might take them; it must have been a memorable sight for the uncomprehending audience. They had probably been hoping the entertainment might have been Cliff Richard or Moctakobny at least.

THE WHIRLIGIG OF TIME

A mere forty-eight years later Sue and I booked a cruise around Britain and France. The highlight was supposed to be the visit to Monet's garden in Giverny, a short trip from our mooring in Le Havre. It was indeed beautiful but not as intriguing as the brochure for the *Marco Polo*. Sue noted that the aging vessel we were on was a Lermontov craft from Russia, whose maiden voyage was in the mid-1960s when she was known as the *Alexander Pushkin*. I searched in vain for the tiny dance floor and the hoped for blue plaque celebrating Martin Young's ground breaking performance in *Shakespeare at Sea*. Somewhere in those forty-eight years some heartless and uncultured re-fitter must have removed both.

EARNING A LIVING

I duly applied to read English Literature at Cambridge. As so often in Britain there was an old-boy's network, literally and metaphorically. Any Dulwich head boy was virtually guaranteed a place at Oxbridge. I was determined to get to Cambridge on my own merits, so I worked hard and earned an Exhibition to Gonville & Caius College in 1966. I was summoned to the austere, i.e. boring Science block at Dulwich by the equally boring Careers Master and Head of Statistics. As I entered he was secreting his still smouldering pipe in his desk. "In my business" he confided, "you read a lot about late developers, Young. It's very good to meet one at last". I left, a walking statistic on its way to a big boy's university.

Along the way I had to earn a living. I discovered the harsh, unbridled capitalism of the "cold sell". "Good morning, madam, have you ever considered central heating for your lovely home?" The home was usually fairly grotty and central heating was the double-glazing of the day. I was the front man for the engineer who would follow with the hard sell. He wasn't an engineer at all, of course, he was a pushy salesman who wouldn't leave the woman's house without "closure": her signature on a contract for central heating she probably couldn't afford. The company was "Warm-Glo" or "South East Heating" or something else next week as the creditors closed in. My boss was Australia's answer to Arthur Daley. He even had Arthur's Jaguar. He proudly told me in that open, engaging Australian way that he always kept the Jag full of fuel 'cos you could then get three hundred miles away from your problems on any given creditor's day. Naturally I became one of his creditors. I was pretty good at getting my foot in the door and arranging appointments for the so-called engineer to do his chat up and sign here routine and I was always owed a lot of commission for my efforts. The system was that we would all meet up on a Friday evening with the boss at a designated boozer in the territory where we were working and he would pay us our commission, or not as the case may be. "I'm really sorry fellas but this week I've got grief and I can only pay you a fiver each".

Welcome to the world of work. I moved on. Next on the list was an intriguing advert in the *Evening Standard*, offering untold riches to successful salesmen of their product. There was no mention of what the product actually was, not even when I rang to fix an appointment in posh South Audley Street. The smell of rat was overwhelming. Yes, the rewards could be great but the "product" was encyclopaedias. Sixty punters turned up on day one, by day two there were just fifteen of us left. I stayed because I was intrigued by the nature of the con, written up for us in a script we had to learn by heart. Conning the script was easy for me; I'd been learning screeds of Shakespeare and Pinter for years. The territory we had to cover would be aspiring working-class with little money. Mum would always answer the door: "Good evening, madam, actually it's your husband I've called to see…" "Ah, good evening, sir, I was just talking to your wife…" Now I am friends with both madam and monsieur and the way is clear to their sitting room. If you are offered a cup of tea you must accept it and drink it slowly, however horrible it is. It gives you more time to get through the sacred script and move towards the even more sacrosanct signature. The hard fact in the late sixties was that a

Colliers' Reference Library would end up costing the punter £167.00, a sizeable sum of money, never to be mentioned any more than the dreaded word "encyclopaedia". Indeed, this was what the script said about the money: "By this time, madam and sir, you are probably wondering how much this wonderful reference library is going to cost you. (Do not pause.) Well, it is no more than the cost of a daily newspaper, to have this distinguished library in your home for the education of your children and indeed yourselves." All this was, of course, morally corrupt. In other words, bollocks. I had already decided that I couldn't do it for real, but the nascent journalist in me wanted to see what happened during the rest of the course. By day three we were reduced to about six hopefuls and the gloves came off. No more Mr Nice Guy from the salesman/tutor. I got up to deliver my script and he kept interrupting me with questions, some stupid, some very much to the point. When I reached the critical subject of cost I did not pause as instructed in the stage directions but he barged in with: "'ow much is it then, in total? What'm I gonna have to fork out altogether, eh?" Without so much as a maiden blush, I slid back in: "Sir, I'm not looking for your reaction to a price, I want to see your reaction to our fabulous reference library, doesn't it look impressive here in your main room?" (I had already hung up a real size colour photograph of the books in an MFI style bookcase which would come free with their purchase of the books). "and all this prestige will cost you no more than the cost of a daily newspaper every day" and I was safely back on the script. God, I was good, a full scale spiv. Not to be outdone the salesman started to show off his manipulative skills with the punters: "I walked in and asked for a glass of water. I didn't drink it; I just put it on the mantelpiece and carried on with my spiel. Then I asked for another and another. By the end I'd lined up eleven glasses of water on the shelf and not touched one. Then I got my signature and left". He was brighter than them and he'd conned them and, worst of all, he was proud of it.

I was soon called in by the main honcho, who presented with brylcreem hair, superior suit and lots of bling. He lit a cheroot with his gold Colibri lighter and said: "I like the way you walk into a room, the way you sit down, all that confidence. You could make a lot of money at this game, hundred, hundred and twenty pounds a week, maybe more. When can you start?" "I'm not starting. I think the whole thing is exploiting poorer people who are not as sharp as you are. I think it stinks. I hope the way I walk out of a room meets with your approval too". I left. I have always been glad that I went through the training, but always relieved that I never inflicted my clever spivdom on the residents of Acacia Avenue, Deptford. I would soon have to pit what wits I had against the best brains of Cambridge University. But first:

COMING SOON TO A CINEMA NEAR YOU...

I had managed by some clever stratagem to get myself a membership card for the Film Artistes' Association. I don't know, perhaps they liked the way I walked into a room. Anyway, it was a prized Union membership in the days when the unions practically ran the country. "Who runs the country, the trades union or the Government?" Prime Minister, Ted Heath would ask in the early 1970s. And the answer came loudly back: "Actually, mate it's us."

Armed with this magic ticket, (I particularly liked the "e" in Artiste, it sounded so much better than "extra") I could earn at least £5.00 a day on the lot at Shepperton Studios. I was to be an extra in the background of an episode of *The Avengers*. In the foreground was our hero, Steed, and a stunning, white E-Type Jaguar. Somewhere over there was a young Martin Young just discernible in the far distance striding across the set with his new best friend, another film extra, setting out on the yellow brick road to Stardom. I remember being particularly impressed by the gossip among my fellow "artistes" that this was the second E-Type of the shoot. The first had destroyed its chassis and all four wheels as an over-enthusiastic stunt man flew it over a humpback bridge the day before.

My fellow extras were not an entirely inspiring advert for the noble art of acting. They were the has-beens and the "never-will-bes" of the profession, plus me, a "wannabe". I was, however, suddenly popular, because I had a car and could ferry them to a local Shepperton pub in the lunch break.

My second screen breakthrough was a far grander affair. An entire stage at Shepperton had been transformed into the Berliner Sports Palatz for a scene in Guy Hamilton's film *The Battle of Britain*. You've probably been dazzled by the likes of Laurence Olivier, Ralph Richardson and Kenneth More in the main roles, but I am there, in the audience, shouting "Seig Heil" and giving the Hitler salute with the rest of them. Unfortunately, there are several hundred of the rest of them, who are to be matted into a crowd of five thousand Hitler worshippers. For Adolf is among us and has brought his toothbrush moustache with him. He is, appropriately, an Austrian and plies his trade as a Hitler impersonator in the clubs and pubs of Europe. He launches into the Adolf Shout with gusto:

"Gesternacht, haben die Englander bomben auf Berlin geworfen", declaring that, "we will stop the handiwork of these air pirates, so help us God". He is announcing the start of the Blitz.

We extras are now whipped up into a frenzy of retribution and of adoration for the Fuhrer. (I am the one shouting in one of the pixels bottom right and top right and top and bottom left, since the shot has been matted to increase the size of the crowd. You can't miss me). There are two highlights to the day. After prolonged Union/Management talks we are to get an extra pound a day for delivering our lines in a foreign language. Riches indeed.

The second highlight, though, is priceless. In a break in filming I am outside, by the catering tent, taking tea with Adolf Hitler. He has loosened his uniform and his morals, flirting and laughing with female extras, done up like little Eva Brauns. This was more than forty years ago but, you'll agree, it's a pretty difficult image to shift.

Those who had admired my "pixel" phase could follow my thespian burgeoning at Cambridge where I got to be:

A murderer in *The White Devil*

Laertes in *Hamlet*

Costard in *Love's Labour's Lost*

Mick in *The Caretaker*

Puck in *Midsummer Night's Dream*

Giovanni in *'Tis Pity She's a Whore.*

And a 2.1 in Finals

In John Ford's tragedy I got to sleep with my sister, Annabella, to kill her and then appear at Soranza's banquet clutching her bleeding heart in my bloodied hands. Life was so much more interesting in the seventeenth century. My audience in the Arts Theatre, Cambridge, didn't know whether to laugh or cry. My friends in the acting clique fell back on that great theatrical catch-all: "Darling, what can I say?"

This was the Marlowe Society's main production and in those days the major agents and studios would send talent scouts from London to look at the latest crop of young hopefuls. I was offered a year's contract to play bit parts for Associated British Pictures at the princely sum of £1500.00. I would not be playing too many princes, they would probably be paupers and I was cheap at the price.

I had, however, come to a decision about acting, after years of treading the amateur boards. In order to succeed, I reasoned, you had to believe sincerely that you were the best actor in the world. You didn't have to be any good you just had to believe you were the best. I was an optimist but not an idiot. Television journalism would have to sublimate my innate need to show off.

ACTUALLY LEARNING

At Caius we were taught by the tall, elegant figure of Jeremy Prynne, an academic Christopher Lee playing Dracula in an elegant Georgian room next to Honoris, the Gate of Honour. The gates to each of the quads bore proud Latin names, including the gate beside the toilets on which some wag had chalked the title Necessitatis. Prynne's room was obviously designed by the BBC Props department. It had a whole wall of built-in bookcases stuffed with tomes, all of which you just knew he had read and understood. He sat behind a professor's desk, peering at you over a pile of manuscripts. The low table in the middle of the room also contained a tumble of papers which on inspection turned out to be Argentinian poetry, a subject in which he was, of course, an expert. The Props department had come up with a final surreal flourish. This high-powered man of letters did not appear to have a telephone. When a phone rang we were all quite startled. He opened a drawer in his antique desk and withdrew the offending instrument, reluctantly acknowledging the existence of the outside world. During afternoons we deduced from careful deciphering of his answers that he was agreeing with his wife what they would be having for dinner, which was a bit of a letdown. He made up for this unseemliness by performing one of his best party tricks where he would introduce a writer, say Boswell, and while looking at us walk towards the wall of books, select Boswell's *Life of Johnson* without looking at the bookcase at all and begin to read out loud. Good God, not only had he read all those books he even knew instinctively where each one was. Prynne naturally had a magnificent vocabulary, he was fond of "prototypic alienation" "retro inferential criticism" and, "the discourse on the surface of the language" We used to rush back to our rooms and check his more esoteric utterances. He was always right.

Apart from the dissection of Prynne's prosody, how did we pass those long, languid days by the Cam? We were very busy in fact. Mick had a lot of training to do in preparation for the Varsity Boxing match and I had a lot of rehearsing to do for the several theatre productions – oh, and then there was the incidental need to come away at the end with a decent degree. We also had to make a house a home. We were on "O" staircase, with a metal circle pronouncing that fact. With judicial application of two bright eyes and a wide smile we became the Happy Staircase. We were an eclectic bunch: some were happy on a selection of questionable substances, the scary LSD and the less harmful cannabis. One of our number was famous for his hash omelettes. Another, Marcus Bicknell, was a born entrepreneur and set up his own sandwich business for those many undergraduates who didn't know how to cook. Where was Mummy? Where was Nanny? I had chosen my room with a scrupulous impartiality of which the Beeb would have approved. Beneath me was a boy I had been at school with, Wyber, who had risen to the giddy and irreproachable heights of Chairman of the University Conservative Club – you know, a nerd. Above me, at the top of the imposing Waterhouse tower, was Andy Reid, who had not been at school with me and I can therefore remember his first name. Wyber would always be just Wyber. Andy was the head honcho anarchist of the time, plotting how to bring down the government in between spliffs and bouffanting his Dave Spart hair and beard combo. I came back to the happy staircase one afternoon to make sure my Mum was OK on her visit to see her boy at University. She said how nice the young man upstairs was. She had met the friendly anarchist and had mentioned that she was out of cigarettes. "He was awfu' nice, son, he gave me one of his". Oh, God, I thought she'll be flung out of Bromley Presbyterian Church, if found stoned on the streets of Cambridge. I kept shtum and prayed that Plod didn't turn up at our door. Keen to get her back on her intoxicant of choice I bought her a bottle of sherry with a "specially selected for Gonville and Caius College, Cambridge" label. She was really pleased, not just with the sherry, but with the bottle and its label. For years she would refill it with VP sherry or some ghastly equivalent and serve it to her ladies' circle with the "Keeping up Appearances" remark "It's from Martin. He's at that college in Cambridge right now, you know". She never knew how close she came to having her collar felt by the local constabulary for smoking dope.

She never knew either about our bouts of mountaineering on the face of Waterhouse's fine old Victorian edifice. My room had its own little stone balcony, on the edge of which I would sit while reading some of the books I was supposed to have read three years ago before coming up to Cambridge. So to liven up this rather dry experience, Mick and I undertook some experiments, which we later realised were groundbreaking work towards the science of bungee jumping. There was a schoolboy craze at the time for rubber pencil tops with scary monster faces and waving arms so, naturally, we attached one of these to a very long piece of rubber and, by empirical reasoning, designed the mini-monsters to stop in mid-air at head height. Innocent passersby would be confronted for a split second by a googly-eyed monster waving its gnarled, green arms at them. Not one of them ever looked up to see where it had come from to see the giggling idiots who had launched the apparition. They all spun around looking confused, bemused or terrified. Breaks the ice at parties. The next way we made the most of our one hundred foot drop to the ground was an exploration of the famed robustness of Victorian architecture and mechanics. Waterhouse had topped his brickwork with a large Italianate cornice that ran the whole length of the building, taking in my stone balcony. We discovered that by climbing up on the balcony we could walk along the cornice and climb into other people's rooms through the windows overlooking the street below. Marcus Bicknell, the famed sandwich man, was a regular victim, his room being the nearest to mine, so minimising the amount of death defying walking required by us. We started by wallpapering his window on the outside so when he threw back the drapes to welcome a brave new dawn, there wasn't any. As we got more adventurous we would climb in by the window and wire up his entire room, so that when he returned and opened his door, all his books would fall off his bookshelf.

FROM HERE TO ETERNITY

My room was also the custodian of the so-called fire escape. This ancient artefact was a metal cylinder containing yards of rope; this was designed by Heath Robinson to enable you to descend to King's Parade below. We decided we needed to test its efficacy. Well, it would be rude not to, wouldn't it? Our guest was Gavin Stamp, who must have been brought up in Victorian nappies and had now graduated to the full Victorian gentleman. We each tested the apparatus by scrabbling our way down to the pavement. Gavin brought his umbrella, without which a well-dressed Victorian gentleman would not deign to be seen on the public highway. He descended like Mary Poppins, stopping at Wyber's window and knocking to attract attention. The Chairman of the Cambridge Young Conservatives then met the Chairman of the Cambridge Victorian Society who was dangling in mid-air. "Good evening, Wyber" said the magical male Mary Poppins and carried on his journey southwards. The Conservative spluttered and said nothing. We did not, you may have inferred, have much regard for 'Elf and Safety' but once the fire escape began to pull away from its bolts even we had the sense to stop. With considerable insouciance we reported that the device was broken and that they stood in loco parentis while we were under their care.

These days we read all too often in the hallowed pages of the *Daily Mail* of students lying in bed watching *Countdown* and no doubt ogling the Lady With The Letters. It is good to look back to our university days and note how diligently we experimented with the Laws of Physics in our spare time while studying English Literature so assiduously.

I never did finish that book.

Fast forward three years to our farewell dinner in hall. We had become favourites with the waiters, probably because we weren't stuck-up like some of the silver spoon brigade they had to serve. Their generosity to us with the college claret was unstinting. I became particularly "unstinted" and decided that Jeremy Prynne needed a bit of my wisdom after I had listened to so much of his over the last three years. Here in the gilded halls of English Academe, the wee Glaswegian spoke up for the common man:"You sit here high up in your ivory tower" I slurred at him "and you've no idea what real people actually do or say. They don't all talk in iambic pentameters, you know – they're not all bloody Piers Plowman or Shakespeare's rude mechanicals. You and your prissy Argentine ditties, you don't know what you're on about half the time". My faithful friends dragged me away and put me to bed with a bucket by my side. The following morning the bucket stared balefully at me as I dressed up in all my graduation gear. As I emerged from the Senate House Jeremy Prynne was there to congratulate me, "Well done, Young, glad to see you made it". To this day I shall never know if he meant through my degree or just through the night.

Hang on, this is the swinging sixties, you know sex, drugs and rock 'n roll. So far all I've done is describe the professor's study. Is there something wrong with me? No. On the sex front Cambridge was not the place to be, the ratio was ten eager young men to one female, so you had to kiss a lot of frogs before a princess came along. As your first loveless year turned into year two you became more eligible and I found my first princess, Jan Harvey, later to become a telly star in the soap opera, *Howard's Way*. Don't imagine for a moment that Shakespeare was making all that Capulet and Montagu stuff up from old Italian texts. He based *Romeo and Juliet* entirely on the world's greatest love story, which was "Martin & Jan". No two people had ever been so in love (that sounds like the cue for a song). This was the sixties, lying on the banks of the Cam in the spring sunshine, just loving each other, blissfully unaware of the immense privilege we were being offered. Jan and I came together through the acting mafia. I had cut the throat of a perfectly nice girl nightly at the Arts Theatre in *The White Devil* alongside my friend, Mike the Murderer, who later on was to act Horatio in *Hamlet*, while I played Laertes. (You're wondering how I slit her throat, aren't you? I slid a blunt but evil-looking knife along her elegant neck while squirting a bag of false blood concealed in my free hand, five times nightly and two matinees. As I stared down on her ample bosom each night as she squirmed beneath me I couldn't help noticing what nice breasts she had). I also played Mick in *The Caretaker* at the ADC Theatre, directed by Kerry Crabbe. And therein lay my nemesis. Therein lay the final act of *Romeo and Juliet*. Kerry also went on to direct *Hamlet* and cast the love of my life as my sister, Ophelia. The first sign that all might not be well came when she started smoking again – Jan, not Ophelia that is. Over the seven romantic months we spent together I had persuaded her to give up smoking. Why had she taken it up again? Just a few days before the first night at the Arts Theatre I found out. I sat with Jan in Kerry's room – he was a chain smoker – and, amid a cloud of cigarette smoke, I found out. I was being dumped.

This broke my heart. Allied to the fact that I was about to play her brother in *Hamlet* my heart was in pieces. For seven nights and two matinees I had to kiss Ophelia in a brotherly like fashion as Laertes left for France. By this stage there was nothing left of my heart at all. I was so distraught that one night I left for France but actually left the theatre to go up the road to see my friends in *The Threepenny Opera*, music by Kurt Weill and words by Berthold Brecht. Since all the trendy theatre talk in those days was of alienation, the audience was invited on stage in the interval to mingle with the players. Perhaps the audience assumed that having Laertes in full Elizabethan costume wandering among them was just a further extension of the alienation technique. Anyway I got back to the Arts Theatre in time to be killed.

A few months passed and miraculously my broken heart had begun to heal. I seemed to have survived the most magical romance and thorough tragedy of any two people ever known to man. Better still my soul-mate, Michael Dutfield, was preparing to welcome an old Shropshire school friend, Caroline, who had just come up to Homerton College, the teacher training college, full of girls. Yes, girls. By this stage, in our third year, we both had some pulling power. Mick had gained himself a Boxing Blue and I was President of the Marlowe Dramatic Society. We duly paraded ourselves in Carrie's room in front of a bevy of young girls. Sitting there in modest mini-skirt, knees tightly together, looking demure and clutching a file of lecture notes was Susan. She was very attractive and reading English and Drama, so I showed off as much as I dared about my life in the Cambridge Theatre scene. I thought I was superb, Susan thought I was just bumptious. The flamboyant chiffon scarf didn't help. Nonetheless, despite her initial rejection we became attached and stayed so for the next two years of my job with Tyne Tees television. I would finish the Friday edition of *Today at Six* as early as 6.15. My less than glamorous Triumph Herald would be parked right outside the studio and four and a half hours later I'd be in Cambridge for a weekend with Sue. But I could not be with her overnight without sullying the reputation of Homerton College, Cambridge and the entire British Empire. Queen Victoria may be dead but her strait-laced Puritanism lived on. Riding to the rescue on a broken-winded steed was our very own Falstaff, Jonathan James Moore. As President of Footlights he had a flat above the Cambridge branch of Mac Fisheries. So J-J gave us sanctuary and a private room for romantic interludes infused by the smell of kippers from below. J-J was a striking figure. He had a long body and short legs and a flowing shock of hair and huge beard like Thor, except Jonathan's hair was ginger. He dressed like a badly-tied parcel. That's how he looked as President of Footlights in 1970 and when he became Head of Light Entertainment (Radio) that's exactly the way he looked then. He and his flatmate, Stephen Wright, were born impresarios and brought all manner of performers to the Cambridge stage. It was a bit unnerving to wander in for morning coffee and discover you were sharing it with Alfred Brendel. We were disturbed to see that Brendel had Elastoplasts protecting each finger. Presumably the piano lid had crashed down on his hands. That would be one weekend in Cambridge, culminating in the long journey back to Newcastle, crossing the Tyne Bridge at three in the morning. Some weekends Sue would make the journey to Newcastle and stay in my humble room in Jesmond which didn't smell of fish. It smelt of damp. On one of these occasions I asked her to marry me and, this time, she said yes. We were married in 1971. The vicar at that time in Ealing was the Reverend Fred Secombe and, yes, he was Harry Secombe's brother. Sue and I were married by Neddy Seagoon's brother. What a thrill for a lad brought up listening to The Goon Show. The wedding was a thrill too, except for the bit in my speech where I described first meeting Sue with that bunch of girls in Homerton College. Sue I described as "the best of a bad lot". Most of the bad lot were sat there in my audience. Oh dear.

Just a few months later Harry Secombe himself came to the North East to perform his travelling show and, to my delight, I was sent to interview him for Look North. I couldn't wait to tell him about the wedding. "Your brother married me", said I proudly. "Oh good," said Harry, "I hope you'll both be very happy together."

The early years of our marriage were dominated by BBC *Look North* and then *Nationwide* which, by that stage, had become a rite of passage for all aspiring reporters and film-makers. In those days there was such a thing as a career path; a spell on local radio and/or television, a stint on *Nationwide* and on to *Panorama*, real big boys' television. When I was still at Dulwich I was brought up on the *Tonight* programme presented by Cliff Michelmore and Derek Hart. I would eat my tea and do my homework while watching stars like Fyfe Robertson (It's a very funny thing but…), Trevor Philpott and Slim Hewitt as the proper BBC man and the scruffy cockney in the dirty old mac. Most of all, though, I wanted to be Alan Whicker. I saw him walking and talking on a beach in Fiji, dressed in his best Gieves and Hawke's suit and thought I can do that. I can travel the world at the BBC's expense and just tell stories. As it turned out I found my story in Fiji in 1987 when Colonel Rabuka staged a military coup there just for my benefit. I duly strode my beach walking and talking in true Whicker style. There was a problem though. Yes, I finally was Alan Whicker but in the meantime between being a schoolboy and becoming the roving reporter Whicker had become a millionaire and I hadn't. Before I could travel the world I had to travel Britain, recording the minutiae of everyday life, some serious, some slight and some just plain daft.

PEOPLE AND PLACES ON
NATIONWIDE

Dramatis Personae: director Dave Rowley, two dogs and me.

D ave and I were in Wiltshire, casting around for a good local story. We went, of course, to the nearest pub and read the local paper. We found a Greyfriars Bobbie story about a black Labrador who could not be moved from the crossroads where his owner had died in a recent car crash. Dave was affecting to drink pink gins at this stage, which went down a treat with the locals clutching their big, hairy pints of ale. We ordered another round and chatted up the landlord about the dog at the crossroads. Yes it was all true and the village was so upset that they were taking food and water to the distraught animal. Being a highly trained observer I noticed that mein host had a golden Labrador behind the bar. I asked him if we could borrow his dog for the day. Weighing up the profits he was making from all those pink gins, he agreed. (No animals were harmed during the making of this film). The following morning I set out in front of camera explaining the story and that, unfortunately I did not speak dog, so I had brought my own doggie translator with me.

We filmed the morose labrador orphan and persuaded my labrador to appear to talk to him and then appear to talk in my ear, explaining his sad plight which I then translated for the benefit of the viewers. That worked surprisingly well but we still needed a final act. Dave went to the local restaurant and came back with all the kitchen staff and a chef in full toque bearing plates of food for the bereaved dog at the crossroads. Thus were *Nationwide* films brought from all over Britain to an expectant nation, ten to twelve million of them at the programme's peak.

Dramatis personae: Dave Rowley, little old lady and me.

Another night on the road in the West Country and another search for a good local story. (You may have noticed en passant that I was filming in Somerset while still living in Newcastle. Doubtless the Brighton reporter was at that minute filming in South Shields. Why? The London film desk had a pre-Copernican view of the world in which there were only two locations, London and Elsewhere. It stood to reason that anywhere in Elsewhere was close to anywhere else in Elsewhere. "Ah, Martin you're in Aberdeen, can you pop down to Aberystwyth for us and do a quick film?" Many a long night on the road was spent cursing the London Time Lords who had no sense of space or time, just as James Cameron had done thirty years beforehand).

In the Somerset pub things were looking good. Dave and I had found an "Ah, poor soul, wicked council story" that was bound to engage the viewers. Tucked away in a rural corner of Somerset was a tumbledown cottage drawn by Hogarth or Gillray. In it there lived a little, bent old lady, still forced to live as her ancestors did in the seventeenth century, no mains water, no electricity, nothing in fact that we would consider essential in the modern world. The cameraman was ecstatic; here was his chance to show his skills in costume drama. Little old lady duly hobbled out of her hovel carrying an empty bucket. She made unsteady progress down the cobbled path to the ancient well, filled her bucket with water and struggled back to the cold cottage. She made some tea and settled down by the embers of yesterday's log fire. Looming over this whole medieval shame was the spectre of all the people we love to hate, the Council, the complacent public sector and the fat energy companies. All we needed now was the tearful interview with the victim and an official response from the evil councillor, who I hoped would have a balding head and an officious moustache. First the formality of the victim interview. I put on my caring face and said: "Mrs Mcconachie, it must be terrible for you living here, having to draw your water from an ancient well and having no electricity…" I let my voice tail away so that the old lady could bemoan her lot. "Oh no, no no," she said, vigorously shaking her unkempt white locks. "No, this is the way I like it, this is the way life has always been for me and I'm very comfortable here in my cottage". "But surely," I said, now unsure of my ground "you must want the council to put in the services you need?" "Oh no they're always round here trying to lay a lot of cables and such like but I'll have nothing to do with all that new-fangled nonsense. I keep having to tell them to go away and leave me in peace. Now, will you have another cup of tea dear?"

Dave said "cut". I looked at Dave and he looked at me and we both knew we were beaten. We said thank you to little old lady, wrapped the gear up and scrapped the film. Back, as they say to the drawing board or in our case back to the pub. On *Nationwide* you got good at making bricks from straw but this was a step too far. Pink gins all round and a rethink.

Looking back at those days now I'm surprised to discover just how many films Dave and I made together. He said to me at the time that he really enjoyed working with me, because I was so good with the people we were filming he could more or less ignore them and get on with the serious business of organising the film crew and the logistics of our trip, which he was very good at. I remember that Dave was particularly pleased one year in the seventies when out of the 365 days he made two hundred and sixty odd films. OK, none of them was exactly *Ben Hur*, but then I was no Charlton Heston. Hundreds of little films were the lifeblood of *Nationwide*. And Dave and I gave our blood generously, like the day we had a plane to catch from Le Havre back to Gatwick. Dave was uncharacteristically late, having flooded his bathroom in the hotel, somewhere in Normandy. We set out late and I had to drive like a maniac in our rented Renault 16. When we arrived at Le Havre airport the plane for London, an old Twin Otter, was doing its power checks on the runway. I drove straight up to it like an Algerian terrorist, and we opened all five doors and got all our luggage and exposed film out onto the tarmac. The pilot powered down, the side door and steps were lowered for us and we boarded with all our bags and footage. As we took off I looked back at the runway and saw that some idiot had left a Renault hire car thoughtlessly in the middle of the tarmac with all five doors open. That was 1975. For all I know the Beeb may still be paying for it. Dave really wanted to become a naval officer but he failed on the eye test and, ludicrously, became a film editor for the Beeb instead. No eyes needed I suppose. So, David was never happier than when he was "on holiday" with an army to direct.

Location: The tank training ranges of BAOR near Hamburg.

Dramatis Personae: Dave, assorted tank crew, strippers at the Taboo Club and me.

We were looked after royally by the best PR man I ever met. His first act was to get us access to the NAAFI where we were able to buy spirits and cigars for knock down prices. We filled the glove box of our hired Mercedes with a big box of King Edward cigars and assorted booze. Then Dave got to film with his own private tank regiment. One of the most arresting images on the muddy churn of the tank training grounds was a Chieftain tank bouncing like a multi ton beach ball straight towards us. The barrel of its big gun was so stabilised that it never wavered from a direct line until the driver helpfully stopped just a couple of metres away from the camera lens. We were literally staring down the barrel of a gun, a big gun. After the shoot the world's best PR man filled us full of champagne and then, at the request of our randy cameraman, directed us to the Reeperbahn in the red light district. This story goes downwards from now on, literally and metaphorically, because in those days the prostitutes gathered in festive little displays and festive little, skimpy nether garments in one of Hamburg's more attractive underground car parks.

"Go on then, Martin," said Keith the cameraman "you're the only one of us who speaks German, go and find out how much it is". I imagine that a few hand gestures would solve this problem with prostitutes anywhere in the world so I knew I was being wound up. But it would never do to let the crew see any weakness, to see any signs of my Scottish Presbyterian prudishness, so I selected a girl who obviously didn't own any proper clothes and had had to come to the car park in black bra and lacy black knickers. "Entschuldige, bitte, aber wieviel costet es?" I asked in my best schoolboy German. She said: "fünfzig marken". "Ja" I said meaning oh, indeed as if I was considering her price against all the dozens of other prostitutes I had negotiated with in the past. But she took me much more literally, believing me to mean "Yes". She said: "Ja? Sehr gut, kommen sie mit" and she grabbed my arm to drag me away to her lair. At this point, with the crew giggling in the background it was collapse of stout party as I backed away putting my hands across my crotch and saying "Nein nein". Keith was delighted to have engineered this humiliation for me. He had, of course, been to Hamburg before and when he suggested to me that we all adjourn to the Taboo Club, I was in no position to protest. The Taboo was not at all like a gentleman's club in Pall Mall. In unabashed pink neon it announced that we could see "real fucky-fucky" within its gilded entrance. We were settled down at the front of the stage for some full on action. A succession of young men and women came on stage, wearing very few clothes which they rapidly discarded to free themselves up for the real fucky-fucky. Dave said through a cloud of Gitanes smoke and brandy fumes: "I hope they've got a lesbian scene coming on". And they did as two young women appeared on a bed and began to take a serious interest in each others' naked bodies. Things were definitely hotting up and I glanced at Dave. He was drawing so feverishly on his latest Gitane that the ash was falling off the end of it as it does in a cartoon. The Master of Ceremonies liked to keep us up to date with proceedings on stage in his three different languages. "Und jetzt die orgasmus... Et maintenant, l'orgasme... and now, the orgasm". The two girls now grunted and squirmed as required. Dave's cigarette had gone. He exhaled a huge burst of fag smoke and clapped enthusiastically. So unlike the home life of our own dear Queen.

SCHOOL FOR STRIPPERS

Venue: an upstairs flat in Gateshead.

Dramatis personae: Madame, assorted nubile girls & me.

Continuing my Blue Period took me from the fleshpots of Hamburg to the shipyards of Gateshead. One way of defining "news" is that it must be new, true and different. Girls taking their clothes off certainly wasn't new but it was true. Filming a School for Strippers in Soho would not be different; it might even be regarded as rather glitzy and exotic. But Gateshead? That would be new, true and different. The North East did not disappoint. The den of iniquity stood in a humble row of terraced houses, presided over by a Madame who was straight out of Central Casting, big, blousy and once bonny. Her students were young Geordie Girls eager to escape the shipyards, throw off their clothes and embrace the world of the Arts. They presented in their best C&A tops and skirts, looking frightened. We set up our camera and lights, looking only a bit less frightened ourselves. The girls went next door, discarded the C&A numbers and reappeared in a variety of naughty kit, baby-doll nighties, dominatrix vinyl and school uniform. Someone had to go first. I remember her well, a flurry of pink chiffon which rapidly was discarded until she stood there in her pink knickers, which were obviously about to join the pile of pink on the floor. The cameraman and I had not expected such a bare-arsed display and, to cover our embarrassment, engaged in earnest talk about the lighting and the editing and anything that looked detached and professional. The Dansette Junior record player was reaching its climax and so was our stripping student. Off came the knickers. Now, I'm no expert, but I believe that after the "reveal" the lights are supposed to go out to save everyone's blushes and leave the punters wanting more. No, the poor girl was left there, stark naked in front of us all, while Madame delivered her critique of the performance. It was excruciating and due to continue with baby-doll, whiplash and assorted schoolgirls and nurses being taught how to remove a bra in the most provocative manner possible and how to step elegantly out of your pants. By now, the Dansette Junior was wheezing a bit and so were we. We "made our excuses and left".

While on the subject of naked women, and why not? I was sent to some fashion show in central London to cover, or should it be uncover the secrets of the posh fashion world.

Venue: a catwalk in trendy London.

Dramatis Personae: twelve top models, headed by Marie Helvin, a lascivious film crew, a positively leering "sparks" and me.

Who was the most alluring model of the seventies? It was, apparently, the question across the tout London in the fashionable salons of W1. Just how many painters and plumbers were talking about it in The Dog & Duck, Deptford, E13 was not part of my brief. We arrived and were immediately taken backstage where these fashion goddesses were whisking themselves into and out of some of the finest fabrics known to man. This involved them being naked for much of the time. I had always assumed that the notion that top models didn't wear any knickers or bras was designed merely to titivate (sorry) the aforesaid plumbers in the Dog & Duck. Not so. Now I could see for myself, as these near anorexic visions of female pulchritude floated before us that they were, in fact, bare arsed. My education had taught me words like "pulchritude" – I could even trace it back to its Latin roots, but it had not prepared me for a dozen beautiful women striding about starkers in front of me. We all busied ourselves with our suddenly very important film roles. Except the sparks. Bert was young and ugly with bad teeth and simply stared, leeringly at these Swiss Finishing Schools' finest as they showed off their naughty bits. For Bert, it worked. He trailed in the following morning looking like he'd been on the nest all night. And, indeed he had. The only one of us brave or stupid enough to ask the question "How's about it, then, darling" had got the result and the dame in question. "Well, they like a bit of rough, don't they?" was Bert's final word on the matter. My final words were to Sue: "No, I didn't".

ROBERTO TESTES

In the early seventies the above named and falsely named Roberto Testes, or was it Pedro Penis, I forget, was playing for Chelsea against Sunderland on Wearside. The crowd got on his back after some calumny he was deemed to have committed. Being a bear of little brain he chose to demonstrate against the booing by dropping his designer shorts and waving his willy at the good burghers of Sunderland. This brought the Wrath of the North East upon him and a charge of indecent exposure against Signor Testes. He duly turned up in Sunderland Magistrates' Court in an expensive crotch-hugging seventies suit and sat with his muscular thighs wide open in front of his accusers, who had already seen quite enough of the crutch his trousers were hugging.

We had all seen the offending incident on telly but the Defence knew that the Prosecution had to prove in court that someone had actually been offended by the incident. Chelsea's first mistake was to hire an expensive London QC to plead Roberto's case. It was a mistake because people in the North East don't like rich, smart-arse Londoners swanning up from the Capital to tell them what to do. Nonetheless, Sir Rodney Featherstone-Whittingby, complete with gold-rimmed half glasses, stood to cross examine the Prosecution's first witness, Mrs Agnes Bonnielass:

Sir Rodney: "Mrs Bonnielass, what exactly did you see on the date in question?"

Mrs B: "Well, I saw his thing like".

Sir R: "So you saw his 'thing' like? Can you describe it?"

Mrs B: "Well, it was a thing".

Sir R: "I think we've established that to the Court's satisfaction. Might I take the liberty of suggesting that what you saw was his penis?"

Mrs B: (who is now red-faced with embarrassment and clearly thinks that "penis" is the dirtiest word she has ever heard): "Yes".

Sir R. (who is warming to his task as if he were prosecuting a serial rapist at the Old Bailey): "So, you saw his penis. Can you describe it?"

Mrs B: "Well, no".

Sir R: "So you claim to have seen his penis and to have been offended by the sight, yet you can't describe it. Let me see if I can help you out. This penis, was it long or short? Was it fat or thin? Did it have any distinguishing marks on it? Perhaps you could enlighten the Court?"

And so on until Mrs Bonnielass was reduced to blushing incoherence. Sir Rodney sat down, satisfied that he had destroyed a main prosecution witness. Indeed he had but he had misjudged the twelve good men and true on the Sunderland jury, who found overwhelmingly in favour of the decent Agnes Bonnielass, leaving Roberto to carry his testes back to London and me to stand outside the Court and tell his tale to the *Six O'clock News* without delving too deeply into his nether regions.

THE BOYS IN BLUE

Dramatis Personae: Dave, the entire Merseyside police force and me.

From time to time the programme took on special projects. It fell to Dave and me to do a series of films about a regional police force. We chose the Merseyside force and persuaded the Chief Constable, Ken Oxford, to give us carte blanche to follow his officers around for several weeks. Mr Oxford was an unreconstructed copper. Picture the scene: the police Jaguar, the Chief Constable in full uniform and me with flared trousers and long, ridiculous seventies hairstyle sat in the back seats. Sitting in the floorwell of the front passenger seat was the cameraman, Paul Berriff, filming the great man as he was driven through his domain. A great deal of small talk was required as we toured Liverpool looking for suitable backdrops for the interview. Somehow the subject of homosexuality cropped up. The Chief had a view: "You can always tell a homosexual, you know" he declaimed with conviction "their upper lips sweat". It was now very hot in the Jaguar and my upper lip started to sweat, so the interview was a bit muffled from time to time as I strove to wipe away the tell-tale beads. But we weren't there to discuss the Chief Constable's latent homophobia, however quaint that might be. We wanted to meet the men on the front line. The police offered us two, clean-cut Hendon graduates who, we assumed would neatly toe the party line. We went with police to an emergency call-out where an old lady had died and was lying in the pathetic pose of death, near naked on the floor of her sparse bedroom. On the grounds that this suspicious death might turn out to be murder the murder squad of hard lads had been summoned. The detectives were bustling about looking for clues. Except for two who appeared to be avoiding the action as much as possible, Geoff and Tony. Geoff was the little, squat one with the shifty look and his oppo was Tony, tall good looking and obviously the Good Cop side of the duo. I said to Dave, "look over there, I think we've found our stars". Indeed we had. Tony liked the camera and Geoff loved the celebrity. Much later I introduced Geoff to John Stapleton. You would have thought he was meeting royalty. Let's face it, John, you are good, but not yet in the line of succession. Geoff and Tony gave us a real feeling for detective work on Merseyside which our Hendon graduates were never going to provide. In that soft, caring way of prime time television they were cast on the scrapheap of failed celebrity. Geoff and Tony though, if they delivered, were set for stardom. They delivered. They introduced us to the Bridewell, originally a Napoleonic prison, now the cells where they kept the drunks and the tramps overnight. I spent hours there watching the flotsam and jetsam of Liverpool's sub-culture traipse past me to the charge officer. Drunk and disorderly; actual bodily harm; grievous bodily harm; punch ups outside the pub; a touch of domestic violence here and some petty thieving there. Begging in a public place and obstructing the police in their inquiries were two favourite catch-alls. One image remains firmly in place. A pretty young policewoman came in with a disgusting old drunk half hanging off her. She had good, shapely legs and an immaculate seam down the back of her stockings. She was trying to scrape something off the back of her right leg. We don't want to know what it might have been.

One morning we were sat in the Bridewell waiting for the next episode in our prison soap opera when Geoff came up to me and said "we've caught a fucking animal overnight, a fucking black animal. Tony and I are gonna give him a bit of a kicking. You can come too, but you'll have to kick him or he'll realise you're not a detective". I was deliberately dressed as a detective, Marks and Spencer suit, Rael Brook shirt and tie but kicking drunken black men was not in my Contract of Employment. I politely turned down the kind offer and sat outside listening to the muffled sounds of a"damn good kicking".

On another occasion we filmed a prisoner being brought out of his cell, covered in blood. He had allegedly been beating up his wife and was, therefore covered in blood when he was brought in late at night. I had to write that part of the script with particular care but it was pretty obvious that the wife would have to be built like Mike Tyson to have inflicted all those bloody injuries on her own. Ken Oxford had given us total editorial control over the final cut. All he had asked for was a chance to view the film before transmission so that he could prepare a defence when he was attacked as he surely would be. The viewing of this episode ended with what appeared to be a prisoner who could have been beaten up in his cell. Both Dave and I were really nervous, as the film finished. Oxford turned to his driver and said, "Well, Bert, what do you think?" Bert said "I think it's great, sir, – that's exactly what it's like out there". No changes were requested and none made. Geoff and Tony were well into their stride now. Would we like to film them arresting and questioning a suspect? Yes, we would. We duly wired them up with microphones (Permission for clandestine filming had to be personally approved by the Director General in those days). The two detectives picked Vinny up as he was leaving the Magistrates' Court after being tried for another minor, brawling offence. Vinny gave low-life a bad name. It seemed that he couldn't have such a thing as a quiet pint. Every pub he entered involved a fight of some sort. The particular fight that Geoff and Tony were interested in had ended with Vinny "glassing" his opponent. He was brought from his cell by two warders who had, presumably been hired because they had no sense of smell. I have never smelt such a pong from anybody's socks before and never wish to again. Geoff did the bulk of the questioning but Vinny had played this game many a time and his only contribution was "I wanna solicitor" in a slurred voice that made him sound drunk, as indeed he was and had been in the Magistrates' Court before he was re-arrested. (He had insisted on telling the woman prosecutor how much he fucking loved her, which may or may not have helped his cause.) After several further cries from Vinny about his need for a solicitor Geoff thought it was time to make the position clear. He said: "You'll getta solicitor when I say you can have a fucking solicitor". This was good enough for us and we withdrew. Just a minute or so later Geoff and Tony emerged with Vinny. "Did he confess?" "Oh yes" said Geoff" in that Scouse "but of course" sense. "That was quick, wasn't it?" "Oh yes" said Geoff "You see my friend Tony is a big lad. After you left he picked Vinny up high against the wall and said to him: Now, fucking confess and d'you know what? He fucking did".

Dramatis Personae: Dave Rowley, Sir Charles Forte and me.

Location: Georges Cinq Hotel, Paris.

As usual, Britain was struggling with its balance of payments and its debt problems. *Nationwide* decided to ride to the rescue with a series of programmes under the title "Captains of Industry". Dave and I made two of the programmes: one on Saxon Tate of Tate & Lyle and the second on Sir Charles Forte of the Forte Hotel dynasty. The first was full of 100% undiluted Capitalism and endless boring shots of sugar wharves. They were making a lot of money. Enough said. The Forte extravaganza was much more fun. We had exclusive access to Sir Charles's private offices in the Grosvenor House Hotel on Park Lane and to his excellent PA, the real power behind the throne. One day I happened to mention to her that a regular stopover of mine in my life on the road was the Forte Red Roofs near Doncaster and that standards seemed to have fallen off recently. I later discovered that a fast car with two high-powered executives had been dispatched overnight to Doncaster to examine in detail just what had gone wrong with Mr Young's baked beans on toast. Having heartlessly dumped on Doncaster's management and their sub-standard baked beans my undoubted culinary senses were now to be tested at the Georges Cinq in Paris, one of two top establishments owned by Forte in the French Capital. Dave and I flew to Paris and took a taxi straight to the famous restaurant, Le Fouquet's on the Champs Elysée. We were determined to check out Sir Charles's competition in France. Dave was abroad, and back in holiday mode, so we dined well, but not wisely. Even less wise, once we had settled into our sumptuous suites at the Georges Cinq was the decision to empty the contents of our mini-bars into our maxi-tummies during the remainder of the afternoon. I fell drunkenly asleep, to be woken by a phone call from Dave, reminding me that we were expected to be dining with Sir Charles in an hour's time. I sat up on my heavy brocade bedspread and took stock of the sorry wretch who stared back at me from the Louis Quinze mirror. The thing looked awful, debauched and unkempt. And it had the hiccups. The only thing for it was a deep bath full of the fine emollients so thoughtfully provided by the Hotel. When Dave phoned again the thing looked a lot better, but it still had galloping hiccups. When he phoned a third time to say that Sir Charles and entourage had arrived I was still burping away merrily. Suddenly, there was a knock at the door. I opened it to discover a very pretty young girl who threw her arms around me in a tight embrace "Martin, you old bugger, you should have told me you were in

Paris, we could have spent the day together in bed just as we used to do, you naughty boy…" I was shocked and bewildered. I had never met this girl before. Nor did I know that she was Sir Charles's daughter, well up for the challenge when Dave had enlisted her help. My hiccups had gone.

I went downstairs with Dave and my 'new lover' to dine with Sir Charles in the top hotel in Paris with beautiful food and premier cru wine and liveried flunkeys emerging from the woodwork. No premier cru for me, a nervy attempt at every course and a desperate anxiety to suppress any chance of the hiccups resurfacing. I began this meal still slightly drunk and ended it stone cold sober with a splitting headache. I said my goodbyes and thanks and returned to the scene of the accident in my suite upstairs. I let out a final, huge belch and fell into bed. I am not asking you for your sympathy, a simple "what a prat" will suffice.

PERMANENT RESIDENCE

The transient life of the reporter on the road brought with it many delights from the occasional five star suite at the London Hilton to the insalubrious bri-nylon sheets of the bed and breakfast in the Gateshead Industrial Park, which came with free-standing plastic shower cubicle and the last man's dirt. On the rare occasions when we stayed in the same hotel for a long period of time, it was important to make it in our own image as much as we could. During the filming of *Merseybeat* we stayed in the Holiday Inn in Liverpool for about a month. Every night a group of thirsty detectives would turn up (collective noun a gumshoe of tecs?) and the bar would be drunk dry at the BBC's expense. My room, 212, became Club 212 and Dave and I stocked it from the local offie with everything that the well-dressed detective was flinging down the neck of his Rael Brook shirt in those days of wine and roses or rather days of cheap scotch and cigar smoke, which was the ambience in which I woke up each morning. I learned more about the average detective in Club 212 than I would ever have done while officially filming. Subsequently, I was glad to see the Met condemned as "institutionally racist" after the appalling treatment of the Lawrence family. It was certainly true of the canteen culture I encountered on Merseyside. These men were dealing most of the time in the gutter, but that was no excuse for seeing all blacks and Asians as a sub-species to be despised and yes, beaten about a bit from time to time.

Life on the road also meant a stream of practical jokes. The Holiday Inn, Birmingham was a favourite haunt for the practical jokers, who were often led by assistant cameraman, Alex Hansen and sound recordist, Tony Yeaden. On one occasion I passed Tony in the corridor and said I was just going out to buy some toothpaste. He immediately volunteered to get it for me. I was so grateful. Until I squeezed the tube and the paste came out in about fifty pre-punctured holes. Never trust camera crew. Quietly I got hold of the keys to the camera car and took my useless toothpaste to the underground garage and the crew Volvo Estate. You have to work from the inside out. First, I smeared paste behind the gear stick then all around the rim of the steering wheel again from the rear, out of sight. Finally I clambered out and ran tooth paste behind each of the door handles. The following morning we went filming. Not a word was spoken. Honour was satisfied.

I got off fairly lightly in the practical-joking routines. John Stapleton was not so lucky. The same crew, Alex and Tony, had by now become experts on the intricacies of Holiday Inns. Most importantly they had discovered a way to open the panel that gave access to your room from the corridor, giving them the power to cut off your lighting and, better still, make your toilet flush at will. They waited in the bar one night until John had gone up to bed. Then they went to his corridor and imagined his routine "he's taken off his shirt and tie… he's clambering out of his trousers… now he's thinking I ought to go and have a wee before I go to bed and now, flush…" John reports that their timing was immaculate and he couldn't understand why his toilet had a mind of its own. They then took it in turns to sneak up the corridor and flush John's toilet every twenty minutes or so. They were losing out on their beauty sleep but so was John. Eventually, John was driven to phone the Night Manager. "I think I've got a ghost in my room…" "Oh yes, sir and what is it doing?" "I think it's got the runs" said John, a broken man. "I'll send someone up straightaway, sir…" The man duly arrived, checked the room, gave it the all clear and left, passing two giggling oiks, Alex and Tony, further down the corridor.

Brian Gibson was a super film director and a fully paid up Geordie. He could stand at anyone's front door and say "Canna just come in 'n have a bit of a natter? Thanks very much, pet." And he was your new, best friend, which was a great advantage when doing investigative filming. Brian's introduction to *Nationwide* had been abrupt. One day he got a call from Frank Dale, the film operations manager asking him to go to Belfast to cover the Troubles for a couple of days. He bunged a spare shirt, knickers and socks in a plastic bag and set off for the troubled province during the bomb laden 1970s. Six months later he was still there. After the first week he had tired of re-washing his two shirts and bought himself an entire new wardrobe for the duration, – clothes to be shot at. Brian belonged to the alcohol shall be taken brigade. 1970s Belfast was not exactly the scene of a quietly insouciant and sober approach to the business of staying alive. Alcohol had its uses. One night Brian had put away enough of it to kill a horse and the crew decided they'd have to put him to bed yet again. Dragging him to the lift they passed the huge festive Christmas tree in the foyer and took an executive decision that it should accompany a tired and emotional Brian to his slumbers. It was a bit too tall for the lift and left a couple of top branches and the Angel behind as the doors closed. The crew got Brian safely into bed and tastefully arranged the Christmas tree at the foot of the bed, lights flashing merrily. This was the sight to greet his befuddled brain when he came to some hours later. Merry Christmas.

Brian worked with the Belfast crew and Bernard Falk, a Liverpool Irish Jew who sadly died early but not from an IRA bullet but rather a surfeit of Glenmorangie and naughty living. I still miss Bernie. When I made my first two *Nationwide* films he sent me a memo saying something like: there's nothing I despise more than some jumped up little college boy barging his way in to a sacred place like *NW* and showing off all his pipsqueak linguistic skills Well, try some of these linguistic skills for size: Fuck Off. He signed off "Great Films, cock, Love, Bernie. Ah, I thought, I have a friend at court. Bernie was always a dangerous friend to have and, particularly, to meet on the road. One fateful day we bumped into each other in the Lake District. I was filming with my good friend, Ken Stephinson and fulfilling a claim that if you could climb the Fell, go round the dragon rock and descend in less than an hour you would become a Freeman of Ambleside or some such nonsense. Bernie was engaged in similar major events just down the road. We met up in a lovely lakeside hotel. In the bar, of course, and the Glenmorangie began to flow from the optic with pleasing regularity. Bernie and I were minor celebrities at the time and had been clocked by the travelling members of the British Timber Society, who challenged us to a card game. They could clearly spot a couple of first class mugs from 500 metres. What they didn't know, however, was that I didn't even know what two hand brag actually was. I reasoned that I was fairly bright and would work it out as I played along. Indeed this happened but not before I was about forty quid down. I slowly clawed my way back to solvency and, in due course, to bed, not entirely sure of the financial outcome of the great clash between the Timber Commission and the BBC. The following morning I woke to find a message by the bed saying "I owe you £25 and I am a very silly man. Signed, Ken Stephinson." Many miles away in a small but precious office in Lime Grove Studios sat Sheila, the saintly provider of advances on expenses for those of us toiling so hard on the road. She must have wondered why Falk, Young and Stephinson all needed funds so urgently that day. What had her boys been up to? I bet she had a pretty sure idea.

Bernie, among his many other vices, was an inveterate gambler. Indeed Ken Stephinson, who liked this loveable rogue as much as I did, only stopped gambling with Bernie after a film in a slate mine. There was a minor roof fall, but bad enough to make a mess of a miner's leg. As the man lay there bleeding Bernie bet Ken that he'd need at least twenty stitches to sew up his wounds. Ken didn't take the bet.

On another occasion Bernie was filming the fabulous new Concorde at Filton or Toulouse and said to the crew: "As soon as we can see the plane I'm going to do my piece to camera. It goes like this: 'Concorde with its two giant Rolls Royce engines throttled back for landing is still producing four and a half thousand horsepower and a torque ratio of seven thousand psi to reach a landing speed of two hundred mph as opposed to the mach 1.5 she was cruising at just a few minutes ago'. And then," Bernie concluded with a flourish, "the plane lands alongside me". Well, the challenge was obvious. The cameraman said "You've only got one take, Bernie, are you sure..." In the end the whole crew bet him ten pounds each that he'd never do it. Concorde appeared on its final approach and the camera lens widened to reveal Bernie at the side of the runway. There was a pause before Bernie turned to camera and declared: "And here she is, Concorde". First take, forty quid, thank you.

Investigative Reporting

Dramatis personae: Peter Hill, George de Chabris and me.

Location: Miami. Florida

Peter Hill knew more bent coppers than a Metropolitan Police osteopath. Over the statutory half pints of bitter (detectives would never be seen downing pints) one of Peter's snouts handed him the entire accounts of the National Liberal Club, a venerable institution bought for some unknown reason a few years earlier by a mysterious Canadian "millionaire", George de Chabris. Why rich men choose to buy their way into politics is an eternal mystery but on this occasion it had nothing to do with politics and everything to do with the assets of the National Liberal Club. The accounts revealed how de Chabris had been systematically extracting money and artefacts from the Club during his term as owner, artefacts including a large Gainsborough which had for years adorned the atrium. De Chabris had long ago handed back the keys of the Roller to the hire-car company, tucked away his ill-gotten gains and fled to Miami. The Liberal Party was not having a good year. It had just emerged rather stained from the Jeremy Thorpe sex scandal, whose main victim was the innocent dog shot by Thorpe's lover on Barnstaple Moor. Poor old Rinka met his end in 1975. Among the great regrets of pranks never carried through this one stands out. There had been great sorrow from children throughout the land when the "Blue Peter" dog had died and a plinth was erected to Shep in the horseshoe car park at the front of Television Centre. On top was a sculpture of Shep's much-loved woolly head. A couple of us wrong-thinking people wanted to change the plaque underneath the animal to read: "In memory of Rinka shot on Barnstaple Moor, 1975". The switch-over would have been completed at the dead of night and the change only noticed years later. But we never carried it through which was a great shame.

We drew a blank with all the obvious London contacts. The Club's accountant politely suggested that we desist from our inquiries but we staked him out nonetheless. We did eventually get to talk to him in his expensive bachelor flat just off Marylebone Road. He was the essence of gentility but quietly declined to tell us anything. I think the recent homosexual scandal and the sudden arrival of two hacks purporting to be interested in the stewardship of the club made him think that he was being set up for yet another sex story. We set off for Miami and knocked on the door of George de Chabris' impressive mansion. There was little gentility here. De Chabris appeared at an upstairs window and said "Fuck off". It took us a week to convince him that an interview with us might be his only way out. We staked him out, followed him around and kept phoning him several times a day. Our researcher back in London phoned as well. Soon, de Chabris started answering the phone in Spanish, Miami's second language. Unfortunately for him our researcher's boyfriend spoke Spanish and he now joined the party. Unfortunately for us, all we learned was how to say "Fuck off" in fluent Spanish. We needed back-up and Her Majesty's finest corps of journalists was there in the Street of Shame to crawl out of the gutter and help us. De Chabris was now getting calls from all sorts of British hacks. We hand delivered a letter to the Miami mansion telling de Chabris that the game was up and half of Fleet Street was climbing on flights to Miami to demand interviews with him. There was, however, an elegant way out: if he would grant us an exclusive interview we would call off the approaching posse of scribblers. He agreed to an initial meeting with a promise of a television interview to follow.

Conning a con-man is such a delight. It was, however, only a promise so we resolved to wire me up for the initial chat so that we would, at least, hear some of de Chabris' answers. Our American film crew, who already thought we were certifiable, parked their van out of sight near de Chabris' mansion and put a microphone up the sleeve of my jacket. I discovered that by clutching a pair of sunglasses in my right hand and waving them about as I spoke there was little chance of noticing the small mike where my watch might have been. This whole "chat" was, of course, a parlour game. He wanted to know how much we knew and vice versa. By this stage I knew everything down to the numbers on the offending cheques he'd signed to embezzle thousands from the National Liberal Club but I was keeping most of this until later. We parted on good terms with him agreeing to come to our hotel at two o'clock that afternoon. As we were leaving, I said to de Chabris;

"Don't worry, Mr de Chabris, this afternoon the questions will be the same". "Don't you worry, Mr Young, the answers will be quite different". I realised that he was beginning to enjoy himself. Vive la Chasse. As we were leaving through the vast hallway the Gainsborough peered majestically down upon us.

While all this is going on there is a minor sub plot. A day or so earlier I had gone to downtown Manhattan and returned without my wallet, which was stuffed full of BBC dollars. It didn't need a Kojak to work out what must have happened to this innocent abroad. I phoned Auntie for some more cash and carried on.

My prey had arrived at the Holiday Inn, all smiles and confidence. I had read through my research notes yet again. As the interview progressed de Chabris' confidence increased and my mountain of damning facts increased. In truth, I nailed him. We both went away convinced that we had done well. Peter went with the crew to get some "wallpaper" shots of Miami to back up my script. Keep the crew on your side at all times is my advice. There is an apocryphal story about a crew in New York who felt they had been badly treated by a dictatorial film director. At the end of the shoot he lazily told them to get some local wallpaper shots while he retired to the bar. Back at Lime Grove he called up the background shots to cover the commentary and found two rolls of film of wallpaper in a New York DIY store.

I retired to my room to reflect on the minor scoop we had obtained for *Panorama*. We had the evidence now that de Chabris had systematically defrauded the National Liberal Club of tens of thousands of pounds and conned the upright British Establishment into believing he was indeed an eccentric Canadian millionaire with money to burn. They just hadn't realised it was their money he was burning.

The phone rang. It was the voice of an elderly New York Jew. She and her husband were wintering in Miami and had found my wallet on the sidewalk. It was in the hotel safe. Would I like to collect it? I jumped in a taxi and went to see these good people. I found them lying in the sun outside the hotel in the midst of a host of similar pensioners. It was God's waiting room with Florida sunshine thrown in. They were a delightful old couple who had gone through all my receipts and established that I must be staying at the Holiday Inn. "Don't worry, Mr Young, all the money is there". I believed them. I returned to my hotel room and summoned up some Holiday Inn champagne. The American crew came back with their rolls of wallpaper and gratefully accepted some champagne. Now they were convinced that the Brits were off their rockers. One interview and a few shots of Miami and here we were rewarding ourselves with the hotel's finest and most expensive brew.

Peter and I bought the old couple an enormous box of chocolates. Their first question was "are they kosher?" I didn't even know whether chocolates could be kosher or evil. Fortunately, I remembered that the window display had included a large, chocolate menorah, so I reckoned we were all right on that front.

VIDEO PIRACY

Dramatis personae: Peter, a bunch of South London crooks and me.

Location: Surbiton, Twickenham and Del Boy land.

From the glitter of Miami to the grime of south London – such is the varied lot of the travelling reporter. By the late seventies the world and his wife had a video recorder, which was fine and set off a legitimate market in videos for hire. Naturally it also set off a bunch of crooks who saw the chance of a cheap buck. Auntie in all her munificence was churning out award-winning programmes for free – you wouldn't expect these thieves to be paying their licence fee, would you? The rewards were enormous. It was rumoured that one Arab Sheikh was sending his private jet to London every week to pick up the entire output of BBC1 and BBC2, for his later delight in his desert kingdom. We started with rather humbler targets. *Monty Python's Flying Circus* was at the peak of its popularity and the BBC was selling it around the world. So was a little man in Twickenham. I had some cards made out that proclaimed me to be Martin Jones,

Video Specialist, put on my spiv suit and paid him a visit. The door was opened by a woman with babe in arms. I said that I had come about the videos. She was very welcoming and showed me into the black vinyl sofa room where another young mother was also nursing her baby. I had obviously overdone the spiv impression, because when I asked to see a sample of her partner's work, she immediately slapped on a porn video. A naked girl was showing an inordinate interest in a naked man's fully erect penis. For Martin Jones this represented a collapse of stout party. Porn I could handle but two little babies gurgling along with this gross fellatio was too much for me. As they used to say in the *News of the World* I made my excuses and left. But there was still a story there. I had established that what I really wanted was a set of *Monty Python* videotapes and she had said that the man would get them for me if I came back in a few days. The BBC was losing money and John Cleese and co were losing money as well. I went to see John in the BBC canteen at Television Centre and had this Pythonesque encounter. He was playing in a Shakespeare production and wearing full costume. He was deeply engrossed in this high art and just didn't have time for a silly *Nationwide* excursion. He suggested Manuel and when I returned to the Twickenham premises, Andrew Sachs came with me. Far from being the cringing Manuel, once confronted by the man who was stealing his work he exploded with rage: "you are making me poor, you are denying me a decent livelihood. How dare you steal my work? You are a despicable thief..." and so on until I actually began to feel sorry for the feckless idiot who had just passed over the stolen booty to me in the Twickenham car park beside his flat. This did not stop the video pirates themselves, but it did make it clear that the BBC knew what was going on and would prosecute anybody caught stealing their programmes.

The other thriving market for the pirates was the output of Bollywood, all those melodramatic productions coming out of Bombay and much loved by Britain's Indian community. We found an Indian video pirate operating out of his electronic shop in the Edgware Road. We wired me up and parked the crew around the corner. When they heard me say "That's a deal then, here's the money" that was the cue for them to burst into the shop and film the money changing hands, which I did slowly and ostentatiously. Then I did the interview with the miscreant in which he denied everything, a useless tactic since we already had all the evidence on film. The following day we returned and played exactly the same trick on the hapless shop-owner, except that when the crew broke in they were filming the Indian director of the very film he was busy buying. His interview with the video pirate was much more feisty than mine. To this day I have a vision of this little crook looking over his shoulder for the "Return of the Film Crew 3" every time he starts to do a dodgy deal across his counter. Who knows? Perhaps he has gone legit.

In our valiant campaign to rid the world of this pulsating evil of video piracy we now turned our attention to sport, always a money spinner. In imperial days Piccadilly Circus and the statue of Eros was supposed to be the centre of the world. In the late seventies it was video central, where any kind of video could be bought for the right price. We wanted a copy of the European final between Nottingham Forest and Hamburg but we first of all had to prove that it was a rip-off from the BBC, not some tuppenny ha'penny effort from the stands. By this time I felt hard wired with microphones. I sauntered into Mr Isaacs' emporium, a tiny shop stacked high with video cassettes. He had a shifty, conspiratorial air as he confirmed that for thirty pounds I could get my own copy of the match. I said I would only part with money if I knew for sure that it was the BBC's coverage. He said: "oh, yes, it's Motson, init?" John Motson was the BBC's main football correspondent for many years. I said I would return later in the day to pay the money and secure the cassette. In the meantime, Peter had come up with a wizard idea. When the deal was completed and the film in the can I was to turn to camera and say: "And that is how simple it is to buy a stolen video cassette, here in the centre of London…"

We put the camera in a black bag, with black lens poking out of one end and sent the cameraman in to browse through the video cassettes on the shelving. I was becoming an expert at handing out money very slowly. "So, Mr Isaacs you have given me a copy of the BBC screening of the European Cup Final for thirty pounds. That's ten, twenty, twenty-five (by now the camera is out of the bag and we are filming openly) and finally another fiver that makes thirty pounds in all. And that's how simple it is to buy a stolen cassette here in the centre of London. Thirty pounds may not seem a lot but multiply that by the thousands of crooked dealers like Mr Isaacs here and it mounts up to millions of pounds worth of royalties being lost by the BBC and other television companies every year. Let's talk to Mr Isaacs about this transaction…" People often say in an embarrassing moment "I wish the ground could have opened up and swallowed me". Mr Isaacs was the red-faced exemplar of this old saying. As he realised that he had been filmed and then heard my denunciation of him by name, he had been backing away but, as I said, it was a tiny shop and there was just nowhere to go. He decided to tackle me full on. "I didn't mean to sell it to you" he spluttered "here's your money back", thrusting the thirty pounds back into my hand. At that point I thought he was going to hit me. He was a lot bigger than me and looked like he'd probably had a few dust-ups in the past. To my shame I remember thinking, oh good, that'll make the sequence even better. But failing to grab the offending cassette from me he now moved a few inches back and covered his face with his arm as if this would make him invisible to the viewers. Eventually he climbed into a cupboard at the very back of the shop and that is where I did the interview. He denied everything. It didn't matter. The next time I drove round Eros, Mr Isaacs shop was closed. Whether he was still immured in the cupboard was not clear from the road. We had made a tiny pin-prick in a vast illegal industry, but we had also made an entertaining film for *Newsnight* on BBC2. The Beeb was grateful and repeated the programme as a special on BBC1. Fame indeed.

Peter and I found out that a sizeable piracy operation was based in an ordinary suburban home in Surbiton. Looking through the front window you could see racks of about fifty video recorders wired together, so that any tape you nicked off air could easily provide you with fifty copies at a time. (When the Leveson Inquiry was busy revealing the phone hacking scandal and other media excesses, my daughter, Annabel, asked me if I'd ever done anything like that. I replied truthfully that I'd never done any phone hacking, but I had once gone through some dustbins, looking for clues.) This was the one occasion when I violated a dustbin; – to find out how many empty cassette boxes they were throwing away every day. That's how we proved the large size of their operation. They wouldn't answer the phone or the door, even when we drew the crew's Land Rover across their front drive to prevent them leaving the house. Not many people had fax machines in those days but we found out their fax number and carried on a jolly little one-sided conversation with them, revealing that we had them "bang to rights". No reply. Our final fax read: "We know you're in there. Come out with your hands up." Still no reply. We put the story to air. Still no response but then no writs either.

One film I made at the time could have involved writs for defamation but ended up before the Complaints Commission instead.

Venue: A bureaucrats' room in central London.

Dramatis personae: Three members of the Complaints Commission, including Sir Alan Marr, John Gau and me.

I had never been up before the beak until that moment. My alleged sin was making fun of a pompous little man called Norman. The Federation of Small Businesses had appointed Norman as their new boss. His full name was Norman Small. Small of small businesses was good enough. I was dispatched to find out more at their annual jaunt by the seaside. Norman Small was straight from Central Casting. He was small, portly and pompous and pleasingly looked like Arthur Lowe playing Captain Mainwaring. I had gentle fun with Norman, setting him up against the formidable union bosses of the time. In the seventies these men were capable of shaking a government to its knees. Norman didn't look capable of shaking the Blackpool rain off his pac-a-mac. It was innocent fun but not enjoyed by Norman. Not at all. He complained to the Commission about our lèse-majesté in the face of his important public office. Most of these commissions, boards of inquiry or public watchdogs seem to make up for their lack of teeth by a surfeit of oak panelling and sober self-importance. Not so, the Commission under Alan Marr, a former Director of Public Prosecutions, who took away a great deal of the tension of the moment by saying at the start: "Before we start let me just say that all three of us thoroughly enjoyed your film, Mr Young". Thank God for that, I thought, he has a sense of humour and can see that our aim was gentle mocking not defamatory ridicule. We were exonerated. John and I took ourselves and our best suits to the nearest hostelry to celebrate. I shall never forget the first time I received a letter of complaint. It contained twelve points of error in my report. I read it through with dread and gave it back to my editor, Stuart Wilkinson. He read it and said: "Sounds like a Lime Grove lunch to me". And so it was. The aggrieved party is whisked by limo to the BBC's sacred portals, ushered into the Holy of Holies, the refreshment suites on the ground floor, filled up with Beeb booze and food, blandished with apologies for any misunderstandings that may have arisen and purred away by limo, placated. The lucky ones get to hear the anecdote about Val Singleton dancing on the table in that particular room and, better still, being joined by Sir Robin Day, who dances on a table very nimbly for such an ample man. Oh, the laughs we had and the writs we avoided.

CELEBRITY

"Jezza in *BB* sex romp with Cilly", "Bloggo in *Strictly* booze bust-up", "Katikins as cats arrive for *X-Factor* star"... and so on. Recognise any of the names? No, but they are fictitious to protect the stupid and particularly the litigious and stupid. When we had close-ups of Marilyn looking seductively at us from a thirty-foot cinema screen or James Stewart drawling at us or John Wayne through true-gritted teeth saying "I'm not going to hit you. The hell I'm not", that was celebrity. Celebrity that promised to last because it was real talent, not because it had once had a bit part in some tawdry soap opera or talent contest. Good God, even the judges now are celebrities in their own right with carefully-crafted characters, nice and nasty, ugly and pretty. Real celebrity is well worth celebrating and it is not just about Bogart and Bacall, Grant and Hepburn. Here in Britain alone we have some of the finest actors in the world, Michael Gambon, Derek Jacobi, Maggie Smith, Judi Dench, Ian McKellen... and many more. In sport we have Jessica Ennis-Hill, Mo Farah and Victoria Pendleton, David Beckham and a right foot that he has managed to turn into a global brand. Real celebrity is all around us and yet the tabloids bombard us with this ersatz landscape of z-list party goers and the self-invented. Are people's lives really so barren that they have to be consumed by all this tat? Who is sleeping with whom? Who is doing what to someone else also famous for being famous? Who cares? Please don't tell me that it all helps the TV ratings or the tabloid circulation figures. Public executions would achieve a far better result and you could take your knitting along. I know of what I speak. In the seventies and eighties I attained a degree of celebrity myself being a regular visitor to the country's living rooms through the films I made for *Nationwide* and *Rough Justice*. There weren't hordes of screaming girls clawing at me as I was moved from limo to five-star hotel but I did get a lot of "'Ere, you're that bloke off the telly…" "You're the news man…" "Oy, look Daisy it's that Bernard Falk…" Now, anyone who tells you that he doesn't like being recognised or asked for his autograph is lying to you. It's a very flattering experience and makes you realise that this most ephemeral of media does, nonetheless, have an impact on the public. I was standing at the Club Class desk at Heathrow one day, hoping for an upgrade on a transatlantic flight. Indeed I was always standing at Club Class desks asking for upgrades. The girl behind the desk said that she recognised my voice from LBC. Sniffing the distinct possibility of row ten or twelve I redoubled my effort to be charming. She said: "Yes, I always like to leave LBC on, my dog loves it". As I digested this tit-bit of news the Indian lady behind, dressed elegantly in a sari, said: "Yes, I thought it was you. I listen to you on the *Midday News*. I very much admire your use of metaphor". I got row twelve. Happiness is an upgrade. Even then, though, I could see the pitfalls of beginning to believe in your own publicity. Bit worrying, though, that she recognised my metaphors, had she spotted the litotes or the occasional enjambement?

The main presenters of the show were Michael Barratt, Frank Bough and Sue Lawley and they really did belong to the general public. Being recognised here and there was one thing for me but being recognised everywhere was everyday reality for them. Frank used to complain when I was doing *Rough Justice* that I didn't appear on the telly enough. It was true and it was a complement but I never wanted that kind of life. First and foremost I was a journalist, curious and occasionally probing but anxious to tell a story, silly or serious, human interest or investigative. In today's recreational garden the public seem unable to distinguish a Barbara Hepworth from a municipal rubbish bin as a work of art. I am a great fan of *The Sun*; they provide it free in our local, The Red Lion in Kidlington. Nothing nicer than settling down in my corner and reading *The Sun* but these days there is a vast swathe of the paper that might as well be written in Chinese. Who are these people whose sex bits I'm supposed to be so interested in? The paper's political coverage remains very good. I don't agree with Mr Murdoch's stance on many matters but his paper deserves respect for its diligent pursuit of Parliament and extensive sports reporting. The trick is impressive: *The Sun* sells somewhere between two and three million copies a day and the advertisers, who are putting millions of pounds on this, reckon it is read by as many as ten million people each day, including the casual reader like me in pubs and clubs up and down the land. If you strip out the children and those who never read a newspaper, you end up with a formidable political force in one newspaper. Despise *The Sun* at your peril, a memorable headline like "Up Yours, Delors" can put back the European project as far as Britain is concerned by decades. It was a great, shameful piece of *Sun* propaganda. Delors was the President of the European Commission at the time and had made some communitaire statement that *The Sun* didn't like. The front page had a huge two-fingered gesture to Brussels from a man in a union jack t-shirt against a background of the White Cliffs of Dover. The most telling point about the headline was that the English word "yours" doesn't rhyme with the French pronunciation of Delors. *The Sun* was asking us to reject M. Delors' proclamation, his language and culture. It was also asking us to gather at twelve o'clock on the White Cliffs and give the finger to the European

Union. That latter didn't happen, *The Sun* readers stayed in the snug bar and nursed their pints and their prejudices against the "cheese-eating surrender monkeys" across the Channel.

Because this fringe nonsense of celebrity is allowed to develop into an apparently viable, alternative social landscape the proximity to celebrity becomes intriguing. This is not new, think of "I danced with a man, who's danced with a girl, who's danced with the Prince of Wales". When my wife started teaching in Gosforth, Newcastle I often used to pick her up after school. One little boy said to her "Why does that man get out of the television in your house and come to give you a lift?" When we threw a recent party at Upper Farm we naturally invited good friends John and Lynn Stapleton. One of our other guests couldn't understand why these televisual giants were standing on our lawn. I tried to explain that they were mates not items to be gawped at or revered so that Susan and I in turn could gain brownie points for our proximity to the Great God of Television. For, whether it is a God or more likely a graven idol, it does make an enormous impact on people in general. Michael Barratt once asked the distinguished right-wing thinker and editor of *The Spectator*, Peregrine Worsthorne, how he thought the British People would react to the latest Tory sex scandal involving Lord Lambton and Lord Jellicoe and a call girl, Norma Levy. With cool deliberation Perry said: "Quite frankly, Michael, I don't think the British public gives a fuck." This was mid-seventies, well before the watershed and it went out live. Well, the balloon went up, Perry was banished from the BBC airwaves for the next ten years.

The following week I was scheduled to interview Mick Jagger live in the studio. These were his days of wine and roses, cocaine and Mars Bars and anything could have happened. The management were trembling in their pin stripes, convinced that Mick would provide Mary Whitehouse with yet more ammunition for her prudish Viewers' and Listeners' campaign. In the event he was as good as gold, just the sort of nice boy you'd like your daughter to marry. He'd have to have a haircut before the ceremony of course. When we retired to the Green Room after the show I was, naturally, eager to talk to him but I couldn't get a word in edgeways as he debated military tactics with a retired general who was also on the show. You would expect the General to know about such things but Mick was also quite erudite on the subject. The pinstripes had remained unsoiled and were pleased with my careful handling of the potential Jagger explosion of naughty words. I had been to Iran and Lebanon and to Israel and was certainly on my way to being "a Middle East expert", now after one interview with rock royalty I was to become the celebrity interviewer par excellence. Television thrives on such shallow thinking.

The most surprising instance of fame bestowed on me by dint of proximity to celebrity stardom was in Australia. Susan and I had hired a chauffeur to show us the sights in Melbourne. He was a very jolly young man with the most extraordinary hybrid accent, half broad Yorkshire and half Australian or "strine". I shall not attempt to reproduce the accent in print. I wouldn't know where to start. Listening to Sue and me in the back of his limo he divined that I worked for the BBC. Did I know anybody famous? I mentioned a few names. Had I ever interviewed Princess Diana? No, but then I remembered that we had recently had lunch at a corporate do with Prince Edward and his wife, Sophie. I had a really good time chatting to Sophie because we had a few mutual contacts in her PR world and the Media world. Edward was as stiff as a board and had clearly taken lessons from his father in loathing events such as this. Our Yorkshire/Ozzie driver was now dangling from the chandeliers with delight. (I once met a man who knew a Prince who had known the Princess Diana). As we parted later in the day I asked whether he had ever driven anyone famous. "No" he said regretfully, "but my Dad did drive Elvis once." In the name-dropping game trump cards don't come any better than that. I retired defeated.

REAL CELEBRITY

Now, firmly ensconced in my role as "interviewer to the stars" I was sent to interview Muhammad Ali during his visit to London. So, of course was every hopeful hack in town. I had a secret weapon in the imposing shape of my producer, John Coker. John was black and about six feet four inches tall. We were never sure but we thought that he was the son of the King of Sierra Leone. Most importantly from my point of view in 1960 John had fought a young black man, then called Cassius Clay, at the Rome Olympics. This man, towering above me, had fought with Ali. Ali was at the peak of his powers with both brain and brawn. The event was taking place in a large cinema in Lower Regent Street and had attracted the most enormous scrum of camera crews imaginable, what the Americans rather unceremoniously call "a goat fuck". Into this melee we plunged and awaited the arrival of the great man. He arrived and did not plunge into the mass of people. He seemed to float across them; there was a kind of aura about him that denied the usual crass calling out of questions. He was polite, smiling at the throng but quite detached. Bizarrely the only other person that I had seen with that untouchable aura was the mother of the last victim of the Yorkshire Ripper; – her pain was so evident and so enormous that it created a space, a vacuum around her. Ali continued his trance like transit of the room until suddenly his eyes focussed on my producer: "John" he cried out with real affection, "what are you doing here?" It helped that they were by far the two tallest men in the room and their chatter carried on literally above our heads. John led Ali away and we set up the interview in the front stalls of the cinema itself. I had naturally been only too content to play second fiddle but now was my moment. Ali played his part with ease. To any half difficult question he would say: "You're a very educated man, I wouldn't know about that" or "Of course you're a college boy, I'm just a simple street fighter, you'll have to help me to understand your clever question…" He had me reeling at the end of round one and eating out of his enormous hand by the second round. Street fighter maybe, simple, certainly not. He left on a cloud back to Mount Olympus. I got a taxi back to Lime Grove, having thanked my heavyweight producer for providing me with a scoop. I had just interviewed the man who would later be celebrated as the "Sportsman of the Century".

That was true celebrity.

BACK ON THE ROAD AGAIN

Hello again, Holiday Inn, same old four walls, I'm back on the road again. I don't think we stayed in the Holiday Inn, Palermo, but whoever owned the hotel had bought the concrete for those walls from the Mafia. If you bought cheaper concrete from anyone else you would end up wearing it and propping up the hotel forever. And that would have been a false economy. I mentioned earlier that I had written a book about the Mafia in Sicily and New York called *Men of Honour*. This was the *Panorama* that prompted that book. Through the sunshine laws in the United States we had been given access to the confessions of Tommaso Buscetta, a Mafia Godfather who was testifying against the capo di tutti capi, Gaetano Badalamenti in New York. The confessions ranged from the ludicrous; Buscetta describing the Mafia initiation rites which read like a manual from the Ramsbotham Masonic Lodge to the scary: two civil wars, countless deaths and a screenplay worthy of Francis Ford Coppola. Emboldened by the confessions and the obvious schism in the Sicilian Mafia two very brave magistrates, Giovanni Falcone and Paolo Borsallino decided to take the Mafia head on. For a time it worked until Falcone was blown up in a subway on his way to work at the Tribunale, Sicily's main Magistrates' courts. Borsallino carried on the fight. We went to interview him at his flat in central Palermo. Mr & Mrs Borsallino could not have been more hospitable. Their furnishings were all Louis Quinze, plenty of brocade and crystal. Signora Borsallino was a prim little bird of a woman, a house-proud humming bird. We had our coffee and cakes and conducted the interview across an elegant display table full of bric-a-brac from a surely less-violent era. As she perched on her chair watching her brave husband's interview I just felt terribly sad for her. It could only be a matter of time. And it was. A few months later the Mafia got her husband. She was left a widow, as I suspect she had always known she would be.

To understand the levels of tensions in those days in Palermo you only had to come to watch the arrivals of the Magistrates to work each morning. If you had the right permissions and papers, that is. The threat of imminent death was real. On the morning that we filmed our excellent Italian interpreter and fixer had got all the bits of paper that the Italian baroque bureaucracy could muster. The scene we wanted, and got, was both dramatic and comic opera at one and the same time. For the comic opera input think Captain Bertorelli in that wonderful sitcom 'Allo, 'Allo. The overdressed and oversexed Italian police favour screeching Alfa Romeos for a quick arrival at the Tribunale. Out of the windows they wave silly little ping-pong bats at the crowd to warn them of the arrival of their threatened VIPs. This makes a jolly scene for one and all. The scary bit comes when you look more closely at the police bodyguards themselves. They are in fear of their lives. If the magistrate they are carrying is shot or blown up, then they die too. One of the Alfas stopped at the entrance and, as the magistrate scuttled into the building, his guard, fifteen stone of quivering testosterone leapt out of the passenger seat and ran towards us using the international gesture for "get your fucking cameras outta here". At the BBC we have been to non-compliance school and I heard myself saying "keep filming" as Iron Man continued towards us at a rate. He was within a few feet when he raised his gun and pointed it straight at us. If I'm going to be killed could it please happen from a long way away and come as a complete surprise? Not a gun barrel just a few feet from my nose. What was particularly frightening was how scared the man with the gun was. I said testosterone fuelled a moment ago – no, this was fear high on adrenalin. Just in time the cameraman punched the pan handle and the camera swung away from the cop and the car. He dropped his pistol and shouted for us to go. We went. We went as fast as we could out of that piazza and straight into an ornate Italian hotel. Dead men cannot drink cognac but we were still alive. We could drink and did – at eight o'clock in the morning. I had never looked down the hole in the end of a gun barrel before and I never want to do so again.

RESENTMENT STIRS BENEATH THE VEIL

*R*ough Justice began in the late seventies and I entered a kind of no-man's land as far as the bosses were concerned. I had to earn my living, to fulfil my contract but the product, investigative films that would uncover miscarriages of justice was, as yet, unproven. So, in between bouts of research with Peter Hill, I would shuttle between *Newsnight* and *Panorama* or special projects. When Menachem Begin reigned as Prime Minister of Israel in the 1980s the BBC commissioned three half hour documentaries on the politics of Israel, to be directed by Peter Bate and written and presented by me. They would be broadcast at 9.30pm just after the main 9.00 o'clock news on BBC 1. It's hard to imagine that kind of scheduling these days. It might have made a late night slot after a re-run of the important news of the day, the *Strictly Come Dancing* results show. Nonetheless, Peter and I were duly sent off to Tel Aviv for a month's research followed by a month's filming. This was lavish in terms of production. I had destroyed the Mafia in just a few days filming; ending hundreds of years of Sicilian tradition (according to the idiot who had designed the book cover for *Men of Honour*) now I had a whole two months to solve the problem of the Middle East. Bill Clinton had taken eight years and finally failed on the White House lawn when the two parties wouldn't sign up to the deal. I had done extensive research, reading the *Jerusalem Post* in Lime Grove and was confident that I was the foremost expert in the field. In reality I had the wisdom to know how little I knew. I approached the research believing in "poor little Israel" and was quickly made aware that the story might be a bit more complicated than that. You only had to leave the one dimensional world of Tel Aviv or Jerusalem and drive out to the occupied West Bank and Gaza Strip to sense the grievances behind the continuing outbreaks of violence. This we did, encountering many of the Palestinian activists who wanted their country back, and encountering the little Israeli Major in the disinformation department who didn't like Peter and myself at all. My abiding memory of the trip was the constant summons to the Major's office to be berated. This plump, pompous little man would stride up and down his small room, shouting at us. We would promise never to do what he didn't want us to do. Then we would go out and do it again and return for further, shouted chastisement from the Gilbert & Sullivan Major. What larks. The West Bank with its thriving towns like Jericho and Ramallah did seem to offer some hope for the future. Gaza did not. Nobody had even deigned to call it a territory even or an autonomous region. It was just a strip. Indeed it was stripped of most of its menfolk each working day. There being nothing to do in Gaza, most of the sullen Palestinians had to traipse over the border into Israel to earn a living, adding insult to injury. Peter and I and the crew drove to Gaza City one morning from Jerusalem. We drove through the night, arriving in Gaza about 3.30 in the morning. It was good of Peter to save our lives as we careered along empty roads. Empty that is apart from the idiot in the Citroen 2CV who decided to make an abrupt turn directly in front of us. Peter was driving an American hire car that was big and silly and had the handling potential of a jelly.

Nonetheless, Peter managed to swerve and avoid both the idiot and the ditch at the side of the road. The Citroen driver ended up in the ditch. He was shaken but unhurt. We bounced his car back on to the road and still made it to Gaza city in time to film the daily exodus of miserable men off to work in Israel as the dawn was breaking.

REST AND RECREATION

In the midst of the Gaza gloom and the fulminations of the grumpy Major, we needed a Shining Light and we found him. His name was Bill Martens and he was the manager of the most kosher hotel in Jerusalem, the Jerusalem Plaza. He was Canadian and a goy and the friendship was first struck in the bar of his hotel and then guiltily consummated in his lovely apartment in the hotel, where he would cook us bacon and eggs at the end of a long day. We consumed this delicacy like naughty schoolboys let loose in a sweet shop. We were goyim let loose in Jerusalem's most kosher hotel and we were eating pork meat. I wish the shouting disinformation Major could have seen us. He would have burst a blood vessel.

You will have noticed that I have said little about the politics of Israel. This is because there is little to say. We called the documentary series: *Hanging Fire: the State of Israel.* The title sums up the state then and the state now. The most depressing reflection on that series, filmed over thirty years ago is that nothing has really changed. You could screen those programmes tonight, change the names and no-one would notice. Gaza is still benighted, Arabs still have to cross the border to earn a living, Tel Aviv still aspires to be a chic European style city while Jerusalem remains divided, bombs still go off. There is one central truth in this impenetrable struggle. Before I dare to express it I need to quote that urbane and civilized man Chris Patten, who is dramatically more qualified than a mere reporter to analyse the problem of the Middle East, having worked with all the main protagonists over many years. In his excellent memoir, *Not Quite the Diplomat* he "offers a confession that will attract criticism by the bucketload." He continues:

"I believe that in the Middle East there are two legitimate howls of rage, two storylines not one. I also share with Israel's former Foreign Minister, Shlomo Ben Ami, a wise and intelligent man, the view that, in his words: "The Holocaust... should not give the Jews and Israel any moral immunity from criticism, nor is it proper for Israelis to conveniently dismiss all and every attack against their reproachable policies as anti-Semitism... Anti-Semitism is a malevolent sentiment that I find difficult to comprehend. I hope some at least will understand how much deep offence they cause when they ascribe to anti-Semitism any criticism of Mr Sharon or the policies of the Likud Party. Of course, hostility to Mr Sharon's policies and the practices of the Israeli defence forces can drift into anti–Semitism. But it is unfair always to conflate the two."

My memories of the strident Mr Sharon are more clear-cut though hardly diplomatic. Catching him barrelling his way through the West Bank, I asked him if he would do an interview with the BBC. "Fuck off" he said. I think you should rely on Mr Patten's even-handed views rather than Mr Sharon's robust exchanges with the world.

The Jews have been horribly persecuted throughout their history, most recently by Hitler, but the Arabs have had their land taken from them. Every documentary I have seen over the years includes a scene where an old gent stands in a field and waves an old crumpled sheet of paper proving his right to the land, stolen by the Israelis in 1966. I have stood beside that old man. If I went back today I would be there with his son, the same scrap of paper and the same field. The establishment of a Jewish State was a noble and necessary idea. The theft of Palestine land was not.

I could not be that didactic in a BBC commentary, but I tried to get the balance right between Israeli and Arab. There is, however, no rational discussion to be had over this disputed land. It is either the land of Judea and Sumaria or it is Palestine. My attempts at balancing the issue fell on deliberately deaf ears. I was a Jew hater, anti-semitic and just plain wrong. Back at the BBC it was time for "meeting land" to become involved. John Gau, the head of current affairs went to the Programme Review meeting armed with a formidable defence of Peter Bate and Martin Young and their Israeli series. He anticipated fierce criticism, not least from the Chairman of the Governors. In the event there were a number of positive points made about what a beautifully shot film it was. Peter came in for well-deserved praise as a director and the cameraman Colin was noted for his excellent skills. Not a word about anti-semitism until as the meeting drew to a close and some junior head of Rubber Bands hoping, no doubt, to add Allied Paper Clips to his portfolio, suggested that the programmes might be just ever so slightly biased in favour of the Palestinian cause. Gau turned the heavy artillery he had been holding in reserve for the Chairman on the hapless junior manager and with a fusillade of heavy gunfire reduced him to rubble. Nonetheless it had taken Clinton eight years to fail in the Middle East; it took me just two months to fail. Had I won?

The dissent, the olive drab Major and the oppressive State all reminded me of my great friend, Michael Dutfield. I left Caius College determined to become the doyen of television journalists. Mick hadn't a clue what he wanted to do. We'd discussed every possibility including a life of crime. Think about it. It could be a great life, long periods of champagne and swimming pools interspersed with moments of adrenalin-fuelled tension as you stole the next shipment of diamonds. We were probably much cleverer than your average copper and could get away with our Raffles-style life. We had, of course, "parked" the issue of morality. That was only going to interfere with our plan. No, it was the word "probably" that gave us pause for thought. There just might be a copper out there who was cleverer than us and there are no five-star swimming pools or champagne bars in Wormwood Scrubs. We would be dealing with different bars in the Scrubs for the next ten years or so. Mick cut short this unhealthy discussion by disappearing to South Africa and, in the midst of the apartheid era, becoming chief reporter on the *Rand Daily Mail*, one of the few organs that dared to criticise the Government. I was very impressed by this until he explained that all the other reporters who had been above him in the pecking order had either been shot or bunged into prison.

One day, after Mick had written a particularly scathing attack on the Government after one of his regular visits to Soweto, the South-west Township in Johannesburg, a little man came to see him at the paper. He was dressed in what appeared to be a very smart, well-pressed Boy Scouts' uniform. He announced himself as Mr Van der Merwe of the South African secret police. "How do I know that you really are who you say you are?" asked Michael. The little man produced an ID card on which was written: "K. Van der Merwe, South African Secret Police. Mick decided that Mr Van der Merwe had an idea of "police" in his mind but didn't really seem to have grasped all the implications of "secret". "I have been reading what you are writing about Soweto, Mr Dutfield". "Oh, great" said Mick, "I hope you enjoyed it". For the first time, Mr Van der Merwe looked perplexed. Nervously fingering the hilt of the dirk in his long, woollen socks, he delivered himself of the Government's message. "Mr Dutfield, we think that you should desist". Mick was now all charm "I should love to follow your advice, sir, but I would have to clear this with my editor. He is a very considerate man and I'm sure he'd be delighted to see you".

Imagine the editor of the *Rand Daily Mail* at the height of the apartheid regime. He is unlikely to be a pussycat who rolls over in the face of Government pressure. He was in fact a huge wildebeest hunched over his desk editing copy. He didn't look up as the miscreant Dutfield walked in with his secret service nemesis. "Sir, this is Mr Van der Merwe of the South African Secret Police. He has been reading my articles about Soweto and has asked me very politely to desist." At the word "desist" the wildebeest jerked his head up and fixed his smoulder on little Van der Merwe. "Fuck off" he shouted and Mr Van der Merwe left with his tail between the legs of his Eric Morecambe shorts.

MALTA

Over the years the secret police and I have not, to be honest, rubbed along all that well. Even brave little Malta, the hero of the Second World War and now the holiday paradise for thousands of Brits, was no different. Film director and great friend, Ian Taylor and I were dispatched to make a film there about the left-wing Prime Minister, Dom Mintoff, who had taken over this Sussex on the Mediterranean. Because of his politics Mintoff had been attacking many rich establishment targets including the island's private hospitals. The Prime Minister himself would have nothing to do with the establishment figures from the BBC but we managed to find a private hospital doctor who was prepared to act as whistle-blower on Mintoff's tactics which, he said, were endangering his patients and could, in some cases, be lethal. That evening, relaxing in the marbled, baroque suite of the posh Valletta hotel I heard a knock on the door and Ian Taylor cheerfully announcing that the Thought Police had arrived for us and were urgently awaiting our presence in the public rooms downstairs. We rushed to meet this important duo who were charged with upholding the law of the land. They made many mistakes. First, they presented as sub-Cagney hard men in leather jackets and ill-fitting jeans. Second, they had come to our brocaded splendour in our five-star luxury hotel, not summoned us to their no doubt dingy and intimidating offices. Third, and most unfair, the Maltese are quite small in stature, Ian is six feet and I am smaller but still not in the least intimidated by these comic opera gangsters. Finally, they were just not the sharpest knives in the barrel. "Mr Young, when you arrived here in Malta, what did you write on the entry form at the airport?" "I wrote BBC television reporter just so as you wouldn't be confused." "And why are you here?" "I'm glad you asked me that" I said, looking glad "We've come to make a documentary film about your Prime Minister, Mr Mintoff. Actually, you could do us a favour and put in a good word for us with Mr Mintoff so that he agrees to an interview with the BBC. Could you help us with that?" It just wasn't going well with Cagney and Lacey and they soon departed. Ian and I thought BBC: 1 Secret Police: 0. We never did get a sight of Mintoff but I got to interview the Deputy Prime Minister nonetheless, a man who made the two secret policemen look like celebrity mastermind. Think about it. If you want to rule the country as a mini-dictator, you do not appoint a gifted, clever man as your number two and Mintoff had not so done. His deputy was as dense as a Maltese Falcon, except in this case there was no dull exterior to be scraped away to reveal a brilliant interior. It was quite easy to wipe the floor with him, so much so that I began to worry about what to say to him after the interview was over. I shouldn't have worried. He thought he'd done really well and we sat there congratulating each other on how well we'd done. The Chivas Regal was brought out in a suitably Presidential decanter and much was consumed. We had our story and a full, if wildly inadequate reply from the Deputy Prime Minister. The film duly screened on the BBC and made quite an impact. You don't need to take my word for it; Mr Mintoff banned the BBC from entering the island for the foreseeable future.

This story comes with an embarrassing post script. During

that "foreseeable future" a BBC sound recordist, his pretty wife and two tousled-headed children went for their annual hols to Malta. When they tipped up at Luqa Airport the Customs Officer scanned his passport and saw Occupation: BBC Sound Engineer, stuck him back on the plane with Mum and two kids, buckets and spades and sent them back to Britain. I still feel ashamed of that moment caused entirely by Ian and me and the perfidious BBC. Yet another example of how those three little letters can be a two-edged sword anywhere in the world. They have taken me through many an otherwise impenetrable foreign barrier but they consigned Mr& Mrs Sound Recordist to a fortnight's holiday at home in Hounslow, listening to the planes from Heathrow flying overhead to sunny beaches.

THE TELEVISION TRAINING GAME

There were still large parts of the world to explore but the days of the BBC buying the plane tickets for me were clearly numbered. It was time for a spot of self re-invention. Andy Warhol's famous observation that one day everyone would be famous for fifteen minutes was becoming a greater reality by the minute. Michael Barratt left the BBC for what he called the "romance of business". He formed his own company selling himself and the power of television to rich punters. The business elite was waking up to the fact that having the boss on TV could be a triumph or a disaster.

God's gift to the nascent television training industry was a man called Gerald Ratner. If you ask a British audience of top executives "how do you spell Ratners?" the brightest among them will immediately say C.R.A.P. This is the correct answer. Gerald Ratner had been at his most full-blown during the Thatcher eighties. He ran a successful, cheap chain of jewellery stores called Ratners. At the peak of his confidence/arrogance he delivered himself of the following in a speech to the Institute of Directors at the Royal Albert Hall:

"We also do this nice cut-glass decanter. It comes with six

glasses on a silver- plated tray that your butler can bring you in and serve drinks on. And it really only costs £4.95. People say to me: 'how can you serve this for such a low price?'

"And I say, because it's total crap…" (Pause for laughter)

"…We even sell a pair of earrings for under a pound, gold earrings as well and some people say 'that's cheaper than a prawn sandwich from Marks and Spencer' but I have to say the sandwich will probably last longer than the earrings.'"

Pause for more hearty laughter from the fat cigar brigade. Pause to consider the enormity of just one word, crap. Pause to consider the hubris this rich entrepreneur was enjoying at the expense of his customers. Never let it be said that the public is stupid. Ratner lost his business. He now gives after-dinner speeches devoted to his one word notoriety. Well, it's crap, but it's a living.

More recently the Head of the Immigration service was asked on television how many illegal immigrants were in Britain. He said "I haven't the faintest idea". This is the wrong answer. It's true but it needs to be set in context. For instance: "we can't be sure because these people have come here illegally and so they don't show up on any official documentation, but we think it's some tens of thousands and we're strengthening our procedures to locate them and send them home." That may be bullshit but it's going to keep him off the front page of the *Daily Mail*, which is what most sane people would want. So, dramatic evidence of the power of the word but also the power of television to spread that word into sitting rooms and board rooms across the world. When we set up Chevron television training we had a dry accountant who would resist all my attempts to say the magic word, television, would be our salvation. He would not accept my idea of the power of television until it came to his birthday party and I, for perfectly honest reasons, could not attend at the last minute. Our accountant was furious. Clearly he had been telling all his friends that the man from the telly would be there to celebrate his birthday and they had been disappointed that all they got was a load of other desiccated accountants. You don't have to like the power of television but you would be foolish not to acknowledge it.

My first encounters with television training came through a strange little company called Wadlow Grosvenor, run by the formidable Jean Wadlow out of a prestigious post-code in Grosvenor Street, London. It was in a basement beneath a hairdresser's shop but it was in Grosvenor Street close to Claridge's and the American Embassy. The film I most remember making under the auspices of Jean was an interview with Dominic Cadbury in Cadbury headquarters at Marble Arch. The call was early one morning with the thundering Marble Arch traffic flowing by. The director presented himself in ancient tweed jacket and cavalry twills. He was not in the first flush of youth and, one immediately suspected, had not seen a cine camera raised in anger for some time. He instructed me to stand with my back to the traffic and say: "In a moment I'm going to be crossing the road here at Marble Arch and going to interview Dominic Cadbury in the Cadbury Headquarters behind me". I duly crossed the road and reached the front entrance. "I'm here now at the entrance to Cadbury's main headquarters and I'm about to go in to interview Mr Dominic Cadbury". The camera, aquiver with excitement follows me in to the front desk. I walk up to the Commissionaire and say "Good Morning. I'm here to interview Mr Dominic Cadbury." "Certainly, sir, come this way" and I follow him across the foyer. At this point the cameraman, a smart young Canadian, said in my ear "Christ, Martin this could set cinematography back thirty years". I agreed with him but like the unhappy prostitute I had taken the money and now must perform my task. The next shot is a door with Dominic Cadbury written on it and my hand comes into shot and... I can't go on; this is so dull that I'm even boring myself. The interview itself was no problem, Dominic was pleasant and relaxed and articulate. Jean Wadlow sat perched like a vulture over the proceedings lest I should do anything to upset her precious client and offered some suggestions of further questions which were completely superfluous but still got asked. The film was duly cobbled together and deemed acceptable. The good thing about being a celluloid prostitute is that, having done your first task well, other tasks follow. This was the beginning of my reinvented self as poacher turned gamekeeper, teaching senior executives how to handle themselves on TV. A further bonus was a trip to the Cadbury's factory in Bourneville where I was proudly introduced to the "Curly Wurly Managing Director", a decent cove who gave me a box of curly wurly and a box of assorted Cadbury sweets to take home. It was the first time my young children, Jonathan and Annabel, had realised what a worthwhile job their Dad was doing. I was the Curly Wurly Dad par excellence. Back beneath the hairdryers in Grosvenor Street I had discovered a whole new source of income, training executives to give interviews on telly. I had also discovered a lady who was going to become an important and valued colleague and friend for many years to come, young Adrienne Reynolds, whose father had been Indian Army through and through and presumably called his daughter by an almost male name in his disappointment that his little girl would not be much use facing the Indian hordes. How wrong he was. Addie was a blonde, mini-skirted star of the seventies when she worked in PR with the Charles Barker Company. Her eye-lashes no doubt helped to seal a number of deals and to attract eager young men in Cuban heels and flared trousers to the doors of Charles Barker. Then she worked in the Wadlow Grosvenor empire and somehow survived not the Indian hordes but the far more terrifying Jean Wadlow. Looking around the basement jungle, where Addie was the only one to have a window, where she could look through the security bars onto the small, squalid backyard, it was clear to me that she was the only one who knew what she was doing and what she was selling, the power of television. Not long after the Wadlow experience we set up a company called Chevron to concentrate on television training. Addie found some genuinely prestigious premises in Bloomsbury, half way between the West End and the City and oversaw the construction of a purpose-built studio in the basement of this fine Georgian building. This time though she could work on the ground floor and we had a conference room on the first floor. The premises were good enough to impress bigwig chief executives and flexible enough to run two courses at the same time. Business was booming and we rented a similar set up across the road. Picture the scene: an attractive woman would be seen regularly leaving number 13 Great James Street and crossing the road to number 8, followed by a gaggle of men in suits. After an hour or so the same men would re-cross the road clutching their own personal video. I can report that the Vice Squad never came to investigate. The Scarlet Woman of Great James Street got away with it. Addie has been the valiant mainstay of Chevron over a quarter of a century although, remarkably, she, like me, is only 28 years old. During this time she has had to deal not with the Chief Executives of big companies but with layers of boot polishers, PRs and PAs planted in her way to obstruct access to a succession of Mr Bigs. As we moved into Crisis Management, it is perhaps best personified by the airhead PR who rebuffed her with the confident assertion: "We're not planning to have a crisis this year."

Journalism is just common sense. So is training people to be on the telly. I had no training on how to do it. Like Topsy it just growed. Let's start at the end. There are only two words you need to remember; be honest. There are two reasons behind this advice. First, it's the correct and ethical thing to do but, far more importantly, I just might know that you are lying and have the evidence to back it up. At which point, collapse of stout party. The camera doesn't lie. Yes, certainly today the technology exists to morph a boring man in a suit into Marilyn Monroe and twist his words to say anything you want him to say. You have to take me on trust here for a moment. We don't do that. The image would be ridiculous and the twisting of meaning would be a sackable offence at the BBC and any other serious broadcaster. No, the problem is your face and your eyes, the windows to the soul. The camera can simply see when you are lying. Even the great communicator and serial charmer Bill Clinton couldn't conquer the camera. Look closely, "I did not have sexual relations with that woman". Just at the last second his eyes flick away from the camera. It's a lie. He knows it's a lie and now you know it too. The only part of that famous Nixon/Frost interview that you sincerely believe is the confession, when the weight of the months of deceit are finally lifted from Nixon's sagging frame and he admits that he has let down the Office of the Presidency and the American People by his behaviour over Watergate. In my days of regular interviews with politicians I introduced the FOTMI index. The acronym stands for "the fact of the matter is…" As soon as you hear that you just know that he or she is not going to answer the question. The public is not stupid, it can spot a wrong 'un at 500 metres. These simple truths came as a great shock to the many senior private and public executives who came through the doors of 13, Great James Street over the years. In that famous interview between Michael Howard and Jeremy Paxman, where Jeremy asked him the same question thirteen times, Howard thought he had successfully avoided answering, but throughout the land the sofa audience just thought "answer the question, for God's sake". A transcript of that interview reads like a poem. Howard begins with a fresh cadence each time he refuses to answer: "The fact of the matter is… I told the House of Commons that… the most important fact to remember is" and so on. The starkness of Jeremy's question, requiring just a yes or no strikes in to Howard's sinuous responses like a hammer blow. Many people regard this as strident and awkward. I think it is pure theatre and perfectly valid. Jeremy himself has said of politicians in general that whenever confronted by them, his first thought is: "why is this lying bastard lying to me?" How interesting those same politicians are once they've retired from the fray. Heseltine was all smarm, Tebbit was all chainsaw massacre, but in their later years when all political careers end in failure we suddenly see a transformation into elder statesman status. We learn from Tebbit that, as they all plotted to remove Thatcher, he drew the short straw and had to go on *Newsnight* to defend the Tories and stress how solidly the Cabinet supported the Iron Lady. As he left the Commons cabal who were all hunched over the gunpowder barrels and the slow fuses, Tebbit said to them "This is the last time I go out to lie for her on television". Now there is a political statement you do know to be true, don't you? Lord Heseltine has settled into the role of grand elder statesman with ease, Lord Tebbit has settled for grand old acerbic critic of his own side and, of course, the dreaded socialists on the other side. I used to be terrified of them both, now it's a delight to hear them talk candidly. The late Tony Benn still had the same faultless logic as ever, up to the end. In latter years he became more of a music hall "turn" than a fiercesome force. Ah, the pleasure of interviewing them all now, as opposed to thirty years ago.

THE BRUTAL TRUTH

So, how does television training actually work? It must not be just psychobabble; it must be practical, sitting in front of a real journalist with real questions and a real camera. I used to do elaborate research before each session just as if the finished product was going to air. PR people always send you the annual report which is full of cheerful, hygienic employees of every hue and colour and gender. Everybody is having a ball working for Bloggins and company. The annual report is useful though since it tells you how much money the Chairman and Chief Executive are earning. Then it goes in the bin with all the latest press releases that the spin doctors have also sent. A press release merely tells you what excellent new thing that excellent company, Bloggins & Co. have done recently. I want to know where the bodies are buried, so press clippings are the kind of research to focus on, not press releases. It's remarkable how little management knows or cares about television. They are, of course, perfectly entitled to dislike television and journalists but they must learn how to deal with them, particularly in the event of a disaster. The crash of Pan Am 103 over Lockerbie was a terrible disaster and Pan Am's response was a disaster in itself. Once you make the Chief Executive aware that a bad response on TV can drag down that shibboleth for all bosses, the company's share price, you have them by the balls and their hearts and minds will surely follow, as the Green Berets said in Vietnam, embellishing an original LBJ speech. In Pan Am's case an independent report into the aftermath of the disaster concluded that it was not the fact of the crash that destroyed the company, it was their late and tawdry response to the disaster that finished Pan Am. It took them three days to dispatch a vice president of the company to Scotland to face the cameras. British Airways had been so embarrassed by the behaviour of the American company that they had actually dressed up some of their own employees in Pan Am uniforms to deal with the media on the ground in Lockerbie. Yes, the company already had severe financial problems but the PR gaffes seemed to indicate that they didn't care. This is not psychobabble – this is the death of a multibillion pound company. There is a huge traffic across the Atlantic, why would you want to sit at 33,000 feet above the ocean on an airline that doesn't seem to care about its passengers, that doesn't seek to reassure them in the aftermath of a crash?

Compare that with the behaviour of British Midland after the crash on the M1 as the plane tried to reach the end of the runway at East Midlands Airport. Sir Michael Bishop, the Chairman, had a plan to be put into action in the event of a disaster. The first plank of the response was to get the Chairman to the scene as fast as possible, whether that be Honolulu or, in this case, the end of his own local runway. Second, get what facts you know out as quickly and accurately as possible. Bishop stayed there all night answering questions from journalists from all over the world. He could only really say three things: how desperately sorry he was for the victims and their families, what the latest death toll was, and how the company would immediately launch a full-scale inquiry into what went wrong and ensure it could never happen again. It was an obvious message but the boss of the airline had rushed to the scene and was clearly moved by what had happened. And he had got the message out quickly. This is the harsh reality for chief executives faced with a crisis. During the Boer War the great foreign correspondent of his day, Howard Russell was sending home dispatches that took weeks to reach the pages of *The Times*. Today, those dispatches would be back on the Foreign News Editor's desk with one satellite phone call – instantaneously. When the bomb went off at Downing Street during a Cabinet meeting it was 10.08, the first report was on a newsflash at 10.16 on the BBC. (The times are approximate, but fairly accurate). This is not just the development of startling new technology it changes the game completely. What? A bomb. Where? Downing Street. Who? The entire cabinet. When? Eight minutes ago. Then the big, vital question why? Today the facts are immediately available, so the difficult question "why?" gets asked straightaway at a point where no-one actually knows. You must have a plan. Pan Am did not and went under. British Midland did and is still flying today years later. The irony is that Pan Am did nothing wrong on flight 103, they were the victim of a terrorist bomb, British Midland's pilot did do something catastrophically wrong – he had already lost an engine and in the flight deck confusion he shut down the good engine on his approach. In media terms though perception is nine-tenths of the game. Pan Am bungled its response, British Midland reassured the public.

If the senior executive you are training still thinks that a television interview is easy, he doesn't think that after you've put him through it. He has to sit through a replay in front of his peer group and watch himself sweat and shuffle in his seat. On one memorable occasion the executive I was interviewing lost his train of thought in the middle of an answer and stuttered to a halt, saying "oh, sorry…" This was quite funny on replay but, we agreed it would be better not to repeat a lapse like that in the second interview. He was still pretty dire in the next interview and lost it again, saying "oh, sorry… oh shit…" we agreed that if he had to say anything to cover his shortcomings "oh shit" was not ideal. Television is an unforgiving medium. What you look like matters almost more than what you are saying. To that extent if you have the audience at home saying what a nice chap or what a pretty woman you are, then you are well on your way to a successful interview. If, like Nixon, you sweat under the lights and the beads of sweat glisten on your five o'clock shadow, you are on a hiding to nothing. On radio Nixon won against Kennedy because of what you could hear him saying, on television Kennedy's movie star looks won the day every time. Going from the sublime to the ridiculous I remember training some little man from a water company. He was very keen on television, knew a lot and was very articulate. I've no doubt he was very nice to Mrs Waterman and his two tousle-headed children. Unfortunately, he was diminutive, with greasy looking salt and pepper hair and matching beard and glasses. The piece de resistance was his nose, a big fistful of pink mud in the middle of his face. It didn't just dominate his hairy face it practically took over the studio. It was a great shame because he spoke very well on television and was very enthusiastic. The problem was what he looked like. In pubs up and down the land they'd be saying "did you see that bloke with the big hooter on the box last night?" In my subsequent report I suggested that he would be good on radio interviews for the company and let him down as gently as I could. This is not just a trivial point. If you are distracted by someone's looks, you tend not to listen to what they are actually saying. Communication between the man on the telly and you at home has broken down; your mind is full of distracted thoughts: "Is he wearing that false nose for a bet? Has the makeup artist stuck it on as an afterthought? Or for a laugh? Does he think that horrible stringy beard is covering it up? He speaks very well, very confidently, oh God does he really believe he looks like George Clooney?" These are not the thoughts you want to be going through the viewer's mind as you try to defend your company.

THEY SHALL NOT BREED

Genetic engineering is not a cuddly subject to set before the viewer. Yet if it is what your company does for a living you have little alternative but to defend it. I went to Berlin to train a couple of executives on how nothing could go wrong... go wrong... go wrong. They apparently learned a lot from the German session and invited me to their headquarters in Philadelphia to teach the evil arts to the big banana, their chief surgeon. Now surgeons are excellent people and can rummage around in your insides and make you better, but they can be a bit odd. The very fact of cutting open another human being and sticking your hands in him or her to do the rummaging is often essential to keeping them alive, but it's still a bit odd. I asked the Belgian surgeon who was busy genetically engineering animal embryos what he could do if it went wrong and a seriously damaged embryo were to be born. "We would know of the mutation long before birth and we could terminate the embryo". And if a damaged human embryo were to be born, what would you do? "Look after them in special camps". This is getting worse. "Or, of course we could neuter them so that they could not pass on any genetic mutation to the next generation". By now the word

Mengele is at the forefront of my so far unmutated brain but I draw the line at that and say instead: "Doesn't that smack of eugenics?" The question goes right over his head and he bumbles some sort of reply, but the game is lost. I put in my subsequent report "Never, ever put this man on television or let him speak on radio". I felt like adding, send him to a camp but resisted the temptation.

BIG TOBACCO

That was a rare encounter with Big Pharma, my relationship with Big Tobacco was to be much more protracted. My involvement with Big Tobacco began with a debate, a prolonged debate with myself. Did I want my company or myself to be associated with a product that kills? Would I be seen as an apologist for a foul trade? I had never personally smoked cigarettes, but would my right-minded friends in the liberal elite, who had probably smoked other substances but not tobacco, be appalled by my taking the nicotine money? In the end it was that word "liberal" that made up my mind. As you will have gathered from *Rough Justice* and other stories recollected above, I have always been suspicious of the Establishment and those who wield power. The Government of the day has a duty and a right to levy taxes. With that money I am perfectly happy for them to exercise the rule of law, protect our safety, educate our children, deliver the NHS and empty our dustbins. Then they should stop. I don't need the Government to tell me what to eat or how to conduct the minutiae of my life or that of my family. The decision to take on the tobacco training was, ironically, spurred by the anti-tobacco lobby. Knowing that they had effectively won the battle against active smoking, they switched their attack to passive smoking. It had been clear since the 1950s that active smoking was linked with cancer. The scientific evidence that passive smoking could damage the health of non-smokers was much more tenuous, but also much more dangerous as a line of attack. If the anti-smoking lobby could prove that the very existence of tobacco in society was damaging everybody, including non-smokers, then it could banish smoking as a pariah.

It was passive smoking that Big Tobacco wanted to defend. I reasoned that the next thing was going to be smoke-free pubs, which has indeed come to pass and that the next target would be alcohol, my drug of choice. "How do you fancy coming out for a wild night down the pub with no alcohol and no fags?" it's not much of a come-on, is it? I said that Chevron would take on the work. Then they told me where they wanted the training to take place. They wanted courses in Barbados, Hong Kong, Johannesburg and Budapest to start off with. It was another trip around the world that, this time, wasn't being paid for by the BBC, but by Mammon and Mammon travels business class. The first trip, to Barbados, was very instructive. I remember one grizzled old black man with white hair, who had obviously worked for the company since God was a boy. He just couldn't believe that his company was opening itself up to the media. It was as if he had been protecting the secrets of a Barbadian Bletchley Park all his life and was now being told to blurt it all out in front of the cameras. The truth was that the big Tobacco companies, confronted by the overwhelming scientific evidence against their product had battened down the hatches and refused to talk to the media for fifty years. They reasoned that a significant percentage of smokers would continue with their addiction because they couldn't or wouldn't give up. They maintained, of course, that tobacco was not addictive, a stance severely undermined by one of their American vice-presidents saying in a board meeting: "We are, therefore, gentlemen, in the business of selling an addictive substance, nicotine". When it came to passive smoking, though, the companies realised that they had to fight their corner at last.

I decided to tackle the tobacco course just like any other training, except that this time it wasn't difficult to find out where the bodies were buried. In every parish of the land. There were to be no patsy questions. Sample questions from company PR representatives can often fall into a blinkered line like "And what other excellent things has this excellent company done recently that are excellent?" You can just hear that tripping off the tongue of Jeremy Paxman or Jon Snow can't you? Chevron courses always strove to drill down to the nub of the issue. It wasn't hard to find with Big Tobacco. All the venues, all the executives on a series of training courses tend to blur together over time, but some stand out. I was interviewing a very handsome Dutchman with dark eyes, a manager in one of the company's far flung territories. The company had recently been exposed as a pusher of free cigarettes to young people on some exotic beach. He was frantically denying that his company aimed their product at the young, so I said: "Of course, it makes sense for you to target young consumers since your product is steadily killing off your older customers who contract cancer, emphysema and heart disease. You must get some new, young smokers on board so that, in time, you can kill them off too with your lethal product. That's the brutal truth. Isn't it?" It was a long question and, as it evolved, I watched his dark eyes get even darker until he looked as if he was staring into the abyss, looking deeply into his own soul. He had no reply. I let him sit there until the camera had had its fill and then, politely said "thank you". In some parts of the world, notably in South America, my assertions about cigarettes were fiercely contested. In Columbia, a fiery-eyed little man just couldn't take my heresy any longer and burst out with: "Whatsa the big problem? In Columbia everybody smokes, the women all smoke, the children smoke. Whatsa wrong with that?"

For the tobacco companies there was, indeed, no problem. As

the First World market declined in the West, the Third World market was burgeoning in the East. As India and China started on the road to world economic powers they developed an affluent middle-class who would willingly pay a premium for the status of smoking Marlboro or Benson & Hedges. The share price just keeps going up. It's a shame that people have to die. It took me five years but I got the tobacco spokesmen from a categorical "there is no link between smoking and cancer" to the admission that "smoking causes cancer". After the blatant denial of the first statement no-one sensible is listening to anything else you say, after the second admission you at least have the chance of being heard. Having said that, I saw the Chief Scientist of the company rehearsing the new defence of passive smoking on *Newsnight*. My two grown-up children, Jonathan and Annabel, almost fell off the sofa laughing.

BIG OIL

My involvement with Big Oil began with Chevron's own little crisis. A former director had left our board and made an attempt to steal our major client in the oil industry. I duly went to the headquarters in Paris to meet the man he'd written to, Chris Lajtha. Straight off Eurostar I gratefully accepted Chris's offer of a cup of coffee. He reached across to the bookcase and extracted a bottle of whisky to make the coffee more interesting and I thought "I like this man". He showed me the rather grubby letter my erstwhile colleague had sent him, offering to take over the training and to undercut Chevron. He said he didn't like receiving letters like that and I agreed. That's why I'd come to Paris. In due course he took me to the canteen for lunch. It was a short walk away and, of course, was nothing like a canteen. It was the kind of unexpected little family run bistro that the French do so well. Chris was clearly a favourite son and the food was superb. "I like this man very much" I thought. He was a good friend to Chevron over the years and, when he moved on, he made sure of our succession with the man who took over his job.

It was a perfect day, a trip to Paris, well wined and dined by Chris and mission accomplished, a client retained. It reminded me of another perfect day, this time in Amsterdam to research some training for Philips, the electrical giant that works out of Eindhoven. I was picked up from the airport by a very civilized Dutchman who drove me to his elegant houseboat. He had to go off to collect another executive so he left me in the hands of his lovely daughter, who plied me with wine, before we all went to a chic little restaurant just a walk away from the houseboat. After a good lunch we retired to the houseboat and did a modest amount of research on Philips before they returned me to the airport and I flew back to London. God, it's tough at the top.

You naturally imagine that oilmen are tough guys, lashed to their posts in North Sea gales or Arctic wastelands. There is a truth here but they are not all built like wellheads. They are, however, very tough intellectually and, as I was to discover all over the world in the coming years, teaching them was very satisfying but mentally exhausting. These men and some women had been selected from the best of Harvard and Yale, MIT and Oxbridge. They had sat through a few lectures in their time and suffered or enjoyed many business courses from advanced hydro-carbon studies to company accountancy. They could be forgiven for wondering what they were doing in the Shangri-La hotel in Hong Kong or the game lodge in South Africa, listening to some faded actor drone on about the power of television until the first question, sprung upon them as they arrived at the session, sometimes as they were climbing out of the taxi from the airport, sometimes in the corridor leading to the conference room. "Why is your company, supporting the Burmese government, described by the United Nations and Amnesty International as the worst military dictatorship in the world?" "But we are non-political; we don't support any specific government." "Yes, you do, you provide billions of pounds in oil revenues to a government that supports slave labour, summary executions and horrendous human rights abuses. Why do you do that?" I defy any oilman to come up with a pat answer to a question like that. It mixes morality with business in a fight to the finish. Since the release of Aung San Suu Kyi Burma seems to be opening up and the question may now be out of date, but it doesn't matter. There will be another murderous regime along in a minute which happens to have vast oil and gas reserves which need to be exploited to keep capitalism afloat on a sea of hydrocarbons. Therein lies the difference between tobacco globalism and oil globalism. Oil is geopolitical; its huge revenues contribute vital dollars to all manner of questionable regimes across the world. The Energy Minister in Machete land or wherever is every bit as important as the Prime Minister, President or King for Life. The way oil companies behave can influence regimes. They therefore become a target for Human Rights Watch or Amnesty International. As one top executive pointed out to me, it's not their fault that oil springs up in the most unfortunate places. But they are the businesses who have to take the flak. Back to the car park in the Sheraton, Bangkok. The white-faced executive standing in front of me, rubbing his early morning eyes, straight off the plane from Heathrow or Houston, just can't deal with this moral dilemma and they all fail. The result is that the day has started, not with a tedious and formal introduction to the three-day course, but with the candidate being rocketed back to 33,000 feet, suddenly realising that this is a dog that can bite him. When it is played back to them in front of their peer group the reaction is a mixture of laughter at their discomfiture and fear as you wait for everyone to witness your own faltering efforts in front of the camera. I'm not saying this is fair, but it's damned effective and rams home the power of the lens to reveal sloppy thinking. So, where to from here? There is an old tabloid boast which says "We build 'em up, we knock 'em down". In decent TV training the opposite is true, we knock them down and then build them back up again. The doorstep interview is a real hatchet job; the rest of a successful course is a reconstruction job, so that the candidate leaves feeling that he or she is capable of facing the camera. I remember a little man called Kevin, who was the marketing director for the sofa people, DFS, based in Doncaster. He was due to appear that evening to face the formidable Anne Robinson on *Watchdog* and I was jetted in to play the role of the sneering Ms Robinson, hauling Kevin over the coals for some defect in his sofas. The whole factory was at Def Con One, trying to get Ms Robinson's tanks off their lawn. The phone kept ringing for Kevin. It was the product manager, the health and safety manager, Kevin's boss all trying to help. Exasperated by all the conflicting advice he was getting, Kevin finally said in his heavy Northern accent: "I'm sorry, Geoff, but I'll have to go. I've got this chap from t'television in London teaching me how t'carry on". Eventually I got the phone banished and put the first stinging Anne Robinson question to him about the faults in his sofas. God bless him, Kevin stuck both arms in the air and said:"I'll have to plead guilty to that," I said to him, "do that tonight and you'll win the public over". He did and the following day I heard some people in the pub saying "did you see that DFS bloke surrender to Anne Robinson last night?" I determined that we should have a new motto for Chevron Television Training: We'll teach you how t'carry on.

Unless the executive or his company is crooked it is unlikely that he will ever face a doorstep interview. There will be time to prepare. Homework is the key to success. If you enter into a television interview without knowing what you want to say you will almost always fail. If you have done your preparation it can be as simple as ABC. Answer the question, bridge to what you want to say and then communicate. ABC. Don't miss out A, if you don't answer the question the audience will get annoyed or stop listening to you or both. Walk up any High Street and ask people what they think of politicians and I can guarantee that among their top complaints will be "they never answer the question". What after all is the point of accepting an invitation to be interviewed and then not answering the questions? Let me give you an example: "why, Mr Young, did you decide to become poacher turned gamekeeper and set up your own company?" A: "because I was fed up with being under the control of media managers and I thought I could earn a decent living", B: "but the more I did it the more I enjoyed it and, ironically, I learned more about interviews than I had ever done while I was actually plying my craft". C: I found it very satisfying to turn the tongue tied into confident spokesmen. Everyone improved because the lessons are basically very simple. The reasonably articulate became very good, even the pathetic got better and a very few got a report saying "never put this man on the television". What's more, the men and women taking part in the courses really enjoyed them. It was not a load of business theory. It was hands-on practical learning. You can't learn it from a book; you learn it from sweating in front of the camera.

WILL YOU WELCOME PLEASE...

I was holding forth in Smith's Bar one night after *Nationwide*, when Frank Bough asked me whether I ever did public speaking or after-dinner speeches. I said that I occasionally did it for family and friends. Did I ever get paid? Well, Frank, I occasionally got my petrol money. Frank immediately got me installed with Associated Speakers, which sounded suitably grand. In reality it was run out of a suburban semi by Dabber Davies and his wife. Dabber knew his audience, his clients. You began with ladies' luncheon clubs and worked your way up to Rotary clubs and corporate functions. Once a year all the blue-rinse ladies who lunch would be invited down to the Dorchester in London and we speakers would be there, so that they could feel our flesh, test our fetlocks and decide who was worth £100 or so for their annual bash in Bolton or Billericay. Then they had time to go shopping in Oxford Street before returning to Huddersfield or Harrogate with Giles Brandreth or Russell Harty safely tucked up in their handbag for their big regional lunch later in the year. Very shortly after joining Associated Speakers I got a call from Dabber. Could I go to Sutton Coldfield and take over a gig from Glyn Worsnip, who had been taken ill? I drove to the venue and found myself in the function room of a faded Midlands Hotel, facing about three hundred women. Could I write an intro about myself for the whalebone encrusted Madame who was their Chairwoman. Certainly, and I did a brief intro about Martin Young, who read English at Cambridge and was now nearly fluent and other such feeble but serviceable chat. I need not have bothered. The Ship in Full Sail rose to her feet and said the following: "those of you like me who don't have a television probably think that this (dismissive gesture, no eye contact) is Glyn Worsnip. Well, it's not, It's (check notes) Martin Young", She sat down on her fat arse and I stood up in front of six hundred eyes that had basically been told that I was a nobody. I so clearly remember what went through my head at that moment: anybody with an ounce of self-respect would get up now and leave the room, preferably tipping a glass of Bristol Cream over the old bat's perm. At the same moment I realised that I had become a prostitute and must provide the service for which I would later be paid. It was an interesting if excruciating example of the way organisations are run. They do function from the top down. My hostess was so rigidly encased in corsets her austere presence permeated the entire room. It took me five minutes to warm them up but by the end they were laughing heartily at things that go wrong on the telly. I also realised that in order to survive you need what is essentially a cabaret act. What I didn't realise was that there was a potential telly series there, called "It'll be All Right on the Night". I could have beaten Dennis Norden to it. There was a strange, atavistic satisfaction in the whole public speaking experience. I graduated from the cuddly animals of the ladies' luncheon clubs to the hairy mammoths of the cigar-smoking industrialists of the metal-bashing lands of the Midlands and the North. Having slain them, sung my song and got off I would duly collect my fat cheque from the Treasurer and drive back to Oxford where I would wake Susan waving the cheque in front of her. The children shall have shoes after all.

It was important when you arrived at the venue to check the

place where you would be speaking. Did you always need a microphone? Standing up and tapping the microphone smacked too much of commentating on the egg and spoon race at the local Primary School. Get a look at the menu and see if anyone is speaking before you. He or she is probably a well-meaning amateur. You are the paid "turn" – you have to be good.

I went through this routine when I arrived in the heart of Middle England in the Royal Borough of Tunbridge Wells. I looked with dread at the lady billed to precede me. Her topic was the celebrated town itself. Oh dear.

I can still recall her exact words as she stood to address her fellow Tunbridgers: "It gives me great pleasure tonight to talk about the Royal Borough of Tunbridge Wells at length." And she did to the point of somnolence among her audience. Those two words "at length" made my heart sink and ensured that, after her, I would be stuck yet again with five minutes to warm up the audience who either wanted the toilet or another large brandy or both. The by now well-rehearsed cabaret act came to the rescue. They got a big laugh and I got a big cheque. Mrs Tunbridge Wells probably went home a happy woman and dreamt about the Borough "at length" under her candlewick bedspread.

NOTHING CAN GO WRONG

The pricking of pomposity is one of the staples of comedy. What can be more pompous than a man or woman standing up in front of a camera, pretending to be talking to us in our own living rooms? That's why it's so funny when everything goes wrong, when Toto pulls back the curtain and reveals the Great Oz as the charlatan he really is.

I became a great admirer of those who were born to speak, apparently effortlessly, after dinner. At the annual Dorchester horseflesh convention, a few of the speakers would be chosen to entertain the ladies. A rather grand, David Lloyd George of a man, who was Professor of Linguistics at Bangor University, rose from his seat and said in his deep, Welsh accent: "Ladies, I would like to tell you how at home I feel here in the Dorchester Ballroom. It reminds me so much of our own dining room at home. Except that our curtains are green." Standing there against the acres of blue velvet curtains and the enormity of the Ballroom itself, The Professor held the entire audience in the palm of his hand.

The actor, Ron Moody, famously Fagin in the musical *Oliver!* gave the annual speech to the Variety Club at another huge

London Hotel. The text of the speech was excessively dull "like to thank… great honour… worthy cause… good works etc. etc." but, as he spoke about the essence of charity and how he was only too glad to be able to contribute to the Variety Club's Good Works, a spoon fell out of his sleeve onto the table, followed bit by bit by a whole dinner service of stolen cutlery. "… glad to be able to give my services for free… tonight a very worthy cause… (clink, clink)… aware of those less fortunate than ourselves… (clink, clink) until the whole table in front of him was heaped with what he'd pinched. Nobody will remember what he said, everyone will remember the speech. After dinner speaking is flummery.

People want to laugh, they are full up with food and booze and they don't want a lecture on palaeontology.

They want to be told about that great reporter, Philip Tibenham, who stood beside the canal and said: "perhaps the most historic and memorable fact about the Trent and Mersey Canal is so historic and memorable that I've just forgotten what it is", when Frank Bough says: "and now over to Harry Commentator, our carpenter." Or, in the mists of time, when the commentator at some great royal event said "coming round the corner into the Mall is the first troop of the Queen's Royal Arse Hortillery".

NEARLY CRASHED AND BURNED

I t has happened to all of us. *Nationwide* decided to stage an air race from the various regions into Biggin Hill aerodrome. The plane from Scotland, bearing the BBC Scotland presenter missed the runway, flew into Death Valley, so called after the War, and crashed. No-one was hurt but the presenter and the pilot were, of course, in shock. The pilot retired to the hospitality tent to recover and have a few whiskies. This was about eleven in the morning and I got the job of interviewing the pilot at the site of the crash, live at six thirty that evening. He had continued with the medicinal whiskies all afternoon and was now well alight and ready to tell the world, via me, of his dreadful ordeal. "I'm gonna tell them what a bunch of bastards the BBC are, you drag me all the way down here for some damn, fucking race and smash my plane up, you fuckers" he informed me. He had clearly reached the argumentative phase while I had entered the "please will the ground open up and swallow me" phase. Over the sound of him effing and blinding I said plaintively over my microphone "can anybody hear me?" Frank Bough, who was fronting the show, said "don't worry, Mart, when I stop talking you start". I looked at this wretched pilot who seemed as if he'd been badly re-assembled there in that muddy field and thought "Thanks a bundle, Frank". I can remember my heart pounding as I asked the first question "what actually happened?" Out of somewhere the pilot suddenly found strength: "I was coming into land and the engine malfunctioned and I tried to fly over The Valley but the engine cut out completely and I had to go through the whole emergency landing procedure. Thank God no-one was hurt". I saw his legs begin to buckle under him and handed back to the studio as fast as I could. I could have kissed him, not a "fuck" or a "BBC bastards" to be heard. A man with that level of composure can fly me any day. The programme ended and I sprinted for the hospitality tent. It was my turn for a stiff whisky.

THE DEMON DRINK

Drink was always a problem at these speaking jollies. I remember arriving in Halifax after a particularly hairy drive from Oxford. Would I care for a drink? You bet. I asked for a large gin and tonic, which was proffered to me with evident reluctance. When I had a second, the eyes of the organisers were all fixed on me. Eventually I asked if everything was all right. It turned out that the speaker the year before had got progressively so drunk that when he stood up to deliver his after dinner speech, he collapsed and slid under the table. The treasurer had to make up the time with an impromptu speech of his own.

Their eyes didn't leave me all night. I studiously drank water and all was well. Pretty quickly I learned not to drink any more than one pre-prandial G & T.

It was not so much the fear of sliding under the table, a few drinks can really mess up your timing and convince you that you are the funniest thing since the Marx Brothers, whereas your audience is near to pelting you with bread rolls. That nearly happened to me at a posh corporate do at the NEC in Birmingham, except that this time I was forewarned by Dabber. The year before his speaker had been bombarded by bread rolls.

Helpfully, he added that they didn't hurt much unless they had been dunked first in red wine. I was in Oxford when I heard the good news about how much I was going to be paid for the gig and the bad news that I might emerge as a casualty of war. I went to the ex-MOD shop in Oxford and found an old German tin hat. I secreted this under my chair and when I stood up in full dinner jacket to give my speech I told the audience that I understood there had been a minor problem last year vis-a-vis the bread rolls and immediately donned the German Helmet. The night went well, not a wine-sodden bread roll in sight and I departed carrying my tin hat and a large cheque. I am tempted to conflate that event with another night at the NEC in Birmingham when I was suddenly invited back to present the *Breakfast Show* on LBC. So, conflate them I will. I emerged into the night outside the Metropole Hotel with my cheque for £1000 safely tucked into my tuxedo and switched on my mobile phone, The message from manager Robin Malcolm who had seriously misled me about my future at LBC said: "We wondered if you might be prepared to darken our door again, here at LBC, fronting our *Breakfast Show*. Give me a call". This from the radio station from which a few months earlier I had sacked myself. I was, as they say, "over the moon, Brian". I got into the Porsche (sorry about that, but it doesn't take too many after dinner speeches to be able to afford one) and drove back to Oxford down the M40. You have no idea how difficult that is with two triumphant arms and two fingers in the air for forty minutes. I didn't call Robin Malcolm. I asked my agent, Annie Sweetbaum, to call him and say that I would return to LBC for twice the money: "Not a penny more, not a penny less". They agreed, the fools.

Before I sing my song and get off there is one more story that needs to be told. In the old days the weather forecast was conveyed to an eager public by a magnetic board on which were placed magnetic letters spelling out our meteorological fate for the day. It was a foggy day and Julian Pettifer was telling us all about it when the letter "F" in the word fog fell off the board and went "clink" onto the studio floor. Julian smoothly wrapped up the bulletin; "And that's your weather for today but in conclusion I'd like to apologise for the "F" in fog." You are talking to millions of people, sitting happily with their innocent children on the sofa at home and there is no way out. I mean, you can't say "oh, I'm sorry, I didn't mean the fucking fog" can you? You can't put the words back in your mouth, can you? It's the perfect story for a grey-haired coterie of Ladies Circle women, – risqué without being vulgar. But it is very unfair on the presenter who, I discovered later, wasn't Julian at all but a regional presenter on BBC Wales. Still, always leave them on a laugh.

DIVINE COMEDY

What had happened to my bedraggled broadcast career so cruelly cut short by the perfidy of BBC managers? You might have noticed that I have not ranted against incompetent management for some time. This is deliberate, because I had removed them from my life. Benign management was just around the corner in the comedic shape of Jonathan James-Moore, who was now Head of Light Entertainment (Radio) and the far more stylish shape of Harry Thompson (Thompson with a 'p'), then the producer of *The News Quiz* on Radio Four. Harry was a great fan of the Tintin books. There were two bumbling detectives called Thomson and Thompson. Harry was the one with the 'p'. He wrote a book called "Tintin, Herge and His Creation."

After I had appeared on a few editions of The News Quiz Harry invited Sue and me to dinner with Ian Hislop and his wife, Victoria. Harry and his girlfriend lived on the fourth floor of a rather lovely Victorian house in Paddington with their Vietnamese pot-bellied pig. As you do. The conversation was engrossing and, as I said to Ian at the time, it's quite remarkable how quickly one can settle down to dinner with a Vietnamese pig snuffling away on the carpet just beside the fire.

The pig was called "Lunch". Of course it was. It reminded me of a very old joke about the old timer who had a three-legged hog, who had once dragged him out of a barn fire. "Is that where he lost his leg?" "Oh, no. A hog that good you don't eat all at once." Lunch snuffled merrily away, unaware that the Youngs were about to free him from a life of captivity in a fourth floor flat in deepest Paddington. We invited him with all the News Quiz team to one of our Upper Farm parties. Harry and his girlfriend, the trendy young metropolitan couple, should have been in a drop-top MGB, but arrived in a rusty Vauxhall Viva, with a pot-bellied pig snorting on a blanket across the back seats. Time for lunch, Lunch. He gambolled free in our half acre of garden, rooting around for truffles and other dainty comestibles. The kids were delighted to have a full scale pig to play with and Lunch was, for once, in his element. When, hours later, Lunch had to get back to his Vauxhall it took Alan, Harry and me ages to hoist him back onto his rear seat rug.

Later that week Alan Coren wrote about the joys of the open road in his op-ed column in The Times. He wrote lyrically about driving to Oxford with the hood down on his new BMW, explaining that his thoughts were prompted "by a lovely lunch in a magical Oxfordshire garden with a mob of friends". Sue says to this day that it's the nicest thank you letter that she has ever received.

My run-in with the Lord Chief Justice had lent me a certain notoriety among the anti-establishment figures of the day. Harry Thompson invited me to join the wonderful Alan Coren and the subversive pairing of Richard Ingrams and Ian Hislop on *The News Quiz*. It was the hardest work for the least money that I had ever done. I had the sense to realise that I couldn't be a comedian like the other three, so I determined to be the humble, but well-informed journalist instead. Alan, God bless him, always wanted me on his team. He called me the Swot. And how right he was. Every week, when I knew that *The News Quiz* was looming on a Thursday I would make time to go to the BBC archives and read the whole of the newspaper output for the last seven days. If you had been reading only the big boys' papers, you might have missed the elephant with the two heads or the snake that doubled as a magician. I would spend a whole afternoon at my labours and make copious notes about Arnold Cringeworthy, the man who married his own tuba or Fred Skuttlebuck who lived on a diet of farm manure and smoky bacon crisps. Thus armed I would turn up for the Thursday night recording at the Paris Theatre on Lower Regent Street. What a theatre that was. Everyone had played the Paris and there were pictures all down the corridors: Hancock, the Goons, George Formby, Jack Benny, Sinatra, everyone. This really was my fifteen minutes of fame. It came at a price, all that burrowing in the archives and all that anxiety that you'd mess up on the night. Because no-one gave you any help. *The News Quiz* was genuine; you had no idea what questions the chairman, Barry Took, was going to ask. He started off by introducing me as "Martin Young, who has come onto *The News Quiz* this week as part of his community service, thus avoiding a custodial sentence for cheeking the Lord Chief Justice". The show, as I said, was nerve-racking and paid for at slave labour rates by the less than munificent BBC. When I first did the quiz I think I got £60 and roughly the same for the Saturday repeat. The truth was that most of the guests would have paid the BBC to be on Radio Four's prestigious *The News Quiz*. I was once on the show with Rory Bremner who, I presume, doesn't necessarily get out of bed for less than £10,000. He will have gladly taken the beer money that myself and the others accepted just for the privilege, and the fun of being on the show. He effortlessly imitated my voice and told me afterwards that he'd always liked it because it was so distinctive, so odd. Unfortunately, he also told me that he'd done me in rehearsals for his new programme but the producer had simply said: "Who the hell was that supposed to be?" When Rory told him who it was, he said "never heard of him." I was duly dropped. Ah, the price of fame.

Over the many *The News Quiz* programmes I did I was

constantly surprised by how clever the comedians were. Rory, Paul Merton, Ian Hislop and Alan Coren and a host of others who made you laugh but also brought to the party a kind of Weltanschauuing that, first and foremost, accepted the futility of our posturing on this planet, with no idea of what we were doing here or who we were. Look at the permanently confused state of Paul Merton, furrowed brow, head dodging from side to side, trying to seek help from the audience. When I graduated to *Have I got News for You* I remember us all getting bogged down in some political discussion when Paul took over. If you had any sense, you shut up and just let him go: "What's all this about? What's going on? The people don't want all this intellectual tosh. They'd rather have a knees-up, sing a song not listen to all this posturing. I'm right aren't I? Let's all have a damn good sing-song". The audience were roaring their approval by now, really up for a song and a dance. Ian and the then host, Angus Deayton, looked on benignly at this apparently philistine outburst. Paul was only asking the forever perplexing question posed by the Pythons in *The Meaning of Life*. It's the same question put by Bluebottle to Eccles: "Eccles, what are you doing here?" "Well, everybody's gotta be somewhere". To all of these comedians, Spike Milligan was the genius, born out of the Second World War (*Adolf Hitler: My Part in his Downfall*) and turning comedy from its frilly knickers phase and "Where's my Bike?" to a whole new, surreal perspective. Fifty years on one of the new crop of comedians, Milton Jones, who also looks perplexed and thoroughly confused can walk on stage and say just three words: "Do you think…" and a long pause creates a Cartesian moment in which the same old imponderables fester. Don't take all this psychobabble from me, take it from the wonderful Morecambe and Wise. They came on an afternoon chat show many years ago to talk about the business of comedy. Ernie did his straight man act, talking rather boringly about the psychology of comedy. He droned on but as always with those two you were wondering what the other one, the goofy one with the specs, was doing. Eric had spotted a rather nice coffee pot and cups on the coffee table in front of them and he was clearly worried that the coffee was going cold as Ernie continued to expatiate on the philosophy of comedy. It began as a slight worry, Eric continually touching the coffee pot, developed into a series of whispered asides "it's all right Ern" "It's still hot enough" "It's cooling down" to a full scale obsession as Eric clutched the coffee pot and said "Quick, Ern, we've gotta drink it now or it'll be stone cold". All this silly business completely distracted us from Ernie's earnest attempt to explain the roots of comedy. Eric was doing the roots of comedy right in front of us and making us laugh.

I have seen Billy Connolly on stage for about two hours. I never stopped laughing for a moment, yet I can only remember one sequence of gags: "I'm over sixty now and things begin to change you know, so I've made myself some rules. One, if you get the chance of a wee, take it. Two, remember that ever fart is a potential catastrophe. And three, in the unlikely event that you should get an erection, use it immediately… even if you're on your own".

Equally I saw Eddie Izzard's stand-up routine in London. One sequence sticks in my mind. He needs a loaf of bread, so he goes to the late-night petrol station and joins the queue to pay lining up at the armoured glass and bars of the man at the till. His attention starts to be distracted by the other people in the queue. He is alone on stage but magically makes it seem as though he is surrounded by pimps and prostitutes, weirdos and men with machetes and machine pistols. He's got la condition humaine nailed down. That routine was pure Pinter. Much of the best comedians are more like Beckett in their world view. At the end of the play the two tramps are still waiting for Godot:

Vladimir: "Well? Shall we go?
Estragon: "Yes, let's go."
(They do not move.)

Beckett lived in France for much of his life and wrote *Waiting for Godot* originally in French. You could interpret Godot as God

Zero. Beckett is saying that God is nothing and will not save you after death. You will not be going to sit on the right hand of God the Father or Allah or Buddha or anyone else. Even blowing yourself up is not going to offer you seventy-two virgins in paradise. Krapp in *Krapp's Last Tape* looks back at a fumbled romantic moment in his past. He doesn't look forward. He doesn't see anything ahead except blackness. Beckett is always paring away at his subject until the reductio ad absurdum is "Not I", a disembodied mouth apparently suspended against a black cyclorama, pouring out a torrent of despair.

In the beginning was the word. In the end is the word. If you share that arguably nihilistic world view then you have a number of options. If you are a scientist like Richard Dawkins, you can write diatribes against the religious institutions, books like *The God Delusion*. If you don't want to bother yourself with the great imponderables you can play golf and die peacefully in the nineteenth hole after a game you've won comfortably. If you are full of scepticism and you are clever enough to laugh in the face of seventy or eighty years of experience in a universe that is about fourteen billion years old, you can become a comedian. The sort of comedian who is also intrinsically a tragedian. Dave Allen tells a long shaggy-dog story about the man who sets out on a strenuous trek to meet the ancient guru at the top of mountain. He reaches the old man with the long beard and the ragged loincloth and says: "Tell me the true meaning of life". "Well, my son the secret of life is never to argue, never to get angry with your fellow men and be friendly to everyone you meet in your walk through life". Allen bursts out with indignation "Don't be ridiculous, you stupid old man, that can't be the secret of life", and he storms off down the mountain, swearing and cursing all the way. Stephen Fry, I note, now ends his programme with the words "Be exceptionally kind to each other". That's something we can all agree with, so why is there so much discord and evil? I certainly don't know and nor do the comedians, they can only make us laugh at the absurdity of it all. They are the Dadaists of our day.

I had a wonderful time on *The News Quiz*, meeting lots of great company like Francis Wheen and Matthew Parris and the occasional airhead lady columnist who was daft enough to try to take on Richard Ingrams at his own game. Quite politely she was laid to rest after the first five minutes and said little else thereafter.

DINE AND DUCK

I was lucky enough to become an unofficial member of Ian's luncheon club for those people who, for good or bad reasons had caught the probing lens of *Private Eye*. I approached the first lunch with trepidation, hoping I was there for good reasons not bad. The invitation from Lord Gnome, no less, had come to me on an elaborate illustrated card and very solemnly invited me to this great event. Grand it was not, held in a grotty pub in the 'function room' on the first floor. Our ungracious host was Norman, who slapped down plates of vaguely warmed food in front of us. But no-one was there to eat. They had come to gossip. I was sat opposite Ian and beside a busty blonde hackette. Ian seemed capable of listening to everyone's conversation at once. He broke off a discussion about the vagaries of defence spending with an earnest correspondent from one of the serious papers and turned to said busty blonde on my left: "We're getting a lot of dirt in on you at the moment. A lot of sex stuff". She began to bluster a reply and finally said: "Well, who are you getting all this from?" Ian said, "We thought it might be her", indicating the rather striking black girl sitting on his right directly opposite the blonde. He left them to it and turned back to his discussion on defence procurement.

There was always a frisson about these occasions. Would you be the next one to be confronted with an uncomfortable truth? Would you say anything indiscreet that would inevitably find its way into the pages of *Private Eye*? I did it once when I was talking about LBC. Andrew Neill presented the *Breakfast* programme and I would normally arrive just after nine o'clock to get ready for the *Midday News*. We would often meet as he was leaving and exchange a few words. I had known him since the early days of Nationwide when I would often interview him about politics or the economy. There had long been a fascinating debate about the degree to which Andrew was follically-challenged. *Private Eye* had long ago dubbed him "brillo-pad Neill" out of devilment and, I suppose because he'd taken the Murdoch shilling so willingly. Anyway, all I said at the lunch was that if you wanted to know about the state of a man's hair just meet him every morning after he's spent the last three hours pulling on and taking off his "cans", the headphones we all have to wear in a radio studio. I went away feeling a bit queasy about what I'd said and then worried like mad that it would be in the next edition of the *Eye*, no doubt alongside another excuse to show that embarrassing picture of Andrew en fete with a pretty girl who is taller than him. If they did publish my remarks I could see that our jolly little morning chats might come to a chilly end. They didn't publish. I had escaped my indiscretion. Until now, of course.

Light Entertainment Radio was full of talent, bright young men and women who wanted to produce good radio and possibly transfer to television. The brightest and the best was undoubtedly Harry Thompson who had an admirable habit of delivering a great series and then taking off to India or Cambodia or anywhere exotic for weeks at a time. It seemed to me an excellent way to establish yourself in a big organisation. I'm yours but on my terms, yes I see the greasy pole over there, but I'm not going to clamber up it. I'm going to Sumatra for a few weeks. *The News Quiz* was so successful on Radio Four that there had been several attempts to transfer it to television. Indeed, my great friend, Richard Stilgoe, was in a series called *Scoop* but for some reason it never really caught the public's imagination unlike Harry's inspired pairing of Ian Hislop and Paul Merton in *Have I got News for You*. It's amazing now to think that it has been going for twenty-five years and is one of the most popular shows on television. Being a friend at court to Harry and his literally merry band I was a guest on each of the first three series. After that, I was never needed. By then, the show was already so successful that Harry could have phoned the Queen of Sheba and she would almost certainly have turned up at the studios for the recording, glad to be asked. The pattern of recording the television news quiz was much the same as the radio programme; the frisson and the fear were the same too. Ian and Paul are naturally funny; Ian enjoys being a senior member of the "Harrumph!" Club, Paul enjoys being the ignoramus in the public bar. The game is hard enough but you, the guest, are playing it once every now and then. They practise it every week and they are very good at it.

The television version is actually much easier intellectually. The camera, as ever, is King. There has to be a full-scale camera rehearsal before the recording and during that time you are asked, but do not have to answer, the questions. After each rehearsal Paul and I would retire to his dressing room and search though all the week's papers to find the stories we hadn't identified from the run-through. My permanent anxiety about not knowing the two-headed elephant story was removed in a flash. I could think of a hopefully, amusing journalistic take on the stories, Paul could sit there drumming up his sardonic best or rapping on a theme. You rarely knew who the other guest would be until you arrived at the studios. On one occasion I was checking in at the front desk when a young woman said "I'm going there as well. Can you show me the way?" She was dressed as if the Oxfam shop had just closed and she'd borrowed some togs from a passing bag lady. It was quite clear that neither of us had a clue who the other one was. I was

Martin Young and she was Kathy Burke. I had dressed up like tellyman, she presumably was off to change. No. Kathy had dressed down for the occasion. What I saw at reception was what the viewers saw on transmission. Still, we hadn't come for the London Fashion show and Kathy was great fun. So was *Have I Got News for You*.

MINI CELEBRITY

I had become a mini celebrity in the seventies and eighties, now the nineties rocketed me back to the z-list. It came with privileges and humiliations in equal measure. Taxi drivers in London would rarely recognise my face but I only had to say, "Paddington Station, please" and every one of them would say; "'Ere, you're that news bloke aren't you? I like your programme" or "What's that Angela Rippon really like?" and, on occasion, the ultimate accolade from a cabbie "I like that *Midday News* – you're a bit left wing aren't you?" It was amazing to think that the programme was being listened to and analysed. I did, of course, not believe my own publicity. This new found fame with the hackney carriage trade was all down to the travel reports that popped up regularly and made the cabbie's life easier. At that time they had no real alternative to LBC, so that's what they all listened to. It reminded me of the early days of *Nationwide* when Richard Stilgoe was sent to Fort William and, walking down the High Street, was gratified that everyone seemed to recognise him and many greeted him with a cheery "Och, Hullo there, Richard". Later on, he discovered that the only channel they could receive was BBC1 – his fame in the North of Scotland was entirely due to transmitters and geography, not only his undoubted talents. Dickey and I are small in stature and regularly get the remark "Ooh, you're a lot smaller than you look on the telly". Waiting outside the lift in some hotel, somewhere, the doors opened to reveal a young couple. The man looked at me and said "You're the news man, aren't you?" Before I could say anything his wife broke in with:"Don't be silly, Brian he's that magician chap". I went back to my room and looked anxiously in the mirror. Oh God, I did look a bit like Paul Daniels – how depressing.

I said earlier that the mini-list celebrity status came with humiliations as above, but also with lovely privileges, like being able to play cricket for the Lord's Taverners. As a cricket fan I am ace, as a cricket player I am rubbish. But who's counting? It's a great charity, providing all manner of help for disabled kids, not least an ever increasing fleet of mini-vans with the Lord's Taverners logo painted on the side to ferry them to special events. Along with us Z-listers there were always great cricketers of the past and genuine A-listers like Robert Powell. On one occasion I was sharing the autograph table with Robert when a highly excited young girl presented him with a photograph she'd taken earlier. She asked very politely if he'd autograph it for her. Since he had made a name for himself playing Jesus Christ, Robert had been trying hard to be thought of as an actor first and the Son of God thereafter. The girl's picture was taken of Robert sitting in front of a mini-van with the word "Lord" above his head like a crown of thorns. The rest of us thought this was hilarious. Robert, like Queen Victoria, was unamused.

I was unamused when I spotted the name of the English fast bowler, John Snow on the team lists. John was my hero when I was a teenager and he was bowling very fast for the England Test side, tall, straight-backed and distinctly rapid. I saw him at Lord's when he was cheered after every over and took a sackful of wickets. But, crucially, whose side was he on for this charity game? I didn't mind being recognised as a rabbit with the bat, but I didn't want to be permanently traumatised or have all my limbs broken. I'm all for charity but there is a limit on how much you're prepared to give. Thank Goodness, John was on our side, older but still bowling like a demon. It was an absolute delight to be on the same field as the Greats. I can tell my grandchildren that I played cricket with Colin Cowdrey, John Edrich, Mike Denness and a dozen others. Arriving at one stately cricket field for a game sponsored by Guinness I was cheerfully enjoying some black velvet when I noticed that M. Young was opening the batting with M. Atherton. I sought out the skipper and reminded him that I was a genuine rabbit, whereas Atherton had just scored a load of runs on England's winter tour to Australia. Mike immediately offered to drop down to number two so that I could face the first ball. In the event, I shared in a 50 partnership with the Test player, Mike got 49 and I got 1. Mind you, this wasn't just any old one, this was a charity one. During the lunch and sensing my apprehension one of the other Taverners pledged ten pounds for every run I made. I settled down at the crease and watched the scary fast bowler pounding in to knock my head off. The ball came slowly, bounced helpfully just in front of me, appeared to stop in mid-air, a window opened and a flag came out with "hit me" on it. (All right, I made the last bit up). The quickie had remembered that there was £10 for the charity in that ball. The money was earned and I was able to watch Atherton play effortlessly at the other end. The next time I faced the same fast bowler he got me middle stump. That was one of the great things about playing with real professionals. They had batted and bowled against the best at the SCG, MCG, Eden Park, Newlands you name it. At the charity level they could do anything with bat or ball and they tended to enjoy their favourite strokes. I watched John Edrich play against us in the Channel Islands. John had forearms like Popeye and got to a hundred by repeatedly hoisting the ball for six. Then he simply picked out the safest pair of hands in the field and holed out. All the pros could get to 50 or 100 and then deliberately get out. All the fast bowlers could spot that you were a well-meaning amateur with cross eyes and would bowl softly at you. Indeed they could look at the telly people and see from just one catch or throw that you didn't have a clue. Conversely, when John Price, Middlesex and England, nicknamed "sport" would talk about "bowlin' 'em out", he would make an instinctive curl of his wrist and fingers that he'd done for real millions of times, the batsmen would use the back of their hands in a perfect arc when talking about the 100 they got at Lords or the Gabba.

Back in the *Look North* days I always remember one of my fellow reporters, Luke Casey, being in a pub when someone accosted him with the rather superfluous news that he was Luke Casey from *Look North*. A trite conversation was brought to a sudden halt when the man said: "You must meet a lot of interesting people in your job" "No," said an exasperated Luke, who just wanted to enjoy his pint in peace, "They are mostly boring old farts like you".

This was never the case at Taverners' dos. You met the most interesting and unlikely people. I was playing at the Hampstead Cricket Ground for the Taverners and spotted a fellow amateur fielding near me. Between overs and after the game we got chatting and I discovered Dave was a musician with his own band. When we went home Susan mentioned to our son Jonathan that she'd met this really nice bloke called Dave Gilmour who was a guitarist with his own band. Jonathan was ecstatic. "You've met Dave Gilmour from Pink Floyd? Wow!" It's not often that you get such a reaction from a truculent teenage boy. Suddenly it was as if his Dad did a real job after all, just as he and his sister were bowled over by the boxes of sweets from Cadbury's all those years ago.

The Taverners didn't stint on the hospitality front. We might be there to earn money for the charity but we never went thirsty. On one occasion we were sponsored by Bollinger or Moet and in the hospitality tent we were plied with the sponsor's product to our great delight. The younger amongst us were excited that our childhood hero, Norman Wisdom, was coming to support us. You want me to tell you that he entered the tent, tripped and fell over, don't you? No, it was better than that. Norman sneaked in quietly, borrowed a waiter's jacket, took a silver platter full of champagne glasses from a flunkey and travelled around the tent acting as our personal waiter. That was typical of the Taverners.

Somewhere, deep in the archives of *The Kent Messenger*, there is a photograph of Colin Cowdrey coming off the ground after a charity match. He is besieged by eager young lads keen to be near England's celebrated batsman. If you look closely there is a very young Martin Young waving his autograph book. Twenty-five years later here I am playing with England's legend for the Taverners. By this stage Colin was suffering from heart disease so he'd had to modify his playing style. He'd given up singles and twos and went exclusively for fours, scored through his elegant, favourite shot, the late glance. In the unfortunate event of a single Colin, never the quickest between the wickets, would simply walk to the other end. No-one who'd gone in to bat in a Test match with a broken arm could ever be accused of not really trying, could he?

I couldn't even bat with two arms and try as I might I never improved. With the Taverners in some trouble one day the skipper, ex-England captain Mike Denness, turned to me and said right, Martin you're in. I protested that I probably wouldn't make many runs. "Cometh the hour, cometh the man" said Mike in his trusty Scottish accent. I was out first ball.

I was needed urgently by another captain, Leslie Crowther, to save the day for the Taverners. He put me up the order to No 7 when the Taverners needed a few runs to win the game. I was out first ball. I trudged back to the tent that was doubling as our pavilion and Leslie put a friendly arm around my sagging shoulders. "Martin," he said "You did your best...It just wasn't fucking good enough".

210

I tried so hard in my final innings for the Taverners' side led by Chris Tarrant that I had to be carried off. I actually reached the giddy heights of 15 runs, eschewing all this poncy technique I had been failing to master and simply sweeping every ball that came my way. I began to get carried away with my success and was racing to make my ground when I felt a sharp pain in my calf and heard a loud crack. I thought for a moment that the ball had hit me on the way to the wicket, where I lay sprawled all over the crease. Until I tried to get up and my leg wouldn't work. I had to be carried back to the pavilion. Martin Bell, the downhill skier, was in the bar with his girlfriend, who was a sports physiotherapist. She realised I had torn the sheath of my Achilles tendon and did what she could to ease the pain. Martin Bell has thighs like tree trunks and he ferried me to my car, lifting me into a piggy back position, picking me up as if I were a four year old not a forty year old. I had left the field of play forever, never to return. Chris Tarrant sent out a thank you card to all of us who had contributed to the charity that day. On mine he scribbled "Don't break your bloody leg next time, you twit". A few days later I was almost magically restored by reading in the newspapers that Chris had fallen out of a tree and done himself considerable damage. I took a delight in sending him a Get Well card with the Crowther Consolation: "You just weren't fucking good enough".

OH, HELL

I t wasn't all quaffing champagne with the great and the good. My spurious celebrity also attracted all manner of unexpected invitations, to be, for instance, best man at a Hell's Angel's wedding.

Venue: various clubs and pubs in the North East.

Dramatis Personae: The Sunderland Chapter of the Hell's Angels, Ken Stephinson and me.

News you will recall must be new, true and different. A story about the Hell's Angels may be new and true, but what makes it different? When they are a charity, baring their diamond-studded hearts to the good folk of Sunderland. My friend, Ken Stephinson, was a *Nationwide* "border baron" for a swathe of the North of England. He found the story and we found ourselves filming in a rough looking village hall where the even rougher looking Hell's Angels were diverting the crowd with a truly dreadful rock concert. The aim was to pass the hat round for some donations towards a scanner for the local hospital. Now, there's nothing wrong with little old ladies politely asking for charity money in the high street but it is easy, equally politely, to hurry by with a kind smile. It is something quite different, at the end of a raucous rock concert, to be asked for money by a large, tattooed man in leathers with the word "H.A.T.E." branded on his forehead. It is always a sure-fire fund-raiser. But all was not sweetness and light. Throughout the evening a rather mild chap, dazzled by the sheer brilliance of my celebrity, had been asking for autographs and photos to put on the walls of his humble bedsit. I wasn't at all bothered by this, regarding it as part of the job, but the Hell's Angel, known to the Chapter as "The Prisoner", thought otherwise, invited mild-mannered Joe out to the car park and beat him up on my behalf. Sorry, Joe, if you are still using my photo as a dartboard in the bedsit, I apologise.

In the meantime a marriage was being made in Heaven. The President of the Hell's Angels had taken a shine to me. He wasn't that big but he was wiry, well-built and strong. I was reminded of him, many years later, by the head of a security company, who minded us in Bogota, Columbia, a genuinely scary place. The President was a kind of philosopher King. The charity idea had been his and the money was genuinely going to the Hospital. (I had checked.) He and I talked a lot of cod philosophy and real politics. I think he liked the way I treated him as a person and not a freak. A real marriage was being planned. It's not all bad being a Hell's Angel and the Philosopher King was surrounded by a court of young girls in mascara and miniskirts and he had chosen one of these hopefuls to be his bride. I was to be best man.

I don't remember much about the wedding itself. There didn't appear to be a church or vows or any of that old thing, but rather a succession of dowdy pubs and increasingly raucous, eccentric behaviour as we celebrated the happy couple's Big Day.

To be honest, it did not have the feel of permanence about it, this marriage. There was still a lechery of other mini-skirts orbiting the President. I doubt whether the old Harley Davidson is now de-commissioned, leaning against the rose covered wall of the retirement cottage in Whitley Bay, while the Pres and his missus plan their Silver Wedding thrash. But, who knows? I've been wrong before.

THE NORTH LONDON MAFIA

The other charity I became involved with was The Rainbow Trust, which offered respite holidays to parents who had to look after seriously ill children. It was centred around a North London salon, presided over by the ultimate Jewish Momma, Gay Keogh. Don't let the surname fool you. Gay had married a lovely but long-suffering Roman Catholic called Mike Keogh, a goy like me but adopted by the warm embrace of Gay and her friends. We were a motley crew. Along with Andrew Morton I represented the world of journalism, Trevor Philips was to become the head of the Equal Opportunities Commission, and Jeremy Beadle and Christopher Biggins came from the wilder reaches of Light Entertainment. From the very centre of Radio Fourdom came Shula Archer and Brian Aldridge, old friends Charles and Judy Collingwood, married in real life. We also boasted a lawyer, an accountant and a rabbi, Dame Julia Neuberger. There was also a very sharp, very amusing character called Dennis, who, when repeatedly asked what he did would always reply "Leave it out". I still don't know what Dennis does to this day. So we covered quite a lot of territory. Appropriately, we also had someone in the shmutter trade. This was no East End barrow boy, but Richard Caring, a millionaire who travelled the world making cheap clothing and shipping it back to the big stores in Europe. I never minded Richard having so much money but I got really fed up with him having all those Air Miles. After years of sitting in Goat Class, just by the toilets there in row fifty, I had graduated to a silver British Airways card, whereas Richard was so far above Gold card status that they were probably manufactured for him in the Ionosphere by the Chairman of British Airways himself. He carried a black card that represented millions of miles travelled and was a kind of Knighthood of the Skies. I suspect that flying first class to and from Hong Kong all the time must have had something to do with all this.

Richard is a great guy and, I soon discovered, a "player". There were various parlour games we would play at Gay's salons, some of them quite competitive. It was during one of these, when Richard and I were the last men standing that he recognised me as a natural player as well. I had, as usual, been banging on about cricket and the next One-Day International between Australia and Pakistan. Richard said that we should all join him in his box at Lord's. Except, he didn't have a box at Lord's. I learned later that he had passed that little problem on to his fixer; let's call him Monty Goldbloom, although I never knew his name. He told Richard that the game was sold out, not a box to be had. Richard said: "If you can't get me a box, your name is not Monty Goldbloom". Monty, with his very existence as a human being in question, went back to work. Come the day of the Test, we entered Richard's box. He was greeted warmly by the hostess with: "Good morning Mr Hornby, welcome to your box". I can only assume that Mr Hornby had been on the 'phone all week apologising to his favoured clients, but was considerably richer as a result. Every event with Richard was a big event. He had decided that we would support the underdog, Pakistan, so when we arrived at his house that morning we had all been issued with Pakistani shirts, wigs and moustaches. A stretch limo arrived and we headed for Lord's. At this point the foreign correspondent in me took over. In a moment we were going to arrive outside the Grace Gates in a highly conspicuous rich man's limo and step out into a crowd of excitable Pakistani youths who were already shouting for their team. They would see a bunch of middle-aged Brits step out in fake Pakistani stick-on hair and moustaches, wearing Pakistani Test team shirts. Attack, I decided, was the best form of defence, so I stepped confidently out of the limo, punching the air and shouting "Pakistan, Pakistan" at the top of my voice. The rest followed my lead as we trooped through the famous gates. They didn't lynch us, they loved us. The Pakistani team batted first and got themselves into a terrible tangle. At 70 for far too many wickets it was clear that this powerful Aussie team was going to win. The TV cameras had been favouring us as the only colourful idiots among the corporate suits and bacon and tomato ties in the rich mans' boxes. At this point Richard stood up, facing the suits and stripped off his Pakistani shirt to reveal an Australian Test shirt underneath. He conducted the boxes in a chorus of "Australia". Unbeknown to us he had gone for a walk around the ground and bought an Australian shirt from a supporter. Also, unbeknown to us he had just lost a large bet on Pakistan to win. Unbeknown to us but, it turned out, the bet was quite enough to buy you a decent family car. Don't fret, he still had enough for a taxi home. The stretch limo was waiting to waft us back through London.

Richard kindly invited us to the villa he had taken for a month in the summer at Eze sur Mer, overlooking Cap Ferrat. It began the longest joust of our relationship. I had been filming in India, stopped at Heathrow on the way home, swapped some love and luggage with the children and went with Sue to the airport at Nice, where we hired a car. I had been travelling for the best part of twenty-four hours when I stepped out in front of a car near the Promenade des Anglais coming out of Nice. I had been to a tabac to ask the way to the villa and, pondering the French reply, I stepped out into the road, looking the wrong way. Pretty sophisticated for a World traveller, don't you think? When I came to half of France's emergency services appeared to have gathered around me. Pleasingly, someone had chalked an outline of my crumpled body on the tarmac. I felt as if I was in a *Columbo* movie. More pleasingly still I woke up speaking French to the doctor kneeling by my side. We were in fact within a stone's throw of the villa and my friends soon came running to see what all the fuss was about. Brian Aldridge of *The Archers*, my friend Charles Collingwood, said: "Darling. We all wanted to make an entrance, but this is ridiculous". I had to spend a night in Nice Hospital because the doctors had to check me for a head injury. And what a night. I was incarcerated with a group of mad Algerians, whose idea of a good night out in a hospital was throwing the furniture around and shouting in an impenetrable accent. Meanwhile, I was lying there as stiff as a board, when my friends came to see me. "Charles, what kind of car hit me?" "Rolls-Royce, darling" came the reply. It was actually a Ford Fiesta but Charles's sense of theatre demanded something grander on the Promenade des Anglais. They left me with their love and good wishes. I was left there, among the pieds noirs, with plenty of time to ponder the last twenty-four hours. I had left a whisky reception in Delhi, had a few drinks on the plane to London, a couple of pints in the Dog and Duck at Heathrow, and a couple of those tiny wine bottles on the flight to Nice. Ah, but I wasn't driving at the time of the accident. Happy thought. Then I remembered that, under French Law, you could be charged with causing an accident while drunk and I had been breathalysed at the scene before being red-lighted to the Hospital. Unhappy thought. Richard arrived the following morning in a reassuringly British Range Rover and took me to the car in a wheelchair, which he tried to buy from the hospital porter. The man wouldn't sell the hospital's property so, on the way to the Chateau Richard managed to buy a pair of crutches. And, as they used to say in *The Goon Show*, this is where the story really starts.

Once I had swept through Nice in a wheel chair, with Charles saying "Look pained, darling. The punters standing in the queue are going to love you." I returned to convalesce at home. "Fly by Wheelchair for hassle free travel" was my new slogan. The crutches now stood balefully in the corner, posing a silent challenge. It was incumbent on me to return the crutches to Richard who had bought them for me in the first place. A party at Richard's house proved an easy opportunity. I left the crutches in a downstairs loo among umbrellas and walking sticks. Honour was satisfied. A few weeks later, Annabel was alone at home when a white van arrived and a man struggled up the drive with a plant, an enormous plant in a giant, earthenware pot. It bore a compliments slip from one of my current clients. Why were they sending me a present? I phoned the major people I knew in the company and all denied any knowledge of a giant Triffid in a plant pot. Then I fell in. I unravelled the great mass of foliage and there were the crutches. Game on again. This was going to demand even greater subterfuge. I had two good friends in Oxford who came to the rescue. Professor Sir Andrew McMichael, who travelled the world to medical conferences and John Barrows, who runs Elmer Cotton Sports in the City. From John I got an empty wooden crate for carrying croquet mallets. Come on, this is Oxford, everybody needs a box for carrying their croquet mallets, don't they? Andrew's next conference was in Hong Kong, where Richard had his Asian Headquarters. His staff in London had strict instructions not to accept any parcel for Richard personally. So I was delighted that his Hong Kong office accepted my gift to him and he returned to the Far East to discover a jolly little gift of some croquet mallets. He still doesn't know how the crutches got there or that one of the world's leading medical scientists had hand delivered it. The endgame was approaching. Sue and I threw one of our much loved parties at Upper Farm and invited all our friends, including the North London Mafia, who arrived in a coach. My bet was that Richard would hire a helicopter from Oxford Airport and drop the crutches on our lawn. But I reckoned without the scale of Richard's ambitions. Half way through our party two lorries reversed up our drive and tipped several hundred crutches along the entire length of it. I was snookered. The entire party put their glasses down and helped me to clear the mass of crutches into the barn, so that the North London coach could collect its returning passengers. Jonathan, meanwhile, had found the original crutches and chatted up the coach driver to secrete them in his vehicle. Honours even. Richard had his crutches back and the John Radcliffe Hospital had an unexpected gift of hundreds of free crutches. So at least someone had benefitted from two grown men acting like naughty boys in the playground.

SEX AND THE CELEBRITY

When my daughter, Annabel, first heard that I was going to be filming with Jimmy Savile, she was very impressed. Now, of course, she is as horrified as everybody else. Horrified and baffled by Savile's evil career. Savile was a criminal and chose to brandish his weirdness on radio and television. I wonder whether that was actually a deliberate double-bluff. By appearing to be a silly weirdo in public he could go on to be an evil weirdo in private. Hiding in plain sight. It's easy to forget now just what a big star Savile was. He began on radio when it was just exploding out of the Home Service days into the amazing world of Radio 1, where the teenager was king. The successful DJs knew how to exploit this new phenomenon, Tony Blackburn with his unctuous charm and endless good humour, Simon Bates, another BBC refugee sheltering at LBC ("These are my broadcasting trousers" he would proudly announce as he strode into the newsroom, indicating an ancient pair of moleskin kecks that looked as though they hadn't seen a dry-cleaner in decades) and Jimmy Savile working on the principle "if you can't beat 'em, join'em" dressing up as the world's oldest and wackiest teenager. When Savile made the magical and lucrative move into telly, it was still in the black and white age. Savile's ridiculous peroxide blonde shoulder length hair stood out. When television switched to colour, so did Savile, appearing with a full spectrum of colours on his head over the years. He told me with some pride how all this posturing and the silly hair was a deliberate ploy to hook the viewer. It worked. Remember that there were really only three channels, the well-established BBC 1, practically woven into the fabric of the Nation, a fledgling ITV and BBC 2 for Guardian readers and Radio 4 aficionadas. Savile was getting ratings that would bring tears to the eyes of young commissioning editors in these multi-channel days. (A word about commissioning editors. Behind the acne these are people who can make or break a young independent film-maker. I lost my faith in them when a group of us at United Television Artists made a film for the RAF on its fiftieth birthday. Ian Taylor's film was greatly appreciated by the Top Brass, so much so that one of them said to Ian over the post prandial port "why don't you make a film for the BBC about the Queen's Flight? I can get all the relevant permissions from the Palace". Ian, quite naturally, seized the opportunity and we duly put it to the commissioning editor at the BBC as our first submission. Think about it. It had everything, lots of whizzy planes, exotic locations and it had Royals, indeed it had Royals that actually flew themselves from time to time. And we had the access at the top level. The commissioning editor waved it away, saying, "I'm a bit fed up with Royal stories." I rest my case). Perhaps we should have put Savile forward as the presenter. He liked schmoozing the Royals and men in uniform. And he was certainly bankable.

I first met him in a hotel in Carlisle. He was about to go on one of his charity runs across Britain, this time from coast to coast, Carlisle to Newcastle. Given that the director, my old friend Ken Stephinson and I were in the same business as our guest his attitude at that first dinner was odd. Indeed, everything about Savile was odd. He treated us as if we were fans not fellow professionals doing a job. The dinner was all "Me, me, look at me" and I began to dread a whole week of this man and his ego. I asked him about his charity work, particularly his job as a porter at Leeds General Hospital. He talked about going out with the emergency ambulance and went into graphic detail about the mangled bodies he'd scraped off the road. I didn't really want to know and Susan, who was on half term at the time, can feel faint at the thought of blood. That's why she doesn't remember Savile's most graphic story at all. She has that wonderful feminine ability to blank out things she doesn't want to hear. Savile described a particularly nasty road accident where he dragged the body out but the head was missing. He said he'd crawled under a lorry and collected the severed head himself. I thought "Oh God, I'm really not going to enjoy this week at all". But we had presumably passed some strange initiation test into the ways of Savile and he got nicer towards me and the crew. I ran part of the way with him while the cameraman, Paul Berriff, had to run backwards carrying a heavy camera. Every now and then, to prove his supremacy, Savile would say "change gear" and accelerate away from us. Why he needed to prove his speed and fitness to Paul and myself, was just another oddity of his strange persona.

We had no idea just how strange he was. He had done a deal with a motor home company who provided him with his own movie-style caravan to make the journey. It was great for me, because I could write chunks of script in there as we followed his run and Paul could get plenty of passing shots as the crowds waved from the side of the road in all the little towns and villages we went through. In all the Lower Pudlingtons along the route they could see a telly megastar up close and they loved it.

I had open access to the motor home and it became my office for the week of filming. One day I stepped in and saw that Jimmy was in residence lying on the double bed with a young girl. I don't know how old she was and they were both fully clothed. That's it. I could now no doubt make up some more interesting tale and trouser a big wad of money from a lascivious tabloid. But I didn't. Indeed, after I told this odd but tame story on the *Panorama* special about the Savile scandal, I was approached by several foreign television stations but just didn't call them back. *The Sun* was more persistent; they sent a callow youth along to my house. I opened the door and he proudly announced that he was from *The Sun*... could he come in? No, he couldn't. I said to him that, if he wanted to know what I saw, it was all there on the *Panorama* film and there was nothing to add. He obviously wanted me to talk about Savile and his set of friends and hoped to establish that I was one of them. I thanked him politely and closed the door. As I returned to the warmth of my living room I thought: "What an amateur. I would have got in the house and shared a drink with the target" – that gave me a warm glow.

After the *Panorama* special I got lots of calls from old friends. I hadn't been at all well at the time – indeed I had a skeletal face that could have scared children in the street. I didn't know whether my friends' calls were genuinely to congratulate me on having the bravery to speak up or simply to ascertain whether I was still alive. The programme got five million viewers and I think I got respect for being prepared to share a collective responsibility for the tacit acceptance that Savile had been allowed despite the fact that so many of us found him "strange". Esther Rantzen has also expressed regret for the failure of so many of us to sound a warning. The police set up Operation Yewtree in the aftermath of the Savile scandal and several other well-known media celebrities were charged with what are now being called "historic" sex abuses. As that list of celebrities grew I found myself increasingly "conflicted", a psychobabble word that really means I didn't know what to think. Nobody is going in to bat on behalf of child abusers or relatively old men having sex with underage girls. Nobody should lend a word of support or understanding to Savile, for certain. Indeed one of the most baffling aspects of the Savile case is our inability to understand how anyone could behave in such an evil way. In the case of the historic charges against the other named celebrities I can say nothing specific since, at the time of writing, their cases are either being tried or are pending trial, but I can make a general point about "historic" charges, one mentioned recently by the wonderful Joan Bakewell. The sixties and seventies were a very different society from today's. Joan reveals how women in the media just expected some of the men to pinch their bottoms and act in a sexist manner. They didn't like it but it sort of came with the territory. The wonderful Frank Muir famously dubbed Joan "the Thinking Man's Crumpet". Very funny at the time but you couldn't say that today about a pretty woman on television. You could of course call Daniel Craig "the Thinking Woman's Crumpet". You take my point. Societies and social mores change over the decades and that needs to be taken into account when putting "historic" charges. It's also worth pointing out that the grizzled old faces of once famous DJs and seventies television presenters were good-looking "stars" once. The image of an eighty-year-old man walking into court accused of sex with a young girl is misleading. That's not what he looked like forty years ago. I am not, in any way, condoning any criminal activity but the Savile scandal created a feeding frenzy in the Press and the Law should not encourage that. That's the conflict. I trust the estimable jury system in this country can help to resolve it. Until that time the best maxim to live by is: "Keep it in the breeks".

YOU TWIT

lternatively, you could tweet it to the entire world. If you are Noreen Nobody boasting about a quick grope behind the bike sheds with Barry, nobody is going to care apart from the other nobodies. But if the said grope was with a Premier League footballer in his Lamborghini you could become front page news the moment the presses run or instantaneous news in the nanoseconds it takes for your selfie to reach Facebook. Twenty years ago the second half of that sentence would have read like Mandarin Chinese. The exponential growth of technology in the latter half of the twentieth century has been astonishing and for the most part beneficial. Inevitably, though, there have been excrescences like Twitter. If you are as stupid as my fictional Miss Nobody or as clever and witty as Stephen Fry, a noted tweeter, then it probably doesn't matter. But most of it is drivel and potentially dangerous drivel if trawled through by a tabloid reporter.

To get a true picture of today's information overload, just look back through my forty years in the journalism trade. The esteemed columnist, Alan Watkins (Watney's to *Private Eye*) always insisted that journalism is a trade, not a profession and, more recently

Jeremy Paxman has described journalists as having second-class minds. The first-class minds are running the civil service and the Foreign Office and the Treasury where only the pusillanimous politicians can get in the way. Watkins also believed that the politicians were trade, not professional; "politics is a rough old trade" was a frequent incantation from Alan on the news from Whitehall or the Palace of Westminster. Look back at the way things were in 1969, when I started at Tyne Tees in Newcastle. No laptops, no memory sticks, no mobile phones, no Sat Nav. You had a pad of paper, a pencil and a pocket full of pennies to use any available phone box to report back to the office. In the heyday of the *Daily Express*, before it became the bad joke it is today ("World ends at lunch time today. Government blames freak storm chaos and immigrants for the end of life as we know it"). The editor would send out five or six journalists to a big story. One would actually be writing the story while the others filled up every nearby phone box to prevent the rest of the press pack from filing their copy. Today, of course, you'd go to work on a big story with your own laptop and satellite phone and you can file your copy instantaneously from the middle of the Sahara desert or the Indian Ocean. How did we ever find people without a laptop of electoral rolls and Sat Nav to guide us to Acacia Avenue in South Shields? Her Majesty's Post Office was often the answer. Village postmistresses were a fount of knowledge. They didn't need digital help. They had gossip. Try explaining "gossip" to a logical computer. You can't. The GPO's gossipers in chief would get you to Acacia Avenue. I remember bowling into one such den of information and finding a young postmistress of my own age. As I asked her the whereabouts of Miss Newsworthy I found myself staring at her face and mentally stripping the years away. It was Rosemary Richardson, the mata hari of the Bromley Revolutionary Front, who used to play "Dare, Truth, Promise, Kiss, Cuddle, Love" in the garages behind our house in Palace View. We never got to the Love bit, but a kiss and a cuddle with Rosemary

Richardson was as good as winning *Who wants to be a Millionaire?* Now, the gossip of the day was us and our gang. Rosemary's husband stood guard in case this flash Harry from the telly had any further amorous ambitions on his lady wife. I duly turned up at Dahlia Drive to find Miss Newsworthy. But, at which number? You simply knocked on as many doors as you could until someone told you, an analogue solution that my grandchildren just wouldn't understand. One of the sharpest observations from Stephen Spielberg is that glowing finger on *E. T.* Armed with that anything, all things, are achievable. Yes, escaping on an old bicycle is analogue, but escaping on a flying bike is distinctly digital. My beautiful granddaughter, Jessica is just twenty months old and, I'm sorry to say, has not yet mastered CGI. George, now four years old, has got to grips with the iPad and Molly, aged nine, makes some very good videos on the same machine. What did she want for Christmas? A tripod of course and a green curtain as background for any image in the world in front of which she can sing and dance. The machine comes with a fantastic range of special effects. One of these enables her to create several Mollys on the one screen. I tried to explain to her how we used to achieve a much more shaky example on early television. In one scene a ghostly Martin Young had to rise from the sleeping form of Martin Young in an old, spooky hotel. We used a clockwork camera, a Bolex, to film the rising ghost, physically wound the film back and superimposed it on the sleeping form of Martin. Other film makers at Lime Grove were intrigued by this innovation, just as they had been years ago when Whicker delivered one of his trademark pieces to camera while rowing a small boat across Lake Windermere. The film makers then just couldn't understand how he had managed to get a whole film crew onto a tiny dinghy. The answer was again the faithful Bolex. Originally used to do silent pick-up shots, it had been adapted by Whicker's cameraman, the estimable Slim Hewitt, to take sound. Everyone wanted to know how Alan and Slim had done it. As I explained all this to Molly she looked pityingly at me. What on earth was this silly old codger trying to tell her? And, what's "clockwork" anyway? I'm sure that whatever job you were in there must be moments when you look back and think, how did we do that? How did we take such risks?

In 1983 *Panorama* sent me to cover the Democratic Primaries in the States. Here are the bald logistics. I took a plane from Heathrow to Washington with a three man BBC crew and a director. We made our film and then sent the assistant cameraman back to the airport to ship the exposed cans of film back to Heathrow. The cans were picked up by a BBC dispatch rider, taken to Television Centre, put in a chemical bath to develop the film, dried off and then viewed. After a week's work, this was the first time that anyone knew there were definitely images on the exposed film. One day our prints will come. You had to believe it. This whole process had involved two day's travel across the Atlantic Ocean, motor bike rides and chemical baths. Today, Jeremy Paxman or Andrew Marr can sit in a comfy chair in a warm studio and summon anyone in the world to their presence in nanoseconds. The documentary maker can sit and view his "rushes" on the Syrian border or in South Sudan. He at least knows that he has the makings of a film, not for him the long wait for processing back in London. If the war situation gets worse he can always send his material back home by satellite.

THE QUEST FOR MONDALE

n Washington I still had to find some material. I knew precious
little about the American political system, but I did know that
we weren't allowed to stay at the Georgetown Inn because it
was too expensive. So we booked ourselves into the Georgetown
Inn, phoned Mondale's campaign and asked for an interview with
the candidate. I knew I had already won the looming battle with
BBC expenses back in London. I mean, you couldn't bid for an
interview with the next man who might Rule the World from a
payphone in L'il Abner's Diner and B&B, could you? It had
worked for me at the Paris Hilton, while meeting President
Giscard d'Estaing's entire French Cabinet; surely it would work
again in Washington. The important business over, I turned to the
minor problem of getting an interview with Walter Mondale. The
trouble was there were very few votes for him to worry about in
Britain so an interview with the BBC's *Panorama* programme was
hardly top of the candidate's wish list. The answer each day was
"No". We followed Mondale around on the campaign trail but
continued to get the bum's rush treatment from his campaign
manager. However, I was beginning to learn a bit about American
politics, not least about the "assassination squad". They were not

there to assassinate Mondale but to be sure to get the pictures of him being shot should another Harvey Oswald be lurking around the corner. Mondale would still be dead but there would at least be nice crisp colour pictures of the event for the networks to view immediately and a born again Warren Commission to pore over for years. The assassination of JFK in 1963 had shocked and frightened the world but had traumatised Americans. The man who was to beat Mondale to the Presidency, Ronald Reagan, would be shot but not killed during his term of office. No wonder the President was surrounded by security men ready to "take the bullet" for their leader, whenever he stirred from the White House. No wonder that the networks had their assassination squads who trailed the President everywhere. I had wondered as we trailed around watching Mondale press the flesh, who the camerawoman was who kept as close to Mondale as she possibly could. She was small but muscle-bound through working out I suppose. I had never heard the term "work-out" before but I couldn't help but notice her, wherever Mondale went. She was of indeterminate ethnicity with a splash of American Indian in her somewhere. She had the strength and stamina to carry a heavy film camera on her shoulder all day and had a disarming ability to lean all her weight on one outstretched leg to get under and nearer the action. Now I knew what action she was waiting for.

It rapidly became obvious that I was not going to get a formal interview with Mondale, so I had to scrabble for attention in one of the daily press conferences. I had often noticed that by asking the rudest question you could almost always get a response. Mondale's campaign message was "Strong Government" so I simply said; "Senator Mondale, why have you decided to run as the candidate of strong government when for the past four years you have been Vice President in the weakest government most Americans have seen in their lifetimes?" The Press Corps, I could tell, were quite impressed by this uppity Brit who was dissing the Carter regime in front of the Veep. The point was, it was true.

Jimmy Carter may well have been one of the most decent men to have ruled the White House and his peace-keeping efforts since have been admirable, but as far as the American voter was concerned at that time he had failed to rescue America's hostages in Iran, sent in the lamentable helicopter rescue, Desert One and generally not stood up to the Ayatollah. This was not the smack of firm government. Mondale was unamused by my question but he did answer it. So I had my interview, although hardly the far-reaching geopolitical debate I had envisaged. I did the rounds of the senior statesmen who would talk to the BBC and discovered that they worked out of vast offices on the Hill, as opposed to the broom cupboards our boys and girls got to share in the Palace of Westminster.

The campaign manager remained underwhelmed by the BBC's presence in Washington, so we decided that if you can't beat'em, leave 'em, and leapt ahead on the campaign trail to Atlanta in Georgia, the home state of Jimmy Carter, the peanut farmer. There we filmed the queues of men selling their own blood and the Omni Centre selling every designer label in town. It's too easy and glib to say that this was Carter's legacy, today President Obama struggles with just the same inequities on American soil.

I HAVE SEEN THE FUTURE AND
I DON'T UNDERSTAND IT

The last time I read the news was yesterday. My granddaughter, then aged nine, was the director, the cameraman and the editor. She had recently seen me on a BBC archive film I made in 1977, complete with full head of long seventies' hair and lapels on my Jaeger safari suit as wide as the Amazon. Nonetheless, Molly had decided that grandpa was a star and therefore fodder for her file of videos. So I had to read the news on to her iPad. Like Simon Bates and his broadcaster's trousers I never lost my broadcaster's voice and, sure enough, back it came as Molly cued me. I am probably already this week's choice on "YouTube" or "oldcodgers.com". Molly was quite fierce as a director, no jackboots but an Erich von Stroheim in the making nonetheless. I offered to improvise some headlines but she was clearly determined to do all that herself as Chief Correspondent, so my role was strictly just to top and tail the bulletin, leaving the starring role to her. Quite right, too. The future belongs to the Forever Young club, not the Harrumph Club. Yet, where will it all end? For, end it must as the comedian/philosophers continually remind us. If I, at sixty-seven, am increasingly nonplussed by the speed of technological change, what sort of a world will Molly at sixty-seven and her brother George at sixty-one look out on. Will their grandchildren have developed an E.T. finger with built in computer? Will they know their friends mainly as holograms that they can call into their living rooms from anywhere in the country or the world. They already Skype their friends who live a few doors away. Suddenly, even now, there is the sound of a full-scale conversation going on in the kitchen where you know the child is on her own. But the computer is allowing her to have a chat with her best friend, Charlotte. Will Molly's grandchildren make H.G. Wells' *Time Machine* a reality? Will Charlotte be able to beam up Molly for some playtime? You can dub on William Shatner's voice saying "Beam me up, Molly". Sadly, I shall neither be in Heaven nor Hell. I'll be out there somewhere in a pile of dust, mingling with Richard Dawkins and the man who wrote *The Atheist's Bible*.

ONE-TAKE WONDERS

We've done the present and the far-distant future; now let's go back to the past, in this case the sixties and seventies which do seem to be a very long time ago. In the sixties as I watched Whicker take his moustache and glasses around the world, I admired his style, sometimes florid, sometime quite spare.

Location: the middle of the desert, somewhere in America.

Dramatis personae: Alan Whicker and a train.

It is a simple story told by Whicker in one piece to camera. Rumour has it that if you stand here anywhere in the desert beside the main rail line, the train will stop for you if you wave it down. All this time the train has been thundering down on Whicker. He raises a languid arm. Will it stop or will our hero be left to wither in the vast desert? The tension in sitting rooms from Huddersfield to Hendon is unbearable. The train stops and Alan climbs aboard with a cheery wave. One shot – a film is made. Only a short time later do you find yourself wondering about the film crew left alone and sweating as the midday sun batters down on them. Are they frantic with fear for their lives or are they calculating how much BBC subsistence allowance they'll be able to claim when finally rescued? My bet's on the latter.

The piece to camera, or what the Americans call the stand upper is hardly an art form, but it certainly takes skill. People used to ask me where I did all my writing, imagining some elegant suite in Lime Grove. The answer was anywhere I could find, a garden wall in Grimsby, the bonnet of the camera car in Albuquerque or Shimon's front room or Ahmed's tent near Jericho. Then, you had to commit it to memory while the crew stood impatiently at your side. Then you had to deliver it. I was a favourite with crews, being known as a one-take wonder. Except... on a commercial shoot for a programme called *Inside Urology* (I have often wondered which bit of it I was inside) I was presented with this: "... and other operative procedures such as pelvic lymphadenectomy." I just couldn't get it right. Eventually, after about fifteen takes I made it and turned in triumph to the director. "You said pelfic" he said coldly. I never went back *Inside Urology*. I've no idea why.

Michael Rodd of *Tomorrow's World* was a contemporary of mine and famous for his ability to talk live to camera. I found myself with a cameraman who had recently filmed Rodd doing a long, elaborate piece to camera. Eagerly I asked him how many takes he'd needed. "Two," said the cameraman. I thought, that's not too bad, I could do that. "Yes" he continued, "one master take and one over all the cutaway shots. He was word perfect on both." Another cameraman later cheered me up with a story about Whicker, also known as a one-take wonder in his day. They were filming on the White Cliffs of Dover and Whicker kept getting it wrong. A film reel in those days was about 400 feet and lasted about ten minutes. Alan was having such a bad day that he took up a whole reel of film with his failed pieces to camera. The cameraman took all the film off the take up reel and hurled it over the White Cliffs to oblivion. "Right," he said "let's start again, shall we?"

Nationwide film techniques ranged from the outrageous to the highly predictable. A film that began with a big close-up of the reporter, in this case Chris Rainbow, would, inevitably pull back to a wide shot revealing that our hero was wearing something silly. In this case the reveal showed us that Chris was wearing a tricorn hat and eighteenth-century uniform, complete with knee breeches and a cutlass. I have seen his many attempts to complete his piece to camera so many times that, even today, I remember it by heart, which is more than he ever did. "Customs men, or Excise men as they were known in those days, used to row out to the ships to search for contraband goods" and he was off, rowing like a good 'un towards the unseen clipper. Or, at least that was the plan. On the first take he got as far as "Excisemen" before his eighteenth-century memory let him down. On the second take it was his two hundred year old teeth that got in the way of what he was trying to convey. By the tenth take the assistant cameraman is leaning into shot with glee and announcing:"Customs Men Take Ten". This time he gets as far as the bit where he's supposed to take up the oars and set off. There is a magical moment where you see his brain tackling one of the world's Great Imponderables: Number of things to do, pick up two oars, wave cutlass. Number of available arms, two. "Customs Men Take Eleven" We have made it safely to the oars bit again. With a knowing glint in his eye, Chris sticks the cutlass between his teeth and grabs the oars. Students of this chapter of accidents, and there are many, will have noticed that the tide has been going out so they have had to tie the rowing boat to the jetty. Chris is going nowhere. "Customs Men Take Twelve" the assistant announces, having difficulty holding the board steady while shaking with suppressed laughter. Take twelve comes and goes as it is revealed that the prow of the boat is being held in place by a film crew hand. By take thirteen, things are going swimmingly, if you'll pardon the pun. PTC complete, cutlass safely stowed, no film crew hand in shot and, with a flourish Chris is off, off his bench and head first into the bow of the boat. At the moment critique he has caught a crab. All we can see now is a crumpled mass of BBC eighteenth century wardrobe with a pair of knee breeches sticking up in the air. He finally got it on take eighteen. Not bad for a morning's work, time to go to the Admiral Benbow for a stiff rum or two.

Venue: Vindolanda Roman site, Northumberland.

Dramatis persona: Me.

I was not immune to the occasional lapse into "mumble mouth". To cover my embarrassment and to prevent myself saying "fuck" when I lost my train of thought I used to say "knickers". I was busy showing the viewers some of the artefacts they had found at the recently-discovered Roman site at Vindolanda. I was busy clutching an old pair of Roman sandals when brain fade set in: "And here, perhaps the most exciting find of all, a pair of Roman leather… Knickers". That would indeed have been an exciting and exotic find. But wrong. Take two.

Since I saw Alan Whicker all alone in the desert, I had become mildly obsessed with the one-take film. I never did manage it but I got fairly close.

Venue: Towyn, Wales.

Dramatis personae: the weeping knight, Bill Jones and me.

The story was simple enough. The knight lay there in his tomb with his statue recumbent on top. Some sad and romantic event had disturbed his noble life for, from time to time; tears would trickle down his warrior's visage. What had caused this lacrimony? That was for me to find out and for you to wonder at. It was the perfect story, very few facts and pregnant with possibility. I sat on a tombstone and wrote the story at length, strong on speculation, light on facts. Was he weeping for a lost lover or a lost battle? Did the tears flow for comrades lost on the field? Was his lover a flaxen-haired beauty or the girl with the dragon tattoo? Had he tried to slay the dragon and failed? I delivered all this fevered speculation over the recumbent knight and from various recesses in the beautiful old church. We shot just 265 feet of film, about five minutes worth. Once the flash frames had been edited out and everything was topped and tailed we had over four minutes of final film. But, no tears. Our knight stubbornly refused to weep on cue. Now, Bill Jones had not fought his way through the Vietnamese war in order to be defeated by an ossified Welsh Knight. "Glycerine" he declared cryptically, and the assistant cameraman was despatched to find a tube of the stuff in the local Towyn pharmacy. Please do not write to the Director General or cancel your licence-fee payment but we then perpetrated a minor deceit by making the Knight of Towyn weep pure glycerine. That was our final shot and we left with only one thing on our conscience. The statue did indeed produce water through a fissure in the stone under certain atmospheric conditions. We had merely accentuated Nature's process, hadn't we? Unless, of course, the glycerine bunged up the fissure for centuries to come....

THE LITTLE HOUSE IN AMBLESIDE

Bill Jones was an excellent film director and, as we have seen, resourceful. Ken Stephinson was first class as well and he and I made dozens of films together, mostly in the North of England. Indeed, he was my oldest friend in television, having befriended me in my early days at "Tyne Tees" and taken me home where his wife, Doreen, spotted a starving bachelor and fed me up with proper food, not Vesta Chicken Curry. Even in those early days I was still in search of the one-take film, when Ken took me to the little house.

Venue: Ambleside in the Lake District.

Dramatis personae: Ken, the little house and me.

It was the Cumbrian version of the *Play School* house, four windows and one door. It was tiny. It didn't stand by a romantic, bubbling rill, it straddled one. The whole structure was supported by a lovely stone arch across the water. Ken said: "There you are, do something with that, Mart" "Hang on, what's the story?" "That's for you to write and for me to find out". I retired to my hotel room with the words "Rumour has it..." already forming in my mind. If I were to say it in a Scottish accent I would sound just like Fyfe Robertson from the glory days of *Tonight*. Anyway, rumour had it, I decided, that the little house had been owned by a canny Scot, who was very careful with his pennies – mean, in other words. He wasn't prepared to pay for a big house nor did he want to pay the land tax. So, Mr McGregor built a small house over water. There was, at that time, no water tax (for all I knew there was no land tax either, but I was employing poetic licence or "lying", as we call it in the trade). We decided to film the little house as if it were the TV *Play School* house, with me popping out of the four windows and the front door with my increasingly fanciful rumours about the parsimonious Mr McGregor. Not yet the one-take film but pretty close and five minutes of harmless fancy for the faithful viewer. For me it was a rare relief to be released from the strictures of the truth: from the black-vinyl sofas and the sorry tales of the unemployed or unemployable: from the endless strikes of the seventies and the interviews with the truculent Arthur Scargill. From now on, I thought, I'll just go to my hotel room and make it all up, until they find me out. Lest you think me a liar and a crook, consider the following stories perpetrated on a trusting British people.

CASTRO & CAMERON

Venue, Havana, Cuba.

Dramatis personae: James Cameron, Fidel Castro & assorted gunmen.

James Cameron is one of my heroes, the doyen of foreign correspondents in a bygone age. He worked for the *News Chronicle* and the *Daily Express* in their glory days. I met him once at a "Listener" party as I was preparing to go to Israel to film *Hanging Fire*. I had just been watching an Eddie Mirzoeff documentary on Israel and Palestine, fronted by Cameron. As he stood there at one of the big refugee camps near Jericho, he talked of the endless floods of shattered souls who had flown in one direction or the other since 1948, just a year after I was born and the grand exodus in 1966 after the Six-Day War, when I was still at school. I told him that watching him with all his first-hand knowledge had convinced me not to do any pieces to camera in my forthcoming series. What did I know of all these savage scenes over half a century? James gave me a war-weary look.

In 1956, the Cuban revolution was led by Fidel Castro,

bringing Communism almost to the shores of America itself. It was a feverish moment in the ever-present infection of the Cold War. In those days simply getting to the centre of the revolution, in Havana, was a story in itself and James filed many a colour piece on Cuba while waiting for the promised audience with Castro. He was there for a week and still no sign of a meeting with the head of the revolution. He cabled back to Fleet Street that there didn't look like being any meeting with Fidel, so he was coming home soonest. He drank a bottle of whisky and went to bed, having failed in his mission. As he and Johnnie Walker slept deeply, he was awakened by a series of imperative thumps on his hotel room door. A troupe of angry looking men stormed in carrying machine guns and surrounded his bed. He was fearing for his life until another man followed behind the armed guard. It was Fidel Castro. "So, you want to know about our revolution? I will tell you". And he did, for about an hour, striding up and down Cameron's room, extolling the virtues of Marxist Leninism to the British capitalist dog before him. Meanwhile this running dog of the capitalist elite was trying to wake up, sit up in bed and shake off lack of sleep and a surfeit of whisky. He had become a one-man Cuban peasant army, aroused and whipped on by the gift of the means of production dangling before him and the forthcoming joys of dialectic materialism to improve life back home on the farm. It was a heady mix of rhetoric and bombast and Cameron had heard it all before in other parts of the world to which he probably should not have been admitted. He let it all go over his head as he watched the man giving forth, the man who in a few years would be playing "Who will blink first?" over the Cuban missile crisis and risking Armageddon. Abruptly, Castro was gone, taking his bodyguard with him. James fell back, exhausted, and plunged back into a deep sleep. When he awoke a few hours later, he didn't remember a thing that Castro had said in the middle of the night. It had, literally, gone over his head. So, in the best traditions of British journalism, he made it up and cabled his world exclusive back to Fleet Street: the first interview with the communist leader, Fidel Castro, with the by-line James Cameron, Havana, Cuba. We sent our man. He got the story. Well, sort of.

THE MAN IN THE COCKTAIL BAR

My first foreign news story for the BBC *Nine O'clock News* was a tug-of-love human-interest story about a British mum, Linda Desramault and her French husband who had fled with their daughter to Northern France. Linda had been bought up by *The Sun*, who had her hidden somewhere in Paris. We traced her to the Paris Hilton, where I seriously considered letting down the tyres on *The Sun's* escape car. I desisted. More fool me, since a car chase ensued through Northern France towards Bethune, where hubby was believed to be holding the daughter. It was a frantic chase made much worse by our hire car. We had been met at Charles de Gaulle airport by a tall, elegant man dressed in full chauffeur's uniform. He informed us, in impeccable English, that he was Emmanuel and would be our driver while we were in France. He ushered us towards an enormous Daimler Majestic, the sort of car that you would see the Queen stepping in and out of in Pathé Newsreels of her foreign travels. Clearly, someone at the Paris Hertz desk had an inflated idea of Britain and the BBC. We were, of course, in the airport named after the man who had rallied the Free French from a BBC microphone in London, the man who would later walk down the Champs Elysees in triumph after the liberation of Paris and the rout of the hated Bosch. But we were not driving down a wide Parisian boulevard; we were stuck in a narrow market town in an even narrower fruit market, unable to get the great Majestic through the gap. Behind us the world's press were also stuck, because of the BBC's ridiculous imperial car. When we eventually reached a hotel in Bethune, we were not flavour of the month in the newly-established Press Bar, – and *The Sun* had got away from us all. I did eventually get my interview with Linda and earned some brownie points with the BBC News Editor. Only much later did I hear how it should be done.

Another tug-of-love story, another venue, no names, no pack drill. Henry Hack is summoned to the editor's lair. Henry has recently left the *Daily Express* and been taken on by the *Daily Dirt* to help salvage their falling ratings. The editor says that he's sorry but he's sending Henry on a wild goose chase to Switzerland to try to make something out of this tug-of-love story. The girl, let's call her Linda, has already been bought out by the *Daily Express*, Henry's last employer, and they are planning to whisk her back to Britain for an exclusive splash in the next edition. Can Henry get him at least some colour story to give them a chance of competition? Here are your airline tickets, do the best you can.

Henry flies to Geneva airport and heads straight for the bar, where else? He looks around the bar, sipping his first whisky of the day – apart from those free ones on the plane from Heathrow – and spots a face he knows, drinking an orange juice. It is none other than the *Daily Express* pilot, who greets him like an old friend. They settle down for a chat and Henry realises from the gossip that the pilot doesn't know he's left the *Express* for the opposition. After a while he goes off to the loo, but actually goes to the phone boxes opposite the bar and links up two kiosks together. A Tannoy call rings out for the *Daily Express* pilot, will he please phone the office urgently, please go to kiosk 11 to take the call. Henry is nearby in kiosk 6, imitating the editor. "Come back to Heathrow immediately, the plan is aborted." Henry returns to the bar where the pilot is gathering up his flight bag and planning his imminent departure. They shake hands and Henry orders another drink. A short time later, the *Express* reporter ushers Linda into the bar and goes off to find out where his private plane has got to. This takes some time, during which Henry befriends a confused Linda and takes down her entire story, tears and all. He returns to kiosk 6 and files his copy to his new, impressed editor. He has another drink or two and watches a by now frantic *Express* reporter return to tell Linda that their plane has gone. Soon, Henry has gone too, back to London and a hero's welcome. He has not wasted any money, staying overnight in Geneva. He just submits his enormous bar bill as "hospitality to informants".

SCARGILL

From time to time *Nationwide* decided to devote a whole week's programming to one of the regions. When we went to Yorkshire, we celebrated the famous pudding, did some pigeon fancying and explored the cradle of the industrial revolution. In the late seventies you couldn't come to Yorkshire without presenting your diplomatic papers at the Court of King Arthur, then the boss of the Yorkshire branch of the National Union of Mineworkers. It was quite clear even then that Arthur would become the National leader of the NUM and a political force to be reckoned with. So I gave him a call to say that we were doing a profile of him for our forthcoming Yorkshire week. He agreed to take part under three conditions: he would not allow us to film his wife at home; he would not be filmed down a mine; and he wouldn't do a scene in a pub, downing pints with his mates. I put the 'phone down and had a think. During a week in Yorkshire there could be no show without Punch. We needed Scargill, but we weren't about to dance to his tune and accept conditions. Mindful of the fact that we could put Scargill in front of ten to twelve million viewers, I called back and turned him down. I remember the anxiety on the face of the editor when I told him of this act of youthful bravado. The phone rang. It was Scargill, agreeing to an unconditional interview. I had taken on the bully in the playground, and won. Admittedly, it was a little less significant than Margaret Thatcher's victory a few years later. 'Twas a small thing, but 'twas mine own.

Venue: the Yorkshire coal fields

Dramatis personae: Jane Drabble, Arthur Scargill and me.

I shall start with Jane, my director. Here, the unthinking sexism of the seventies rears its ugly head. So, here I go. Jane was drop-dead gorgeous. Scargill fancied her and so did every hot-blooded miner we met. Indeed, I overheard one of them say to his mate: "'Ave you seen that bird the TV bloke's brought with him. He's bleeding lucky to 'ave a bit of crumpet like that". Everywhere Jane and I went it was just assumed that I'd brought my girlfriend with me for the ride. Jane was used to this and we didn't even try to explain that she was actually in charge of me. She was very bright (the surname Drabble was a bit of a clue) and ended up running the *Everyman* strand of documentaries. Nothing became her in life so well as the leaving of it – leaving the BBC that is. She wrote her own obituary, describing a glorious life devoted to the poor and the needy, inventing all manner of medicines for Africa, running her own political party bringing in liberal laws and tackling injustice. She concluded: "before that, she worked for the BBC". This was the bright girl and hard-headed reporter that Arthur set about trying to convert to Marxism. I had been preached to by the smooth, right-wing zealot, Cecil Parkinson, and stared into the "eyes of Caligula" herself, now I was to be inducted into the inner sanctum of British Marxism. From the start it was clear that, underneath the comic hair-do, a good political brain and driving ambition could be found. He reminded me of Tony Benn. Tony of the great disappearing name. He'd begun as Viscount Stansgate, become Anthony Wedgwood Benn and then gone further down market as Tony Benn. The next logical change was to 'To-be.' And logic was central to both Tony and Arthur which made them both so difficult to interview. Tony would ask you "Do you believe that all men and women are equal before the Law?" "Yes". "Why, then do we have a Third World, why in this First World country do we still have poverty and starvation? Why is there still a North/South divide in Britain? Decent socialism, putting the means of production in the hands of the workers would solve these problems, wouldn't it?" If you tried to argue with Tony or Arthur, they would turn directly to camera to plead their case to the British Public, pointedly by-passing the lickspittle from the ruling classes, who has clearly graduated from the public school and Oxbridge system to keep the upper-class jackboot firmly on the necks of the poor. Did I still believe that all men and women were equal before the Law? "Yes, but that's a simplistic argument". "No, it's a simple argument. Are all men equal?" And so on…

In every generation there are the nearly men, those who were born out of their time. Tony Benn and Arthur Scargill should have been reaching political maturity in the 1920's, Michael Heseltine or Kenneth Clarke should have been the Tony Blair of the 1990's. Both had the same communicating skills to temper the sour after taste of Thatcherism, so well traded on by Tony Blair who turned "social justice" into his personal mantra in 1989. But the Tory backwoodsmen or Shire czars, choose your own cliché, these unreconstructed Right wingers in their safe seats rejected them both. In Heseltine's case you sense he never got over the toffs' insult that he had had to buy his own furniture. There was a whiff of "trade" about him. As for Ken Clarke his unwavering support for the European Union put him permanently out of tune with the Little Englanders on the right of the Tory party. Instead the Tories went for William Hague, extremely able but too young and badly advised to gain the top job; Ian Duncan Smith, a cipher with the voice of a frog: and Michael Howard, who had pleased the Right as a hard line Home Secretary and could have won in 1989 but was up against the remarkable charm of Tony Blair, who was to win three elections in a row for Labour, just as Thatcher had won three for the Conservatives, only to be stabbed by her own Cabinet. Tony Blair could possibly have won a fourth election for Labour but was stabbed in the front by his own policy on the Iraq war. That will be his legacy, which is why he keeps trying to say that it was the right thing to do. What might we expect in the future? Ed Miliband looks and sounds like a loser. Cameron, having had the nerve to go into coalition with the Liberal Democrats, may have the steel to run a minority government against a demoralised Labour party still run by a toxic duo of Miliband and Balls, or he might attempt to continue with a Lib/Con coalition, a conciliatory system that, I sense, the much pursued centrist voter rather favours. Yet anybody who dares to predict the political future risks making a fool of himself. What was Harold MacMillan most worried by? "Events, dear boy, events". His fateful event took place between the sheets when Christine Keeler slept with his Minister for War, John Profumo, who subsequently lied to the House about the affair. Once it was discovered that the alluring Ms Keeler was also sleeping with a Russian spy, MacMillan's government was in its dying throes. So, the future? Look around the arid ranks of the Conservative benches in the Commons and despair. Yes, there are safe pairs of hands, like those of Philip Hammond, Theresa May or Eric Pickles (except who wants to be ruled by a barrage balloon in a suit) but where is the flair? It's up the road in the architectural testicle of the Mayor of London's office. Boris Johnson will be parachuted into Parliament and defeat David Cameron after the next election in 2015. Why? Because he wants it so much. We can understand why the belching old guard of the Shires want Boris. But why would the rest of us accept him? Because Boris is the next iconoclast waiting in the wings and Boris is beyond "events". He has so far bluffed and blustered his way out of various sexual shenanigans, done his share of falling about in front of cameras and even contrived to dangle from a high wire, twisting and turning in the breeze to the delight of those same film crews and political reporters. And what do we do? We laugh and say of this latter-day Cicero, "ah well, that's Boris for you". Ultimately, the laugh may be on us. He is clearly an intelligent man masquerading as a buffoon. But how would he govern? My guess is rather well. I have interviewed Boris many times on LBC radio. It was always a challenge and always entertaining. I have had one personal encounter with him in Woodeaton, where we lived for thirty years. Boris was our constituency MP and the village was facing the threat of the vast quarry re-opening and ruining the village. Boris agreed to listen to our fears, so we waited for him to arrive on our village green. He was late. He finally arrived in a Porsche Carrera 911 and tumbled his way out of this car that was clearly built for a young and athletic type with plenty of money. Boris was wearing about three thousand pounds of Saville Row pin stripe suit but still looked as though he had slept in it under a handy Oxfordshire hedgerow. His flies were undone. He sorted this out before we traipsed up to the quarry and ran into a man in a hard hat who was surprisingly articulate and well-briefed on the proposed re-opening of the quarry. Both Boris and I, who had been gossiping about our recent appearances on *Have I Got News for You,* recognised hardhat as a "plant". Boris had recently been editor of *The Spectator* and I recognised then that I would not have liked to present him with a badly-researched piece of journalism or an article lacking in intellectual rigour. The good burghers of Woodeaton had laid on tea and cakes for the distinguished visitor and he did not disappoint, staying for an hour or so to press the flesh and reassure his voters. And then, he was gunning the Porsche through the village, road testing it for *GQ* magazine, he said, on his way back to London. He left behind a warm feeling among natural Tories and those who didn't share his view of the world, like Susan and me. The quarry was duly quashed at a public inquiry. Whether Boris spoke up for us, we will never know. Was his support just words or did he mean it? We shall never be sure but we do know he left us with that warm feeling and that's quite a trick.

Into this heady mix we must add the United Kingdom Independence Party and its bibulous leader, Nigel Farage. To my shame, Farage was also a product of Dulwich College. For my money Cameron got it right first time when he called them swivel-eyed loons and closet racists and he should stick to that line, call them the Ostrich party, with their heads not so much in the sand as firmly up their own bums. Continuing the zoological metaphors, Farage himself is clearly "'aving a giraffe" and is quite delighted to be in the public spotlight for as long as it shines on him, then it's off to the lounge bar in his tweeds and cavalry twills to become the pub bore in Littlehampton by the sea, until he is reduced to an arcane footnote in Parliamentary history where he belongs. But UKIP is only the latest in a series of electoral oddities; remember Sir James Goldsmith's Reform party, George Galloway's Respect Party and his victor's speech predicting a mass vote. He ended up crawling on the ground playing Rula Lenska's cat in some ghastly reality TV show. These inane sideshows are part of the price we pay for democracy, a method of government which is truly priceless.

ROMANIA

I n 1997 I was asked to train some young Romanian journalists in the ways a free press works in a now supposedly democratic Romania, released from Ceausescu's yoke of tyranny. It sounds like a fairly dry subject – a series of lectures about the nature of freedom and democracy perhaps. Far from it, we were actually on air from the University city of Sibiu each day for a month, broadcasting live to the people of Transylvania. Quite what they made of us, a bunch of confused young students trying to learn how to be broadcasters, overseen by a Brit who didn't even speak the language, is anyone's guess. Romania was grim but fascinating. Everywhere you went was dull and grubby unless it had been built for Ceausescu's use like some of the buildings in central Bucharest. Like Mussolini he favoured the Communist concrete brutality movement, every building at least a storey too high and hundreds of feet too wide for the humble capital city around it. From the exorbitant cash price of the entry visa at the airport, money that I'm sure was never seen again by the municipality, to the venal efforts of the cab drivers to rip you off on the way to your hotel, the whole place stank, it just didn't work. I was given two interpreters, Marian and Sorin who between them told the story of post-dictatorship Romania. Marian was a hood. He was straight out of *On the Waterfront*, short stocky with boxer's shoulders. He had done well under the dictatorship. He must have been a faithful follower of the old regime since he had risen to be the Head of Bucharest Radio, an organ not noted for its independent thought and fearless criticism of the more oppressive actions of Ceausescu's government. Marian was a time-server and I was the next object to serve. He came with a tame government driver and the Romanian car of choice for the lower government officials, a small Dacia, produced under licence in Romania from Renault parts. In it we were driven through the Transylvanian mountains to the medieval city of Sibiu where the grim concrete buildings of the University stood. To someone brought up on Hammer horror films, the location was both magical and threatening at the same time. The real threat was not the wolf packs roaming the hills or the occasional Count with virgin's blood dripping from his fangs, it was the road itself. There were three types of traffic, horse carts with children or animals on board, travelling at about four miles an hour, ourselves in our Dacia bouncing around on the potholes at about fifty miles per hour and the clear beginnings of a new oligarchy, racing at eighty or ninety miles an hour in a selection of elite badges, Audi, BMW and Mercedes Benz. At a mathematical level it was easy to understand the reason for nasty accidents. Around any corner you could find yourself braking hard for a farmer, his family and his horse and cart, while the three-pointed star of Mercedes was bearing down on you at high speed. We made it to Sibiu.

The main square had clearly just been constructed by the Bond scenic designers and distressed by the antique experts at the RSC. It was huge, big enough to house 007's final tank battle against the evil Communist foe, and run-down enough to take the frantic townspeople in their uprising against Count Dracula. There were free beggars in situ to add atmosphere to the piece. I shall never forget one old woman with no legs below the knees.

She had strapped on a crescent of old car tyre to each stump and dragged her body through the square daily as I sat at the only café as the only tourist, drinking my watery beer and wondering what went wrong with Marx and Engel's manifesto for the perfect life and perfect motherland.

The lecture theatre I was given had no character whatsoever. It was big and empty and had just one inadequate neon strip light in the high ceiling. It was suicidally boring so I asked for three new strip lights only to be told that Ceausescu had believed that one light was enough for any room in Romania. No, it wasn't I insisted and gently reminded Marian that Ceausescu was dead. He and his wife had been shot by firing squad in 1989, at the end of the Romanian Revolution eight years previously. The lights never arrived. I taught in the gloom for the next four weeks. Things just didn't get done. No-one was prepared to take the initiative. It was the Communist way, "initiative" implied alternative thinking and that was insufferable to the regime. "Initiative" might lead to questioning which might lead to jail. Anyway, one light was enough.

My second interpreter, Sorin, was a totally different human being. Sorin was an intellectual, a natural free thinker and not surprisingly had got into trouble with the totalitarian regime early in his life. When he got out of jail he became a teacher and a porn baron. That last juxtaposition probably needs some explanation. He needed money and he spotted a hole in one of Romania's illegal rackets. Porn videos were easily available on the black market but all the grunting and heaving was in English so Sorin would dub the scant dialogue over the scanty costumes and make easy money. When he had earned enough he retired to an anonymous village in the Transylvanian mountains and taught English to the children of all the farm workers. I still have this Romantic notion of a group of Romanian serfs up there in the hills speaking perfect English thanks to Sorin. Later, he had returned to Cluj near the Hungarian border and taken a job as an official interpreter for the new, so-called, democratic government in Bucharest. Most of them were, of course, just re-tread communists who now called themselves the liberal freethinkers or the jolly nice party or the Oh no we're not communists at all party. It was, as Sorin well knew, all bullshit. The toughest of Ceausescu's "yes" men now claimed they had been against him all the time and welcomed democracy with open arms as long as they could stay in power.

What of the students themselves? They were mostly twenty-somethings who had lowly jobs in what passed for journalism in Romania at that time. One was much older and had facial scars that celebrated the diligence of Ceausescu's secret police. Like Sorin he had done time for freethinking and demonstrating against the regime. The three of us naturally bonded and would sit in the hotel bar in the evenings putting the world to rights. They accepted me very well, despite the fact that the BBC had not tortured me and that trial by the Mandarins had not sent me to the dungeons. Ah, the hotels of Transylvania… I began in Ye Olde Creeping Cockroach and moved quickly to the New Dead Cockroach Hostelry. I prefer my cockroaches dead and crunchy under foot rather than cavorting about on their several legs. In my new suite of rooms there was just one structural problem, the toilet appeared to have been nailed on as an afterthought and leaked like a drain. My abiding memory of that time is sitting on the bog, wondering if the nails would give way and cascade me with my trousers around my ankles onto the street below, while still holding the towel over my bald spot to catch the water coming through the roof. *Carry on, Cockroach*, starring Norman Wisdom could have been a blockbuster hit in Bucharest. Norman, remember was already big in Albania.

As I continued in my quest to make a silk purse out of the sow's ears I had been given, one damning fact became evident. These able, decent kids had grown up under an evil version of communism and had all the initiative driven out of them. This was the opposite of the can-do society we are so comfortable with in the West. One afternoon in our newsroom a big Sibiu story broke, I said "Phone the Mayor", who was a political appointee. "Oh, no. He'll be busy right now." "Look, I don't care if he's about to slip between the sheets with Sharon Stone, – phone the Mayor". "I can't find a phone". "There's one right in front of you". "It's not working". "Yes, it is, – now phone the Mayor". "But it's four thirty he'll be busy signing all his mail". "Don't you get it, I don't care if he's signing death warrants or completing his Christmas card list. He's responsible for this cock-up, so get on the phone and ask him to explain what he thinks he's doing".

When my frustration had subsided, I realised the horrible truth. Under Communism it was easier and much more safe to do nothing. These kids were supposed to be free but they were still frightened, still trapped by their upbringing. It would take a generation or two to change their mentality and then they'd be dead. It was disturbingly Kafkaesque. I began with the easy bit, trying to teach the young people how to do more than just a sycophantic interview with the Minister for Tourism and Cockroaches, but to punctuate it with sound effects and angry visitors who would prefer to sleep alone without insects cosying up to them. Then I moved on to the difficult bit trying to make my young reporters truly inquisitive, probing, even infuriating in their approach. However, I suspect most of them thought me mad and just could not make the leap from cringing to attack mode. There were exceptions. One rather nerdy-looking young man became an attack dog, turning up allegations of corruption against the Chief of Police in Sibiu. Somehow he managed to include sound effects and stings of music worthy of Hitchcock himself. I couldn't understand it fully, although by this stage of my tour my own knowledge of French and Latin had given me a tenuous grasp of Romanian. I had his corruption report thoroughly lawyered and put to air. He was not incarcerated.

On a rare day off Sorin took me to his home in Cluj via the

beautiful city of Timisoara, where the revolution had begun. But the highlight of my visit was a little piece of America in the heart of Cluj – McDonald's. I can only explain this uncharacteristic lapse of taste to Romanian food, "forty-seven ways of serving Wiener Schnitzel" as a friend had warned me before departure. There in a spotlessly clean and conspicuously cockroach-free environment I attacked a Big Mac with relish. It had relish but so did I for the first and only time. So cleansing was this moment that I treated myself to a trip to the toilet even though I didn't really need to go. The washroom did not disappoint, totally clean, no nails or corrugated iron roof, no need to cover my head with a towel. Sheer bliss. No wonder the Cluj clientele, so close to the Hungarian border, wanted to look west to the European Union, rather than back east to the mind control of dictatorship and the single low-wattage light of Ceausescu's reign. I phoned my son, Jonathan, who had just been right around the world in his gap year and invited him to Romania to meet the anxious young men and women I was trying to educate in the wonders of democracy and free speech. The last time we had spoken he was eating a fried egg from a nice man who'd cooked it for him on the pavement in somewhere Indian and exotic. I reckoned he could tough it out in Romania. He came and was, of course, fascinated to see young people just a few years older than him so dominated by a totalitarian regime that he and his peer group just couldn't imagine. He stayed with me to the end of my trip and we travelled home together.

My friend, Mark Webster has just returned from a similar teaching trip for young journalists from Ukraine. I wondered whether he'd found the same ignorance and confusion about the West. No, said Mark, not at all. They all had a very good grasp of modern life in the rest of the Western world. Today the difference is social media. These young Ukrainian journalists could keep up with the latest trends in London, Paris or New York just as if they were sitting at a café in Notting Hill, the Boulevard Saint Michelle or the Bronx. This has to be A Good Thing.

Sorin had one last task to perform before we left. We had a formal interview with the University Principal and the government sponsors about further such educational trips the following year. At this meeting it was important that every word was correctly understood by both sides, so Sorin did simultaneous translation throughout. It was a weird experience. There is a scene in *Broadcast News* where the blonde bombshell William Hurt, with perfect orthodonty but inadequate brains is drafted in to deal with a sudden emergency in Libya. He knows nothing about the Middle East, but his director, Holly Hunter, knows everything and whispers all the relevant questions in his ear. William Hurt delivers the questions with great presenter skills and the result is a triumph for the network. In the afterglow Hurt says to her, it was just like you were inside me, it was like sex. I had no such homo-erotic feelings for Sorin, but by the end of the encounter I did feel that we had melded together in that brief meeting. Through him, also, I was able to make clear that many other experienced broadcasters would be able to take my place next year, since I would be too busy with other broadcast commitments. Quite honestly, one month in Romania at that time was enough for any individual to take. I wasn't rushing to return.

Nonetheless my trip had apparently been a great success as was heralded by the arrival of Mr Big in not just one Dacia, but two, the second for his entourage, a French word meaning hangers-on. He was the sort of fat, middle-aged nobody I had expected, offering drinks all round for our breakfast. All the alcohol was dirt cheap, even the Johnnie Walker Red Label, but Mr Big drank the only really expensive stuff, the Johnnie Walker Black Label, just to keep us all in our place. Whisky in Romania, Death in Paris, mass hysteria in Britain. It was the morning that the death of Princess Diana in a car crash in Paris was announced to a horrified world audience. I was the one expected to be most consumed by the disaster and therefore expected to consume the most whisky. With a final dramatic draining of his expensive whisky, Mr Big was gone, leaving me the opportunity to phone Susan at home and realise for the first time just what a grief-stricken nation the People's Princess had left behind. Although Bucharest was not a lot further than, say, Milan or Naples it felt like another world. It was, the Third World. In just a month I had forgotten the country lanes of Oxfordshire and could now bump along Romania's ruts with the best of them. It was time for Jonathan and I to go home.

We took the train back to Bucharest, stopping at Brasov, where Scarface jumped off the train and returned with cakes and vodka. Most welcome, but Brasov just about summed up my mood. Yup, Brasov. We found the inevitable crook with a crap car to take us to the airport. He deliberately took us to the military airport and then tried to negotiate a further fee for taking us to the international airport. Jonathan was magnificent. He had just travelled the world, fending off nasty little spivs from himself and his girlfriend. We got to the correct airport with no extra charge. We paid a ludicrous exit charge and climbed gratefully onto our flight to Heathrow. Right, that was it – Romania, been there, done that, but they were fresh out of T-shirts.

Fate has an ineluctable way of dealing you a duff hand. On my return I 'phoned Addie to see if Chevron had any further assignments for me. Yes, the Tobacco company wanted me do a week's work abroad. Great, I thought of the Barbados trip and my Grahame Greene bungalow on the beach, or another trip to the fabulous Shangri-La hotel in Hong Kong or the game lodges in South Africa. No. My course was scheduled for just a few weeks' time – in Bucharest.

Back I trudged, but things were looking up. This was a Club Class trip, not a Dacia in sight. We were picked up by Mercedes and whisked to the brand new Hilton, Bucharest. Unfortunately, it wasn't yet brand new, it was still a work in progress in a country that, I knew, didn't do progress very well. The Hilton was broken, our trip became a sort of *Carry on up the Costas* with Romanian subtitles. The conference room, designed to be a quiet sanctuary for reasoned debate, echoed with strange sounds of drilling and thumping as nearby bits of the hotel were constructed around it. It took all the considerable skills of our faithful travelling cameraman, Steve, to coax the Romanian technology into life. There was a great deal of "vamping 'til ready" from me and my colleagues until we could show the videos we needed to start our course. At least this time I did not have to pay any bribes, no doubt someone else did.

TELEVISION: THE STATE WE'RE IN

U p to our uxters in meerkats, that's where. In the three channel world of television I entered in 1969, I could manage the odd, cute meerkat on a David Attenborough natural history film. Today I can't get through on my thousand channels without being submerged by the little furry bastards trying to encourage me to change my insurance or my underpants or my body shape or whatever it is they're trying to flog. So, here are my helpful and I trust constructive notes to the world of television advertising;

1. Get your heads out of your own backsides and take a look around you. The prized, lucrative market of young people doesn't watch TV the way their Dads and Grandads did. Because of your stupid adverts, inserted at random moments into an otherwise tense dramatic plot, they record the piece and later fast forward through the ads to watch the programme as a whole experience. Your silly but expensive ads just aren't being watched. Go compare yourselves and get that idiot to sing you into submission.

2. Stop trying to be so clever. Do exactly what it says on the tin. What is that coffee ad all about? George Clooney, for it is he, walks into your average coffee lounge, stacked with well-stacked gorgeous girls and sits down opposite one, who is just finishing her coffee. Gallantly, he offers to get her another cup. As he strolls suavely away she indicates to the other beauties that Clooney is among them. She drains Clooney's cup, while he is being mobbed. Why does she steal his coffee, while he is actually getting her a fresh cup of her own? It is one of the world's great imponderables, like why does a man suddenly become a giant bingo ball and look as though he has just ejaculated? Why are all those serial losers so ecstatically happy that they are going to win millions of pounds on the lottery? Why do all adverts for betting have to be shouted at us? Are betting people all congenitally deaf?

3. Give those cuddly toys back to your sons and daughters. When she was little, my daughter, Annabel, had about two hundred soft toys suspended in a hammock from the beams of her room. The collective noun for a clutch of cuddly toys bought at the last minute in foreign airports across the world is a "guilt of soft toys". I've only got a vague idea, she thinks, about who this bloke is at Heathrow who keeps kissing my Mum, but the pressies are great. What's he got me this time? Girls are easy; you can get a Taiwanese My Little Pony just about anywhere in the world. Boys are more difficult, particularly as they get older. Jonathan and I agreed long ago that Annabel should get the giant Mickey Mouse from Los Angeles international and he would settle for whatever currency I had left at the end of my trip. Sadly, he has not grown up to be a hedge-fund manager. He's a really nice bloke. My point is that advertising with cuddly pandas when you're trying to sell to children makes sense. Trying to do the same for bog roll, a necessity for adults, makes no sense at all. Why are all the

customers of one of the "Big Six Crooks" banks strange, android people with elongated necks and stupid faces? Why is another big crook so anxious to give money away to all its ecstatic hard-working customers? Just another small note: stuffed animals don't talk. If I walked into a bank run by talking bears, I'd have yet another reason for never walking into a bank again.

4. Elbow the joyous families on their prized new sofas. First, no family, not even the *Royle Family* are joyous on their sofas. They are screaming for the kids to stop jumping up and down on the prized new artefact, racing to scrub off the red wine they've spilt, kicking the cat to stop it unravelling the weave with its claws, kicking granny for spilling her tea yet again. All is not well in the sofa world. Where do they get those ghastly designs from anyway? Are they the rejects from "The Great British Sofa Event", sent back because they were just too unspeakably ugly? Why are the families wreathed in smiles as a chunk of wood and foam fulfils their every desire?

5. Put charity ads up with a simple graphic and words like: "Are you sorry for the kids in Syria/Sudan/Ukraine? Send money to the address on screen and we'll try to help". We all know what a poor, starving child looks like, we see it on the news all too often. Please don't serve up those awful shots in the middle of *Mock the Week* or *House of Fools*. You are the ones who will look like fools and manipulators.

6. "Banish aching fingers from carrot chopping. Buy Magic carrot choppers. It comes with a list of special features. I'm going to go into them at great length". Oh no, you're not. I've already changed channels. "Sick of that saggy stomach?" No, I've got really used to it over the past sixty-seven years. "Do you suffer from penile dysfunction?" No and I don't want to

hear about it while I'm having my tea. "Do you need panty pads, a cure for pre-menstrual tension or new smooth skin?" No, I'm a man and I'd rather not know about intimate female concerns. Of course we should be free to discuss such concerns, but is this really the forum for it? I'm really worried about all those women who've got rope twisted round their tummies to signify their constipation, blue blood on their panty pads, and those men with silvery-grey hair and lantern jaws who can't get it up any more. "Are you worried by the ugliness and banality of our adverts? Join No more Mad Men today".

The point is the public are not stupid. You, the advertisers, are treating us like idiots. The true cretins are the ones saying to their acne-ridden peer group: "And then, she indicates he's George Clooney, all the other girls go mad and she steals his coffee, – great, isn't it?" "and then the young boy is so enjoying Daddy's new Seat Simpleton that he gets bored with his Space toy and throws it out of the car window, – great isn't it?" No, it's not great, it's stupid and amoral.

What of the programmes themselves? When Clive James first used the term "howling bummer" to describe a programme he didn't like, he couldn't have foreseen whole channels devoted to howling bummers. But they are here today. Who wants to see:

Embarrassing Bodies.
Outback Truckers.
60 Minute Makeover.
The Boy with the Ten Stone Testicle.
Celebrity Guts and Gore.
Bearded Beauty Queens.

All right, I made the last two up but I bet I could sell *Celebrity Guts and Gore* to a cable channel desperate for viewers and frantic to fill the acres of broadcasting hours ahead of them. That's the key. As always, more means less. The more channels, the fewer viewers, the worse the content. So why do people set up these idiotic channels in the first place? Again, I blame the advertisers. They are prepared to put their ads on any old channel, no doubt as part of a package, in the hope that a few of the slack-jawed people watching might buy a Magi-Carrot Cutter. Maybe these channels are designed for viewers who can't find the remote control or are too indolent to pick it up. More likely, the viewers just don't care anymore. My generation was brought up with a fierce attachment to this magical technology that early on brought us the Coronation of Queen Elizabeth II. The whole royal panoply and Her Majesty Herself were there in Acacia Avenue, Bolton, Tulip Grove, Tamworth and Churchill Crescent, Hackney. The community – for there was such a thing – was there, gathered around Mrs Farnes Barnes's telly, since she was the only member of the community rich enough to own the new television machine. In the mid fifties George Whichelow also lived in Palace View, Bromley and he was my window on the world, since he owned an eight-inch screen television in spectacular black & white, with optional snow. We would huddle in George's front room, watching the Range Rider and the all-American boy, Dick West, as they fought the injuns through the snow blizzard. Dick West could hang out of his saddle and shoot his gun from under the horse's belly. Perhaps he was sheltering from the snow. During the late fifties and early sixties the television machine morphed into the goggle box and various do-gooders started to worry that we'd all get square eyes and fat bottoms watching the telly. Oh, and the art of conversation would be gone forever. None of this came to pass, apart from the fat bottoms but that was to do with pies not pixilations. Indeed, what was on the telly last night became a major topic in the pubs and clubs across the land. Today we worry that our children can only interact with their phone or iPad or something else festooned with apps; that teenagers will be losing their virginity on Twitter or Facebook, although as Victoria Wood says in *Dinner Ladies*, when suspected of being pregnant: "I'm not pregnant. Not unless sperm can get through sash windows". So, again, none of this will come to pass. To quote the saintly Victoria Wood again, when asked by Tony whether they'll be happy ever after, she says: "No, I expect we'll just carry on blundering about, buggering everything up like everybody else".

In the sixties and seventies television began to grow up, realising that content had to be king. The initial thrill of seeing human beings walking and talking on a magic box just beside the gramophone in the corner of the sitting room had gone, so television needed really good content to keep the viewers fixated. And television delivered. One benefit of the proliferation of cable channels is that these excellent series are endlessly repeated. During a recent convalescence I had every reason to be grateful to some cable channels, given that, for a time, the height of my physical ambition was sitting in a chair. Top of the list for me has to be *Minder* where George Cole plays the idiot savant, Arthur Daley and Dennis Waterman plays minder to a man who really needs to be minded. It's a mixture of chicanery, charm and sheer buffoonery that just doesn't date. The *Minder* ensemble is a Central Casting Guide to the actor villains of the day. If *Minder* is a Crombie overcoat and trilby hat, *The Professionals* is a Vivienne Westwood flurry of wide lapels, even wider trousers and snipers' rifles. David Croft and Jimmy Perry brought us *Dad's Army*, so good that it can still open the weekend schedules for mainstream BBC. Like all great comedy it is the writing that keeps it alive all these decades later, together with an ensemble performance of great skill. I know so much about these people, how Mainwaring's insecurity is covered by his pomposity, how Wilson is effortlessly upper class, how Godfrey's bladder is dodgy and that Walker can get you anything on the black market. Jonesy fought the "fuzzy wuzzies" in Sudan and Pike needs his scarf. Television is a visual medium but it doesn't work without good words. So, what went wrong? Nothing really, there is still plenty of good comedy writing and dramatic writing on television. The problem is that there is so much rubbish as well ranging from plain dross, like the jewellery channels to the plain offensive like all those programmes featuring girls in trainers falling off bits of mountains and causing the valiant emergency services a lot of unnecessary trouble and danger. On one of these dim-witted programmes I actually saw the aforesaid girl with a broken ankle breaking off from crying and clutching her bloodied leg to smile at the camera and give us the redundant remark: "Ooh, look, I'm on television".

Back in the sixties, when the Beatles were rapidly becoming a British and then American success story, Paul turned to John one day and said: "We're in the hands of the money men now, John".

My pitch for better, more intelligent television:

Soliloquy

An empty stage, bare set. One follow-spot.
Enter David Tennant as Hamlet.
"To be, or not to be: that is the question
Whether 'tis nobler in the mind
To suffer the slings and arrows of outrageous fortune,
Or to take arms against a sea of troubles,
And, by opposing, end them. To die, to sleep—
No more, and by a sleep to say we end
The heartache and the thousand natural shocks
That flesh is heir to 'tis a consummation
Devoutly to be wished. To die, to sleep,
To sleep, perchance to dream. Ay, there's the rub,
For in that sleep of death what dreams may come
When we have shuffled off this mortal coil
Must give us pause.
Pause for first commercial break. King's Cross station, central London.
Lenny Henry is in bed, while London's commuters scurry by,

268

apparently unaware of this famous person sleeping in their midst, even though he is talking to himself and to the television public, reassuring us that we can get a guaranteed good night's sleep at a Premier Inn.

Suddenly a man is shouting at us. A bookie wants to give us money. The man screams "fifty pounds free bet". There is some sort of provision about Silvio Argent having to score the winning goal against Mammon United before this munificent gift will be bestowed upon us.

Equally suddenly a good-looking older woman is worrying about her wrinkles. She applies magic cream. In the "after" picture she looks like an attractive older woman, just like the "before" picture. The only difference is that she has been better lit and mildly photo-shopped.

Soliloquy: Part Two. Sponsored by Viking River Cruises.

"There's the respect

That makes calamity of so long life,

For who would bear the whips and scorns of time,

Th'oppressor's wrong, the proud man's contumely,

The pangs of disprized love, the law's delay,

The insolence of office, and the spurns

That patient merit of th'unworthy takes,

When he himself might his quietus make

With a bare bodkin?"

Have you been injured at work?

(A tall, handsome chap in a reassuring dark, lawyer-type suit is addressing us with great earnestness. He too wants to give us money amid some scary shots of men with chain saws and women falling on slidey floors. Indeed, he's been successful for a happy, smiling gent, now restored to full fitness, is gazing lovingly at a cheque for £5000.)

Suddenly, we are delving back into women's bodies and the thousand natural shocks to which their flesh is heir. They are all beautiful yet that beauty is somewhat compromised by the news that they leak, or that their bowels are knotted in constipation. Oh, here's one who's only got dandruff. Don't worry magic potions are available to all, for a price.

Daddy is a bit sweaty. He is carrying a rather professional-looking toolbox and beside him stands his little Princess, demanding that he builds her a tree house. She is scowling. The house is not big enough. Daddy goes back to work. She is still scowling. By the time Daddy has finished constructing Buckingham Palace in the apple tree, he is just a great big pool of sweat. His little Princess gives him a smile. What she really needed, right from the start was a kick up the royal arse. (This is advertising something but I can't remember what).

Soliloquy. Part Three. Sponsored by Viking River Cruises.
Who would these fardels bear,
To grunt and sweat under a weary life,
But that the dread of something after death,
The undiscovered country from whose bourn
No traveller returns, puzzles the will,
And makes us rather bear those ills we have
Than fly to others that we know not of?
Thus conscience doth make cowards of us all.
And thus the native hue of resolution
Is sicklied o'er with the pale cast of thought,
And enterprises of great pith and moment
With this regard their currents turn awry,
And lose the name of action".

(An eager shouty man is suddenly worried about my grimy gunnels and wants action NOW. He has the Holy Grail in his hand, a dispenser of Cillit Bang that will cleanse my benighted corners. His enthusiasm for Cillit Bang knows no bourn and he bounds about transforming my grubby life into the Elysian Fields.)

Suddenly, the head of a CGI soldier is being torn off by a CGI monster. Action man thunders in, making Prince Hamlet look like a powder puff. The situation is quickly, bloodily resolved. As

Shakespeare so eloquently put it: "Oh, for a muse of CGI, that would ascend the brightest heaven of invention…".

Soliloquy. The end.

This programme was brought to you by Viking River cruises and Stratford-upon-Avon Noddy Boats Ltd.

My industry, the television scenery I entered as a dewy-eyed version of John Reith in 1969 has been taken over by Mammon. My extension of Warhol's famous saying would be: "One day everyone will be famous for fifteen minutes, make a few bob and then be instantly forgotten". Perhaps that was always implicit in Warhol's shorter and pithier version. No-one ever got an Emmy or a Bafta for *Great British Celebrity Chef Vampire Makeover* but they probably made a few bucks from the ever gullible advertising industry, anxious about the falling sales of Multi-jet Carpet and Sofa Solutions. Taste, you might think, is out the window while the cash registers clang.

PARADISE IN PERIL

I made it to my island. A quarter of a century after I sat in Palace Road, Bromley, eating my tea and marvelling at the bright new technology that was bringing Alan Whicker to my front room, I was there following in his tripod marks. Alan's story was that Alan was there. Twenty-five years later I needed something more substantial as a narrative. And Colonel Rabuka was there to deliver it, – a military coup in Paradise. It was a bit like a film I had made some years beforehand about riots in Zurich. Riots in Rio or Rwanda, fine, but riots in the gold-plated streets of Zurich? I don't think so. The film, though, was new and true and different and I discovered that the Swiss do hotels better than anyone else in the world. The Fijians do beautiful beaches and relaxing better than anywhere else. So, what's all this about, Fijians brandishing their Kalashnikovs on the streets of the capital, Suva? I was there to find out. It was already a tiny strike for me. The BBC in their continuing quest to keep me off serious programmes where my fondness for investigation might create further embarrassment in "meeting land" back in London, had put me on *Everyman*. This was a religious strand of programming where, they reasoned, I could make endless enquiries about how many angels could dance on the head of a pin, while real news was left to the big boys. In Fiji I had slipped under the net and found a proper *Panorama* style report. The native Fijians were big and laid-back as South Sea islanders ought to be. The immigrant influx of Indians were hard-working, diligent entrepreneurs who naturally rose to the top of the commanding heights of the native economy. While the Fijians were happy with their bread fruit and small holdings the Indians set about making serious money. The uprising when it came was Methodism versus Mammon. The British Empire had given the native Fijians Methodist evangelists, the religion of unalloyed capitalism had been adopted by the Indian immigrants. Put more simply, it was the Indians who came up with the T-shirts celebrating the revolution, even though they were the target of the uprising. There were in fact two military coups and I have the two Indian T-shirts to prove it. The first one reads "Fiji, Military Coup, 1987" and the second reads: "Just when you thought it was safe to go out on the streets again, 2nd Military Coup, 1987". Both are adorned with a rough woodcut of a film crew recording the events. It was the ultimate in niche marketing. The island is going to be invaded by the world's press for a few days. What do the Brits/Germans/Americans want? They want a souvenir of their visit to the other side of the world, so overnight the Indian who owns the sweatshop bashes out dozens of film-crew themed T-shirts celebrating the coups. I bet he sold hundreds to Dave, Dietrich and Dwayne, the world's press. Meanwhile, in the native smallholdings the bread fruit was bubbling away nicely.

We stayed at the resort hotel directly across the road from the Government Buildings in Suva. Every morning I would emerge into the blazing sunlight and say "turned out nice again, then" to the crew. Inside I was saying to myself, "Thank you very much, God, this is my reward for all those days filming in Darlington". Have you been to Darlington? It's not a town; it's a car park with a railway line running through it. Even the only thing worth looking at, Stephenson's Rocket, is on the platform. The next day

I would be giving thanks for not being in Manchester, not in the Piccadilly Hotel which didn't have rooms; it had rabbit hutches for businessmen. I had a huge room in Suva, looking out on the lavish swimming pool complex.

The British Empire has a lot to answer for, but the gift of cricket to faraway places is one they can be proud of. On day one, as I stepped out of the hotel, I looked out at the waste ground beside the Government Buildings and there were about six games of cricket going on. The most serious was, of course, on the least wasted of the waste-ground pitches. The Imperials were playing the Natives, well of course they were. The Imperials should have been in knee-breeches, top hats and pipes, the Natives in rags. It was rather more up to date than that but it was still clear that the Army & Navy Club were showing what good sorts they were by playing the peasants. As a script writer this was a gift, colourful footage which would allow me to do a short historical piece about Fiji's shift from colonialism to independence. It also reminded me that it was probably "good form" to visit the British Consulate and announce our arrival. This was regarded by the Civil Service side of the Beeb as a *sine qua non* of foreign filming and I had done it in many parts of the one-time Empire, most notably in the Victorian splendour of the British Embassy in Tehran, while the Americans were being held hostage in their Embassy just down the road. I apparently broke some sort of protocol right away by asking our languid ambassador whether he'd been to talk to the students at our ally's embassy. "Good God, no. That would be quite improper" he replied with a rustling of ostrich feathers from his pith helmet. If he thought that I was a trifle direct and uncouth he had reckoned without the feisty Australian correspondent from *Newsweek* who said what we were all thinking: "Can't a fella get a decent gin and tonic in the British Embassy anymore? I mean your 'any more for tennis?' lemonade with bits floating in is all very well but it's hellish dry out there in Tehran. We need a proper drink". The butler was dispatched and the gin duly turned up. I love our Australian friends.

Back in Suva, the British Consulate was more posh wooden shack than John Gilbert Scott but the freshly polished Jaguar and the Fijian chauffeur told its own story. Being posted to the South Seas meant one of two things: you were either a young man with a glittering career ahead of you, or an older man who wasn't the sharpest knife in the barrel. We explained our mission to His Excellency and asked if he knew anyone who might be behind the popular uprising. He seemed nonplussed by this, I would have thought, obvious question. Eventually, he said: "Well, there is some clerical chap on the other side of the island who has been causing a bit of a stink". "Yes, we know, we interviewed him yesterday" I said. Nope, a couple more years in paradise and then a "K" and a bungalow in Bournemouth for you, I think. He was diplomatic and charming but the slip of a girl who was our assistant director had been assiduously courted by MI6 while at University, and intellectually could easily wipe the floor with him. She had been so good that the MI6 offer was still on the table. "So what do I do if I turn up in Moscow and find that you are the cultural attaché?" "Nothing" she said.

The niceties dispensed with, we turned to the serious business of finding and interviewing the opposition to the old regime. It wasn't that difficult and my hotel room rapidly became a makeshift studio where disaffected Indians would come to tell their tales. Together with lots of happy Fijian Methodists, raising the corrugated iron on the roof of their wooden Church, we almost had our story but we didn't yet have the essential interview with Colonel Rabuka himself. We couldn't return to Britain without the key interview or at least some footage of me being bundled away and roughed up by some heavies at the Colonel's headquarters in Government Buildings. We followed Rabuka everywhere and kept asking for an interview. After a few days we were summoned by the Minister of Disinformation to await the Colonel's arrival when he would bestow upon us his wise, Fijian words. The Minister for Disinformation was a sixteen stone, muscle-bound, kilted version of the Israeli Major who so disapproved of me in Jerusalem. We waited. God, we waited. After two hours I decided to push the Disinformation man around a bit. The female producer and I went to his office and I said in my big, stern voice: "We've been waiting here for two hours now. I have an expensive film crew kicking their heels in an anteroom and I was promised an interview with Colonel Rabuka by you earlier today. Where is he?" I call this approach "turning up the gain". The effect on the Minister though was really scary. He took it as an outrageous insult that I had spoken to him so disrespectfully in front of his staff. I watched as his eyes literally turned red and he began to scream at me. I realised that a hundred years ago he would have had me in a cooking pot, garnished with bread fruit, and eaten me in front of the dancing natives. Nonetheless, this was testosterone rearing its ugly head and I opened my mouth to do some shouting back, risking the cooking pot some more. The producer very quietly stood on my foot, shut me up and delivered some palliative words of her own. Soon, we got our interview. A very good reason why we should have more women in the British House of Commons.

Rabuka, when we finally got to meet him, was all smiles and reasonableness. As usual, with these "must get" interviews, I can't remember anything he said, the fact was in the "getting". We had our interview with Rabuka's flashing teeth amid all sorts of good intentions for the future of his islands, all sorts of guarantees about the safety of the Indians. I didn't believe a word of it but we had our interview and a plane ticket from Paradise back to prosody at BBC Television Centre.

EPILOGUE

So, what have we learned over my sixty-seven years and your two hours, while you read, or ten minutes when you decided not to bother?

Rule one: there are no rules. Not entirely true. To disobey some rules would be anti-social, but many rules are just pettifogging and plain silly, dreamt up by bureaucrats who otherwise would be usefully employed sitting at their desks, twiddling their expensive thumbs. Indeed, when I worked at LBC under the Australian blonde bombshell, Charlie Cox, he protected himself from disaffected staff behind a fellow Oz, called Mike. He was built like a nightclub bouncer, with very large pecs and a very tiny brain. When I saw him coming into the wine bar across the street I used to switch into Cambridge mode, using multisyllabic words and as many Latin tags as I could remember. The look on his handsome, well-tanned face was a picture, ranging from sheer incomprehension to slack-jawed admiration of my apparent erudition... eru-what? His empire was a glass-walled cube in the newsroom. I got a clear view from my desk. He was actually twiddling his thumbs.

Rule Two: good management is easy to spot. You can't see it.

Rule Three: Comedy makes you laugh. War makes you dead. Take comedy every time.

Rule Four: Be exceedingly nice to each other. This will be the title of my forthcoming Tony Blair Memorial Tour to the Middle East.

Rule Five: Don't crawl. Chris was a presenter at LBC, during one of its several managements. He took me to lunch at Roberto's, an ancient Italian restaurant near the studios. He paid me a great compliment, although he regarded it as a rebuke: "You're quite soft really, aren't you?" Yes, Chris I am and why are you spending your time looking around for someone more important and powerful than me? Eventually, he found his prestigious target and rushed off to "bump into" him, leaving his linguine pescatori to go cold. When Mr Big's car arrived to take him back to his big desk in media land, Chris ran out after him and ran alongside his limo, reinforcing his bid for stardom. I was a little embarrassed by this. But not as embarrassed as I was about to become, when he insisted that we go for a pint of Guinness at a nearby pub he knew well. After a big, Italian meal and lots of Barolo that was the last thing I wanted. No, the last thing I wanted was there in the pub, a naked girl lap dancing. As she bent over, Chris pulled on his pint and announced: "nice arse". I thought, yes, Chris you are.

Rule Six: Do crawl. If you attach yourself to the right high-flying executive, carry his bags and tiptoe the company policy, never saying a word out of line, you will climb through the ranks of assistants to the deputy assistant and the ultimate goal, keys to the Executive Boot-licking Room, another meaningless title and, at about fifty-eight years old, you will become Deputy Head for Light Thinking (Television), D.O.L.T. (Tel.) You will have left the pesky bug-bites of the audience way behind you and can only be grateful for their munificence in funding your big, fat fund of pension plans.

Alternatively, you can ignore the entire edifice of policies, structures, systems and carry on as a hopefully creative human being, still remembering the limitless diversity of that extraordinary medium, television, that you decided to join all those years ago, when God was a boy. David Attenborough resigned as Controller, BBC2, in 1973. I wonder what happened to him? Of course, this lily-livered logic would imply no management at all.

Good.

Rule Seven: Never forget Rule one. There are no rules.

ACKNOWLEDGEMENTS

The above is the result of bullying. Jonathan and Annabel bullied their Dad to write it all down. Sue, having heard it all a few times in 44 years of marriage, wasn't so sure. But, Saint as she is, she went along with it and helped with the details (never my strong point), and restrained my more elaborate flights of fancy.

But there can be no doubt that the Bully-in-Chief was an ex Lime Grove producer, my friend John Mair. When I was ill and sitting at home unable to understand the complexities of Cash in the Attic, staring at the empty grid of the Times crossword and wondering if I would sink as low as watching the Jeremy Kyle Show, John was a regular and most welcome visitor. When was I going to write that book? When my brain stopped atrophying, John, and I could read more than a paragraph once again. The day did come and the book became a welcome part of my convalescence. I am very grateful to John for all his help.

I could read again. Whole books – imagine that. In particular I re-read:
Point of Departure by James Cameron,
Scoop by Evelyn Waugh,

Not Quite the Diplomat by Chris Patten,

And nihilistic bits of Sam Beckett, and great bits of William Shakespeare.